Queer *Latinidad*

SEXUAL CULTURES: New Directions from the Center for
Lesbian and Gay Studies
General Editors: José Esteban Muñoz and Ann Pellegrini

Times Square Red, Times Square Blue
Samuel R. Delany

Private Affairs: *Critical Ventures in the Culture of Social Relations*
Phillip Brian Harper

In Your Face: *9 Sexual Studies*
Mandy Merck

Tropics of Desire: *Interventions from Queer Latino America*
José Quiroga

Murdering Masculinities: *Fantasies of Gender and Violence*
in the American Crime Novel
Greg Forter

Our Monica, Ourselves: *The Clinton Affair and the National Interest*
edited by Lauren Berlant and Lisa Duggan

Black Gay Man: *Essays*
Robert Reid-Pharr *Foreword by Samuel R. Delany*

Passing: *Identity and Interpretation in Sexuality, Race, and Religion*
Edited by María Carla Sánchez and Linda Schlossberg

The Queerest Art: *Essays on Lesbian and Gay Theater*
Edited by Alisa Solomon and Framji Minwalla

Queer Globalizations: *Citizenship and the Afterlife of Colonialism*
Edited by Arnaldo Cruz-Malavé and Martin F. Manalansan IV

Queer *Latinidad: Identity Practices, Discursive Spaces*
Juana María Rodríguez

Queer *Latinidad*

Identity Practices, Discursive Spaces

JUANA MARÍA RODRÍGUEZ

NEW YORK UNIVERSITY PRESS

New York and London

NEW YORK UNIVERSITY PRESS
New York and London

Library of Congress Cataloging-in-Publication Data
Rodríguez, Juana María
Queer latinidad : identity practices, discursive spaces /
Juana María Rodríguez.
p. cm. — (Sexual cultures)
Includes bibliographical references and index.
ISBN 0-8147-7549-7 (cloth : alk. paper) —
ISBN 0-8147-7550-0 (pbk. : alk. paper)
1. Hispanic American gays—Psychology.
2. Hispanic American gays—Ethnic identity.
3. Gays—United States—Identity.   I. Title.   II. Series.
HQ76.3.U5   R63   2003
305.868073—dc21   2002008752

New York University Press books are printed on acid-free paper,
and their binding materials are chosen for strength and durability.

Manufactured in the United States of America

10 9 8 7 6 5 4 3 2 1

To my *familias,* everywhere

Contents

Acknowledgments

This book is a manifestation of the many gifts of knowledge I have received over the course of my life. Like the different spaces I describe in this text, multiformed spaces have shaped my intellectual formation. I grew up in a home where ideas, humor, *cariño*, and chaos ate together. My grandmother adored me and taught me almost everything I know about death, love, and food. My mother indulged my childhood efforts at theorizing the world, and my father taught me to be curious and kind. My sister nurtures the creative spirit in me and my brother continually affirms my belief in the resilience of that which is good. The aunts, uncles, cousins, kin, and family friends who I grew up with continue to care for my queer self, and I love them for it. Biological families, especially large Cuban ones, can be treacherous. I have been blessed.

Inside the teaching machine, I have been witness to the kindness and beneficence of many scholars who people the machine. Judith Butler, Barbara Christian, VèVè Clark, Johnetta Cole, Juan Flores, Inderpal Grewal, Caren Kaplan, Laura Pérez, and Carol Stack have all generously shared their genius with me when it mattered most. Special thanks are extended to two of the earliest influences in my career: Deborah Britzman, who taught me to read at a tender age, and Patricia Guthrie, my academic godmother. Later in my education, I was fortunate to encounter two visionary scholars who listened deeply and taught me to trust my apparitions: Norma Alarcón, a valued friend who provides unending lessons in the practice of critical creativity, and Gerald Vizenor, the tender trickster who asks questions that spin out in wild ventures of language.

It is also a particular joy when your dearest friends, near and far, are also your trusted academic conspirators and advisors. With that as my aperture, I would like to extend my thanks to Linda Susan Beard, Marisa Belausteguigoitia, Amalia Cabezas, Anne Dalke, Susan Dean, Irene Gonzalez,

Herb Green, Joseph Kramer, Daphne LaMothe, Michelle Raheja, Katherine Rowe, Theresa Tensuan, and Michael Tratner. I take special pleasure in acknowledging the love and support of Kimberley Nettles and Alexandra Seung Hye Suh, two of the best friends and co-conspirators around. Additional thanks go out to José Quiroga and David Román for providing such availing readings of my work. I also want to thank José Esteban Muñoz and Ann Pellegrini, the editors of the Sexual Cultures Series, Eric Zinner, the senior editor at New York University Press, and Rosalie Morales Kearns, copyeditor extraordinaire, for all of their enthusiasm. As a teacher-in-process I am continually inspired by those I teach, so a note of sincere appreciation goes out to my students at the University of California at Berkeley, Hayward State University, Colegio ContraSIDA, San Francisco State University, and Bryn Mawr College.

Several institutions have contributed to the completion of this project. At the Tomás Rivera Latino Dissertation Writing Workshop, Deena González provided many hours of careful, dedicated reading. As a fellow at the Humanities Research Institute at the University of California, Irvine, I enjoyed the guidance and spirited interdisciplinary exchange of many of the scholars in residence; I particularly want to thank Patti Lather and Joan Tronto for keeping it fun. I would also like to recognize the Lindback Foundation for its generous financial support. My unending gratitude goes out to Suzanne Warren, a research assistant who shared with me both her meticulous attention to detail and her warm disposition. Bryn Mawr College and the Tri-College community have been the source of both collegial affirmation and many valuable resources; my thanks to those that have made me feel welcome.

The chapter on activism is dedicated to all of my *familia* at Proyecto ContraSIDA por Vida, because they have all educated me. I would especially like to extend my heartfelt thanks to Jorge Ignacio Cortiñas, Jesse Johnson, Hector León, Marcia Ochoa, Juan Rodríguez, and Adela Vázquez for their hours of inspiring conversation, political insights, constructive criticism, *cariño*, *ovarios*, dedication, and most of all, for breathing vision into life. I am forever indebted to the visual artistry of Patrick "Pato" Hebert, who shared his glorious images with me. I particularly want to thank Ricardo Bracho, who carefully read several drafts of this manuscript, and gave me more gifts of language, memory, and intellectual imagination than I deserve. A femme shimmy-shake goes out to Diane Felix, for all the *música y ambiente* she makes possible, and for being such a fine butch example of *tetatúd* in action. I also want to send *muchos besos y abrazos* to Adriana Batista, Lucrecia and Nela Bermúdez, Connie Boronot, María Cora, Winn Gilmore, Sandra López, Lily Rivera, Natalie Watson, Koko, all of my *amig@s* at Arenal, and *las vascas lokas de Iruña*. I especially want to thank Connie Jackson for always believing I would do this and tatiana de la tierra for sharing so many of my perverse passions. Finally, I thank Frances Grau Brull, *el amor de mi vida*, for sharing what exists beyond words. *Aché*.

Preface

A Note of Caution to the Reader

The reader will already have noted that, unlike ordinary texts, this one
was read first and written later. Instead of saying and writing something
new, it merely faithfully copies what has already been said and composed by others. Thus in this compilation there is not a single page, a
single sentence, a single word, from the title to this final note, that has
not been written in this way.

> Augusto Roa Bastos, *I the Supreme, Final Compiler's Note*

Writing, being essentially excess, struggles at any chosen moment
among restrictions.

> Edmond Jabès, *The Book of Questions: El, or the Last Book*

Writing is silent. Barren white spaces hold the cryptic black marks of text.
Margins impose an imaginary wholeness, even as they establish a border of
difference. They contain the marks and signal their separateness from other
texts. I know something about margins and the centers they create. I know
that the borders of any frame are permeable; other ideas, other texts come in
to flood any sense of originality or ownership. Centers are relative, malleable,
and polydimensional. Margins are continually forming, deforming, and
transforming their parameters. The ideas I present are never completely
mine. They are compiled from a chorus of voices, a story told through other
stories, shaped into a speech/text through a tongue that has been twisted into
an uneasy conformity. In citation, there always exists the error of deficit. The
move from one context to another, from a larger whole to a fractured piece
always involves erasure and excess. Writing is treacherous work; it resists containment. Words spin out in search of their own meanings, ready to turn on
author(ity) at any moment. Edmond Jabès writes, "Any word is a place open
to attack by formidable words ready to usurp the book when nobody is

1

watching" (10). The danger only escalates when the words are unleashed into the space of the public. "The place of the book is a walled-in void. Every page a precarious shelter which has its four walls, its margins. To expose them to light and to eyes means to topple the walls and ceiling" (Jabès 23). As you enter this text, I begin to worry.

At times, I feel like the bemused compiler in Roa Bastos's *Yo/El Supremo*, piecing together scraps of text, cutting, pasting, and arranging the details of a moment that is already gone as I scramble to collect the traces left behind. The innocence of the compiler is a deceptive illusion. S/he, *yo/el-la*, is the archivist, the scribe, the transcriber, *la traductora*, the one who scribbles in the margins, the dictator. No matter how much I resist authority, I am everywhere implicated in this text. The languages I use are borrowed and flawed. They resist my intentions. Yet the words become mine. I am responsible for how I write this compilation of thoughts and ideas. You are responsible for how you read it. The people I write about are like me and unlike me in ways that may not always be clear to myself or to my readers. My own problematic claims to the names *güajira*, queer, transnational subject do not authorize me to speak about others whom I know or don't know. My experience does not authenticate me. Yet I do speak about others, clear in the knowledge that I am not speaking for them, that even if I give their words space, they are framed through a text of my creation, not their own. Still, I continue to interpret and write, always through the traces of other whispers and silences.

Do not believe everything I say. I am learning to feel at ease with ambiguity. Most of this text is not imaginative fiction, but it is a product of my critical imagination. The names and stories that unfold in these pages are haunted by their own shadows; they move in the web of language. Gerald Vizenor writes, "The meaning of words are determined by the nature of language games" (*Manifest* 72). This text is about language games and their consequences, the reality and the fictiveness of stories and storytellers. It is not about truth but about representations, not about inscription but about interpretations. As a critical and theoretical study, this text presupposes a

2

different sort of methodology, one that "refuses explication." Deborah Britzman writes,

> But perhaps you only hear a language game going on, a game of doubt, a narrative that tries to refuse narrativity, a non-narrative narrative. And if this is what you hear, perhaps you will be willing to think against your thoughts, to refuse the uncanny in your own practices, to suppose the equality of intellect in every encounter, to find things in common placed between two minds, to make a practice that refuses explication. (par. 22)

A "practice that refuses explication" demands that you, the reader, read against your preconceived notions of academic disciplinarity, research, language, and scholarship to reimagine the practice of knowledge production. Supposing the "equality of intellect in every encounter," together we will rewrite this text.

Translation as metaphor, as performance, as art form, as the perilous work of reading and writing across difference, haunts every utterance. The act of translation is a process of making legible a foreign symbolic order, of migrating across different dimensions of language, culture, and experience in the elusive search for mutual understanding. This text is not about representing communities or a set of subjects. I am more concerned with ways of looking than constructing credible objects of analysis. In the words of Peggy Phelan, I want "to construct a way of knowing which does not take surveillance of the object, visible or otherwise, as its chief aim" (1–2). Look for multiple, resistant, rhizomatic readings. This is not the text I intended to produce, and it is not the same as the text you are reading. Read the white spaces, hear the silences, peer into the shadows, look beyond the margins. Reach for "[t]hat voice at the edge of things" (Anzaldúa, *Borderlands* 50). I am there as well.

Divas, Atrevidas, y Entendidas

An Introduction to Identities

Identity is about situatedness in motion: embodiment and spatiality. It is about a self that is constituted through and against other selves in contexts that serve to establish the relationship between the self and the other. Places afford preexisting narratives of former encounters; they offer a means of symbolically decoding practices that occur within certain sociolinguistic frameworks. The subject brings to the encounter her own set of decoding practices that are mediated by the regulatory power of a particular discursive space, but not wholly determined by them. The discursive space does not establish which identity practices are available, but it does provide a frame through which these practices are received in that context. The subject's ability to subvert dominant readings is both unlimited and partial. The challenge becomes how to conceptualize subjectivity through both semiotic structures (discursive spaces) and agency (identity practices) by investigating the ways these fields work to constitute, inform, and transform one another.

Discursive spaces exist as sites of knowledge production. The clinic, the prison, the classroom construct fields of knowledge and have historically existed to define subjects. Discursive spaces need not be institutional, however; the chatroom, the bar, the street corner, the computer screen also serve to define subjects and construct knowledge practices. These spaces have their own linguistic codes and reading practices, as they engage in hiding and revealing their own internal contradictions. Objects, art, texts, buildings, maps can also create knowledge, change history, refigure language. Decentralizing the subject in space does not erase her significance; instead it highlights the process through which subjects negotiate a localized time-space framework of knowledge. This work takes as its sites of analysis three contemporaneous spheres of discourse where questions of identity are centrally operative and where the contradictions revealed by their articulation emerge and are negotiated: activism, law, and cyberspace. In each of these contexts, the question "What is identity?" becomes transformed into "What is identity for?" Under what circumstances is it constructed and whose interests does it serve?

In "Conjugating Subjects in the Age of Multiculturalism," Norma Alarcón articulates how discourses on difference and identity create knowledge about subjects and the ways subjects speak back to create new bodies of knowledge. She states that "[t]he paradoxes and contradictions between subject positions move the subject to recognize, reorganize, reconstruct, and exploit difference through political resistance and cultural productions in order to reflect the subject-in-process" (138). Identity, therefore, is not merely a response to culturally defined differences, but is continually engaged in unpacking the stream of "paradoxes and contradictions" that inform the subject's relationship to other subjects and the discourses that surround them. Subjects mobilize identities and are in turn mobilized by those identity constructions. In a way, Alarcón's essay rearticulates the question "What is identity for?" by making central the implications for the competing discourses on "essentialism," "identity-in-difference," "multiculturalism," and the "cultural politics of difference." Drawing on the work of other feminists of color, she suggests that no single term or construct can fully inscribe the historically marginalized subject whose theoretical existence, insights, and ideologies have been "thought out from the site of displacement" (136). Instead, she states that many feminists of color are engaged in a politics of "not yet" as a response to the multiple attempts to determine their subjectivity, even as they construct provisional identities, or what Chela Sandoval names "tactical subjectivities." Alarcón's own term, "subject-in-process," simultaneously moves past the centrality and universality of the unified bourgeois subject or "man" and makes explicit the process through which individuals negotiate the critical terrains that attempt to fix the subject and "produce structures and discourses of containment that resist change" (137). The term "subject-in-process" does not insinuate a progressional, unidirectional development; instead the process is often spastic and unpredictable, continually unfolding without origin or end, an act of becoming that never ceases. Implicit in her method is the need to situate both the subject and the discourses surrounding subjectivity within a specific sociohistorical and geopolitical context, or what she names a "situated contemporaneous horizon of meanings" (137).

Discourse provides the context and the methodology through which both identity and this "horizon of meanings" can be interrogated. Subjects are continually involved in negotiating the accumulated narratives of identity that circulate within these localized "horizons of meanings" and the contradiction revealed within their articulations. Chela Sandoval describes this practice of negotiating "between and amongst" different discourses of identity and resistance as "differential consciousness," an activity that "U.S. third world feminists" have developed and deployed as a response to hegemonic structures. She writes,

> Differential consciousness is comprised of seeming contradictions and difference, which then serve as tactical interventions in the other mobility that is power. . . . Entrance into this new order requires an emotional commitment within which one experiences the violent shattering of the unitary sense of self, as the skill that allows a mobile identity to form takes hold. (225–26n. 25)

7

Identity is slippery stuff. The practices through which subjects construct identity are never singular. We move and speak in ever shifting contexts of meaning. The community forum, the courtroom, the Internet chatroom, the departmental meeting each shape how we talk about ourselves and interpret the words of others. We are continually being read; subjectivity becomes an object of interpretation. There is always an excess that destabilizes, transmutes, or coalesces what we think we know about ourselves or those around us. Manifestations of identity can be mapped within specific fields of knowledge, but cannot be contained by them.

In *The Archeology of Knowledge*, Foucault delineates archeology as a method of investigation. "In archeological analysis comparison is always limited and regional. Far from wishing to reveal general forms, archeology tries to outline particular configurations" (157). As a method, archeology takes theory and practice as simultaneous, with neither one as a preexisting condition or construction. Discourse does not uncover objects, it constitutes them, it takes as its object of analysis that which "'contains thought' in a culture," not a history of that thought or culture itself (*Foucault Live* 9). In this book promotional flyers, legal testimony, and Internet transcripts become the unruly subjects of academic investigation. Yet it is precisely their unsanctioned status as objects of inquiry that opens up interpretive possibilities for the representation of queer *latinidad*, as they announce the contradictory contours of the discursive spaces in which they emerge.

In defining the practice of archeological analysis, Foucault incessantly engages the site of contradiction as a nexus of knowledge.

> By taking contradictions as objects to be described, archeological analysis does not try to discover in their place a common form or theme, it tries to determine the extent and form of the gap that separates them. In relation to a history of ideas that attempts to melt contradictions in the semi-nocturnal unity of an overall figure, or which attempts to transmute them into a general, abstract, uniform principle of interpretation

or explanation, archeology describes the different *spaces of dissension.* (*Archeology* 152)

Not to be understood as merely the location of resistance, these "spaces of dissension," sites of contestation, unmask the process of effacement that makes both hegemonic and oppositional discourses appear unified and whole. The sites I have selected for analysis are not to be read as exceptional or unique instances of these contradictory spasms that yield new forms of knowledge; spaces of dissension sprout everywhere. My goal is to document the processes through which these moments of rupture are articulated and mobilized. Feminists of color have established the numerous ways that contentious oppositional discourses such as feminism, civil rights, and cultural nationalism have maintained themselves through erasure and the melding of contradictions (Alarcón; Lorde; Moraga). Similarly, it is these "spaces of dissension" within oppositional discourses that productively trouble the waters of queer *latinidad.*

Que(e)rying *Latinidad*

> *La búsqueda de América Latina: entre el ansia de encontrarla y el temor de no reconocerla.* (Ansaldi)

I borrow the title of Waldo Ansaldi's text, "The search for Latin America, between the angst of finding her and the fear of not recognizing her," to suggest what it may mean to speak of queer *latinidad.*[1] The spastic contradictions and wild paradoxes of bodies and sites, identities and spaces intersecting are exemplified by the juxtaposition of these two terms, both provisional and immediate. Before attempting to unravel the implications and disjunctures of their union, let me turn first to the problematics involved in the construction of *latinidad.* Here different discourses of history, geography, and language practices collide. *Latinidad* serves to define a particular geopolitical experience but it also contains within it the complexities and contradictions of immigration, (post)(neo)colonialism, race, color, legal status, class, nation, language, and the politics of location.[2] So what constitutes *latinidad*? Who is Latina? Is *latinidad* in the blood, in a certain geographic space? Is it about language, history, and culture, or is it a certain set of experiences?

The most common response to the question "Who is a Latina?" relies on a geographic reference. Contemporary maps of Latin America begin with México and end with the islands at the tip of Chile, with the Antilles cradled between the land masses of the north and south. Under this rubric a Latina would be a woman from Latin America, or of Latin American descent. Geographical namings, however, are constructed by history and politics, ignoring both the national boundaries of México before the 1848 Treaty of Guadalupe Hidalgo and the marginalized Indigenous ethnic communities throughout the Américas that refuse to be subsumed by occupying nation-states. The Mayans struggling for autonomy in Chiapas consider themselves culturally and politically separate from México; does that also constitute a separateness from the larger category of *latinidad*? What about the Indigenous tribes of the southwestern United States? Many tribal members (including those with Spanish surnames) reject a Chicano identity in favor of a Native one. How are national, ethnic, and cultural definitions of identity deployed within different geopolitical sites? How do these different deployments of identity contradict and inform one another?

National identity offers the most immediately available identity category for most Latin Americans, yet it also contains within it the contradictions inherent in any national project. Guillermo Gómez-Peña uses the example of Tijuana as a site "where so-called Mexican identity breaks down—challenging the very myth of national identity" (Fusco 156). A Mexican identity as such only makes sense outside a Mexican context. It is the experience of having to define one's sense of self in opposition to dominant culture that forces the creation of an ethnic/national identity that is then readable by the larger society. "Mexican" is a term that most English speakers understand; *Lacan-*

don, chilanga, or *norteño* is not. The myth of harmonious Mexican national-ism that masks ethnic and social multiplicity and conflict is reconsolidated on the other side of the border, often as a form of resistance to dominant Anglo-American culture. The constant translation between spaces is never absolute. The imposed necessity for "strategic essentialism," reducing iden-tity categories to the most readily decipherable marker around which to mo-bilize, serves as a double-edged sword, cutting at hegemonic culture as it rein-scribes nation/gender/race myths on both sides of the border.

En el norte, Mexican identity can be again transformed to become Chicana identity. This new naming and its transmutations, Xicana and Xicaindia, make a claim from outside the space of national identity to assert a new cul-ture born of Mexican, Anglo, and Indigenous hybridity. It also serves as a claim against U.S. occupation of Mexican and/or Indigenous lands; for many Chicanas/os the states of the U.S. Southwest are their ancestral lands. These are complex and contradictory claims, however: one cultural, articulated through a discourse of *mestizaje*; one tribal, grounded in the language of sov-ereign tribal rights. Manifestations of Chicano cultural nationalism usually invoke an Indigenous past to reclaim a mythical formation of the nation of Aztlán, but it is a path most often traced through the various incarnations of a Mexican nation-state.

The possibility of a "cultural identity" as a means of escaping the bonds of a univocal "national identity" may seem particularly useful for under-standing *Chicanismo* and the cultural formations of other dislocated ethnic communities. Etienne Balibar writes, "[w]hat is called cultural identity is constantly compared to and at the limit conflated with *national identity*, and nevertheless is in some sense 'sheltered' from the empirical existence of na-tions, their borders, their politico-military history" (177). The relationship between these terms is further complicated by the relationship between the nation and the state, because "in practice, individuals 'encounter' the na-tion through the state (through an at least *possible* state) that 'represents' it, through the state's institutions" (Balibar 177–78). The problem of how "cultural identity" is consolidated and written through and against other

11

discourses of nations, states, languages, and bodies, however, remains open to contradictory impulses and practices of erasure.

Questions of the history and implications of *mestizaje, mulatismo*, and their resistance and collusion with state and national narratives seem particularly relevant here and further complicate easy notions of cultural identity. These terms have often served as a means to construct a cultural identity in opposition to stratified colonial Anglo/Spanish/Indigenous/African formations, as well as a way to speak about our multihued families constructed through biology and affiliation. Yet racialized markings continue to serve as discrete and interrelated emblems that inform our individual locations within these familial and social *mestizo* constellations. Terms such as *pelo bueno* (good hair), which is straight or only slightly waved, and *pelo malo* (bad hair), which is kinky or tightly curled; *facciones finas* (fine features), particularly a thin pointed nose and narrow lips; *pies de indio* (Indian feet), used to describe feet that are wide and flat rather than thin and arched; *mancha de plátano* (plantain stain), visually marked as *mestizo*, serve as localized cultural codes for gradations of racialized bodies in Latin/o American vernaculars, retaining the colonial valorization of Europeans.

Spanish speakers, however, have a much richer vocabulary for characterizing physical appearance than do Anglo-Americans, and racial signifiers are often employed and read without biased intent. At times, words such as *negra* or *mulato* are used as generic names for woman and man regardless of the skin color of the referent. Yet these words possess powerful shadows that can be read and received only in context. *Mi negrita* can sound like the embrace of a mother or lover's voice, or as an echo of ownership and servitude. Other times racialized names like La India (the name of the popular Nuyorican *salsera*), El Gallego, El Chino, El Gringo come to replace given names, or to serve as a suffix to personal names. Yet El Gringo can refer to a Latino who merely "looks" like a gringo; El Gallego can be from Sevilla or be a descendent of any region of Spain; El Chino can in reality be Japanese or *mestizo*.[3] These names or nicknames are not predetermined identifying labels, but descriptive or metaphorical representations that emerge and circulate in the context of the familial and the familiar. These names illustrate the linguistic incorporation of the cultural consequences of centuries of immigration and *mestizaje*, but also signal their transformation and resignification within these sites.

In the service of nation building and cultural nationalism, however, *mestizaje* and *mulatismo* can effect the illusion that previous colonial racial categories are no longer operative. Coco Fusco writes,

> It is a cliché to say that Latin America has resolved its problems of identity. What has actually happened is that the state has created ideologies that propose solutions to the problem of identity, but those solutions always occlude the existence of marginalized groups who are not part of the "national project." In this sense, we cannot think that everyone in Cuba, Mexico, or Puerto Rico identifies with the official celebration of *mestizaje*. Things get even more complicated when we take into account that the official notion of *mestizaje* is connected to concepts of nationality and territoriality. (163)

Often both popular and official projects of *mulatismo* and *mestizaje* have been used to flatten or subsume differences, reinscribe margins, and uphold whiteness.[4] As with national identity, these cultural identities are very often grounded in hetero-masculinist narratives and highly stratified categories of racialized gender.[5]

Within a Caribbean context the anomalies posed by a Latina/o "cultural identity" seem to multiply. If Dominicanas are Latinas, are Haitianas? Geographically they share the same island, *el mismo caribe*. And what can we say about those multilingual islands that defy easy classification: Aruba, Curaçao, Trinidad, are they part of *el mundo Latino*? Even when we think of South and Central America, do we forget the English- and Creole-speaking countries of Guyana, Surinam, and Belize, or the polylingual regions of Nicaragua, Costa Rica, and Panamá? How do we categorize the huge Portuguese-speaking anomaly of Brazil? If we decide that Spanish or at least a shared linguistic "Latin" heritage is the common thread that unites us, it is a precarious thread indeed. Clearly there are other official and unofficial languages spoken in Latin/o America and the Caribbean: Quechua, Aymara, Guaraní, French, Hindi, Creole, Lucumi, Papiamento, and English, to name a few. These languages remind us of the Indigenous past before successions of European colonizers, African enslavement afterwards, and centuries of transnational migration.

Perhaps it is precisely this shared legacy of Iberian colonization, massacres of Indigenous peoples, and slavery that defines *latinidad*. Yet Spain and Portugal also spread their colonial seeds elsewhere, in the Philippines, the Canary Islands, Cape Verde, Morocco, Macao, Mozambique, Guinea Bissau, and Angola, for example. In México, the mixture of Indigenous and Spanish blood is considered *mestizo*, yet in the Philippines this same mixture is considered Asian. Italians or Spaniards who immigrate to New York are considered European, but if they or their families migrate first to Argentina, Puerto Rico, or Venezuela and then come to New York, they are considered Latinos. What happens along the way? The cultural fusion of African and Portuguese brought about through enslavement may be considered Latino in Brazil, yet the same combination in Cape Verde is considered . . . something else.[6]

While much can be said about the particularities of Iberian colonialism versus the experiences of colonies under British, French, or Dutch rule, it is necessary to also consider the impact of serial colonialism. Brazil was under Dutch rule before being conquered by the Portuguese. Jamaica was a Spanish territory before becoming a British colony. The Philippines and Puerto Rico were Spanish colonies before they became U.S. territories. And of course, vast segments of the continental United States were previously claimed by the French, the Spanish, and México. National expansion, conquest, and annexation also meant successive tribal deterritorialization for Indigenous peoples throughout the Américas. These complex historical legacies intrude upon facile distinctions based on colonial characteristics as they shed light on a much longer narrative of multilingualism, transnational migration, and colonial geographic imaginings.

Ironically, several regions of the Iberian Peninsula also make claims to being unwilling subjects of Spanish colonialism and conquest. Euskal Herria, the Basque region that crosses the border between French and Spanish states, is home to an indigenous language, Euskera, of unascertained origin, and a cultural tradition rich in pre-Christian iconography and mythology. During the years of the Franco dictatorship, Basques suffered the violent repression of their indigenous culture, language, and traditions. Today certain Basque nationalist factions are engaged in political and armed rebellion for self-determination and autonomy from an occupying Spanish state. Populations in Galiza, Catalunya and Euskal Herria make varying claims for a cultural and linguistic identity separate from an imposed, culturally Castilian, Spanish nationalism, which has historically attempted to consolidate itself precisely through colonialism and conquest.[7] Castilian, or *castellano*, is the language of empire; however, in most of Latin/o America it is commonly referred to as *español*, or Spanish, evidencing the conflation of language and nation achieved through the colonial project. Certainly, not all *vascos*, *gallegos*, and *catalanes* imagine themselves as colonial subjects. The very means by which imperial mandates operate create the conditions where collaboration, assimilation, and contestation as strategies of survival become absorbed as defining features of the colonizing project. Nevertheless, it appears that Iberian colonialism has created a web of cultural influence and domination many times larger than any recognizable concept of *latinidad*.

In the Américas the most glaring example of overt colonial occupation continues to be Puerto Rico, and here again the responses to that occupation represent a spectrum of political strategies. Unlike Chicanos and immigrants from Latin America, whose passage to ancestral or familial homeland is closely guarded by the U.S. border patrol, Puerto Ricans in the United States have unrestricted migratory access to their *isla del encanto*, allowing them to enjoy second-class citizenship both on and off the island. In the case of Puerto Rico, physical geography itself functions as an influential feature of political and cultural ideology. A clearly delineated national identity may be easier to maintain in a small island state than in a larger territory with politically determined borders. Yet the proximity of the various islands of the Caribbean has also resulted in a long history of inter-island migration before, during, and after colonization. Today, Haitians cross the border to cut sugarcane in the Dominican Republic, Dominicans arrive illegally to work as domestics and laborers in Puerto Rico, Puerto Ricans journey north in search of new opportunities.

Yet, particularly within the existing climate of anti-immigrant legislation, Puerto Rico's unique political status vis-à-vis the United States continues to be a heated topic of debate. Though Puerto Ricans hold U.S. citizenship, and thus U.S. passports, and can be drafted into the U.S. military, they cannot vote in federal elections. National plebiscites where residents have been asked to decide whether the island should remain an Estado Libre Asociado (ELA) (Commonwealth), be annexed to the United States as the fifty-first state, or gain national independence have been held in 1967, 1993, and most recently in 1998. Celina Romany writes,

> Being neither here nor there, the repeated attempts to redefine the Estado Libre Asociado turn into a pitiful circus, culminating in the *circus maximus* featuring the plebiscite bill. . . . Being neither here nor there, those from *over here* clamor for a ticket to the circus with a passion that wilts in the struggle for participation in the American political process, which daily confirms their second-class citizenship, while those *over there*, staggering in the peculiar ambiguity brought on by colonial hurricane winds, claim the show is sold out. (95)

The national performance of voting in plebiscites enacts the illusion that political self-determination is fundamentally possible and disregards the festering historical and economic currents that determine the available options. The three major political parties in Puerto Rico break down precisely along the lines of the island's status. The Partido Nuevo Progresista (PNP) (New Progressive Party) advocates statehood, the Partido Popular Democrático (PPD)

(Popular Democratic Party) supports maintaining the status quo as an Estado Libre Asociado, and the Partido Independentista Puertorriqueño (PIP) (Puerto Rican Independence Party) supports autonomous independence. In the 1998 plebiscite two new options were made available: Libre Asociación (Free Association), which represents a new alternative, an independent republic associated politically with the United States, and Ninguna de las Anteriores (None of the Above), which came to be known as *la quinta columna*, or fifth column. This fifth option ultimately won the elections with 50.2 percent of the vote.[8] The paradoxical success of None of the Above and the addition of a new option, Free Association, represent an insistence on rejecting previously imagined solutions. These serve as another example of the articulation of a politics of "not yet" as a response to the existing political strategies for national self-definition.[9]

Just as Chicano identity contains an implicit reminder of U.S. occupation of Mexican lands, Puerto Ricans *en la isla* and in the United States create identities from within the space of U.S. colonization, *en la guagua aérea* of Puerto Rican migration.[10] The geographic distance that separates Puerto Rico from the United States implies a gulf of difference relative to language, culture, environment, and political and economic power. And Puerto Rican identity, whether defined culturally or nationally, must invariably confront the deterritorializing implications of colonization and migratory displacement. In his essay "'What a Tangled Web!' Masculinity, Abjection, and the Foundations of Puerto Rican Literature in the United States," Arnaldo Cruz-Malavé uses the canonical or foundational texts of Nuyorican literature to argue that it "has been written from this *des-tierro*, this landlessness/this banishment, this river of abjection" (237).

These elements—geographic and cultural displacement, desire and rage directed at the colonial metropolis, and the "ruined" formations of a disenfranchised national identity—are central to Nuyorican or Diasporican subject formation. Cruz-Malavé documents how these features of identity often come to be articulated in Nuyorican literary texts through the figure of the male homosexual.

No wonder, then, the insistence on homosexuality in these texts. And if it is true that their characters and poetic personae desperately try to overcome that reversible and ghostly condition that simultaneously emblematizes homosexual practices and the Nuyorican condition, it is also true that they must assume it, incorporate it. . . . To validate masculinity with its ruin, to submit to sodomy, to "buggery," in order to construct a male national identity, there's the paradoxical foundational project that Nuyorican texts set for themselves. (240)

This *des-tierro* is also evident on the island as decades of U.S.-orchestrated unemployment and federal dependence, the imposition of English as the second official language of Puerto Rico, forced emigration resulting from past and present U.S. labor policies, U.S. military presence on the island, and disproportionately high Puerto Rican participation in the U.S. armed services continually remind island residents of the material and cultural consequences of their colonial status. Like the main characters in the texts described by Cruz-Malavé, Puerto Ricans here and there are continually getting "fucked" and "fucked over" by the United States.[11]

This metaphor of sexual submission and conquest echoes the Mexican narratives of la Malinche, the emblematic courtesan and translator of Cortés, who came to be known as *la chingada*, or she who gets fucked.[12] Translation, and particularly the role of women and children as translators, is invariably enmeshed in these narratives of colonialism and conquest.[13] By mediating the space of linguistic difference, translators have often been the symbolic messengers of linguistic and cultural domination. This constant process of mediation is further complicated in a contemporary context by the increasing global mandate of English as the official language of business, scholarship, and international diplomacy, highlighting the relationship between access to language and access to knowledge and power. Bilingualism, or multilingualism, is both a site of privilege that creates access to different discourses and a mark of difference within the English monolingualism of the U.S. state, and very often within the Spanish monolingualism of our own families. The process of translation involves more than merely translating languages, it involves translating cultures, values, and institutions of power. Multiple, syncretic, simultaneous, contradictory translations of languages and cultures form part of the daily strategies most Latinos/as in the U.S. use to navigate the spaces of work, school, neighborhoods, and families.[14]

The question of language and colonization is further complicated within a U.S. context by displacement resulting from generations of immigration—the contemporary cultural consequences of continued U.S. military, economic, and political interests in Latin America or, in the case of Puerto Rico, overt U.S. occupation.[15] Latinas/os in the United States speak or don't speak Spanish, other native languages, and standard English with vastly varying degrees of proficiency. Languages, already accented by regional, cultural, and class differences, become transformed in a U.S. context through their interaction with other languages, accents, and regionalisms.[16] Spanglish in New York's South Bronx is related to the Spanglish of East L.A. only by a shared rejection of "pure" standards of both Spanish and English and the linguistic positionality brought about through (dis)placement.

Rather than a claim to geography or language, others claim *que lo Latino se conoce,* it is an essence that is evident in how we look, talk, dance, eat, play. Is *latinidad* really that easy to spot? How many times have we heard, "She doesn't look Latina"? Who is visible or invisible as a Latina? There are more persons of African descent in South America than in North America, but just how visible are Afro-Latinos in representations of Latina/o communities? In Latino *telenovelas* dark-skinned actors are either invisible or depicted as maids, cooks, and the occasional *santera* or *curandera*, fulfilling the exoticized role of dark spiritual healer for light-skinned protagonists. In the Latin/o American entertainment media, Afro-Latinas/os are visible as singers, athletes, or talk show guests (everyone loves Celia Cruz and Pelé) but rarely as announcers, commentators, or central protagonists. Even in Cuba, which has an established history of at least articulating dialogue on intranational racial politics, media depictions continue to present light-skinned Cubans as the "generic" representative of the nation and Afro-Cubans as something apart. This has led to what one filmmaker, Pin Vilar, describes as "'*negrome-traje*' (black footage): where blacks are depicted in historically specific stories, where race is a central theme . . . but nowhere else" (Mosak 29), perpetuating the centrality of the light-skinned Creole in narratives of *cubanismo*.[17] But aside from daily instances of visual erasure, much of the programming on Spanish-language international stations also recirculates images of shuffling characters in blackface. On the internationally popular show *Sábado Gigante*, broadcast on Univisión, these racially cross-dressed characters make routine appearances, as do "Indians" in full "warpaint" regalia and stereotypical, heavily accented "Confucius"-type characters.

In U.S. media productions depicting Latinos, the circulation of these racialized stereotypes operates on a somewhat different register, attempting to balance the allure of the foreign and exotic with the intelligibility of the familiar as it tries to market itself to both a growing U.S. Latino consumer market and non-Latino audiences. The internationally recognized Afro-Cuban singer Celia Cruz, for example, appears in small acting roles in the movies *The Mambo Kings* and *The Perez Family*, both times playing a *santera*.[18] Meanwhile the current Latin boom in music and film has permitted only the crossover of lighter-skinned performers, and here again almost always within the most sexualized and exoticized terms. Successful dark-skinned Latino actors or musicians are often routinely categorized as African American, ignoring their Latino connections.

In advertisements for North American and European tourist dollars, however, *mulatas* and dark-skinned women play a pivotal role in selling the sexualized exoticism of the Caribbean and the sexual fantasy of a racialized servitude.[19] As Marta Moreno Vega so clearly articulates, within U.S. Latino and Latin American communities, "[t]he image of Black and mulata women remains the sexual, animalistic, primitive creature of desire who is ready to be seduced" (79). Similarly, light-skinned Latinas often fail to fulfill exoticized racial expectations and must therefore continually confront challenges to their status as "authentic" Latina subjects. The intricacies of racialized color, hair, and facial features continue to culturally, socially, and economi-

cally stratify both Latin American and U.S. Latino communities.[20] Not surprisingly, many Afro-Latinas in the U.S. also experience the "tug-of-war" between the competing demands of U.S. African American political and cultural movements, Latino movements, and queer and feminist formations.
The poet and performance artist Avotcja writes,

> Most of the trouble has come from a little tug of war between the self-ap-
> pointed messiahs of the weekend revolution and the self-appointed mes-
> siahs of the Black revolution and the white women's revolution each of
> them trying to claim me and pull me apart into little pieces. . . . I'm not
> ownable. I can't divide myself into different pieces. I'm not only a les-
> bian, but also a Rican who happens to be a Black woman. (14)

This passage, published in 1987, speaks directly to the power of discourse to
lay claim to the body, to "pull [it] apart into little pieces," and voices the resistance to that ownership. The wording of the final sentence is also significant, "not only a lesbian . . . who happens to be . . . " suggests that there is
much more of herself than can be contained by these categories or even articulated in her own self-representation.

Latin America and the Caribbean are also home to large diverse Jewish,
Arab, and Asian communities, yet almost every Latina lesbian event includes
un homenaje a la Virgen, the implied assumption being that all Latinas are or
were Catholic.[21] How are Muslim, Jewish, atheist, or Buddhist Latinas made
invisible within these Latina lesbian imaginaries? How do women of mixed
or multiple cultural heritages negotiate the contradictions and paradoxes of
language, ancestry, homeland, and community involved in the deployment
and displacement of identity?[22]

Identity is more than a list of categories that name our sexuality, gender,
HIV status, nation, age, ethnicity, ability, class, language, citizenship status,
and religion. Even if we expand the list to include all the other significant
features of ourselves, what do these attributes actually explain about our
lives? What aspects of identity exceed the categories we have created to

define our places in the world? How do memories of desire and violence mark us in ways that are similar and different from the ways we have been marked by color and gender? How do street corners and kitchen tables, friends and lovers, lullabies and taunts, private violations and public betrayals leave traces on our lives? How do the many moments of our daily existence determine how we view ourselves and the world around us?

Deleuze describes a method of rhizomatic reading and writing that seems particularly useful here. Like the omnipresent *yucas, malangas,* and *boniatos* of my homeland, a rhizome can be broken at any point and will sprout anew along old lines or create new "line[s] of flight."[23] "The rhizome is reducible neither to the One nor the multiple. . . . It is composed not of units but of dimensions, or rather directions in motion. It has neither beginning nor end, but always a middle [*milieu*] from which it grows and which it overspills" (35–36). A rhizomatic reading of *latinidad* suggests the process through which contested constructions of identity work to constitute one another, emphasizing "and" over "is" as a way to think about differences. So *latinidad* is about the "dimensions" or "the directions in motion" of history and culture and geography and language and self-named identities. Even if individual narratives used to chart these discourses contradict or exclude one another, the site of rupture will itself serve as a new site of knowledge production. Of these seeming contradictions, Foucault writes, "they are not two contradictory propositions about the same object, they are not two incompatible uses of the same concept, but two ways of forming statements, both characterized by certain objects, certain positions of subjectivity, certain concepts, and certain strategic choices" (*Archeology* 153). The contradictions revealed in the various constructions of *latinidad* in fact provide the site of intervention where "the ways of forming statements," the "positions of subjectivity, certain concepts, and certain strategic choices" can begin to be a source of new meanings.

Yet an understanding of the complexities embedded within *latinidad* also makes certain strenuous demands on readers. It calls on what VèVè Clark has described as diaspora literacy and *marasa* consciousness. She defines diaspora literacy as

> a skill for both narrator and reader which demands a knowledge of historical, social, cultural, and political development generated by lived and textual experience. Throughout the twentieth century, diaspora literacy has implied an ease and intimacy with more than one language, with interdisciplinary relations among history, ethnology, and the folklore of regional expression. (42)

Like Clark's *marasa* consciousness, which "invites us to imagine beyond the binary" (43), Anzaldúa's *mestiza* consciousness breaks down the fictions of duality. Anzaldúa does not impose a unity of interpretation, although she suggests a cosmic unity that joins all things, just as Clark's *marasa* consciousness "depends largely on our capacities to read the sign as a cyclical, spiral relationship" (43). Both authors attempt to transcend duality by not only embracing contradiction and ambivalence, but also using them to challenge and transform systems of categorization. Anzaldúa describes the *mestiza* consciousness as "a creature of darkness and a creature of light, but also a creature that questions the definitions of light and dark and gives them new meanings" (81); a constant process of translation and transformation, a movement through and against sites of knowledge. The *mestiza* consciousness she describes is born of hybridity and cross-pollination. She writes, "[t]he work of *mestiza* consciousness is to break down the subject-object duality that keeps her a prisoner and to show in the flesh and through the images in her work how duality is transcended" (80). Anzaldúa invites us to not only "sustain contradictions," but to turn "ambivalence into something else" (79).

Queer Namings

This is not the beginning. I began this chapter with the words *divas, atrevidas, y entendidas*. These are the words, full of *cariño*, that I use for the queer people I love, the queer person I am.[24] *Divas* are a breathing, swishing, eruption of the divine, a way of being in the world, of claiming power as movement, glances, voice, body, and style. *Atrevidas* dare to fulfill desire, challenge assumptions the world has given us. *Entendidas* share a knowledge, understand the significance and nuances of queer subaltern spaces. These identities are rich and real for me. They resonate with an attitude that steps beyond sexual practice or sexual identity into the realm of a politicized passion for liberation and empowerment. These terms also mark a language that is foreign to dominant linguistic norms. They are culturally specific in ways that are not about a discourse of nation or blood but about the language of barrios and bars. *Divas, atrevidas, y entendidas* are all gendered in the feminine, yet they are available to whoever dares to occupy them. In Spanish, there is no direct translation for "queer." These words speak to something that is both the same as and different from "queer": attitude, defiance, knowledge, the excesses of categories.

This breaking down of categories, questioning definitions and giving them new meaning, moving through spaces of understanding and dissension, working through the critical practice of "refusing explication" is precisely what queerness entails. "Queer" is not simply an umbrella term that encompasses lesbians, bisexuals, gay men, two-spirited people, and transsexuals; it is a challenge to constructions of heteronormativity. It need not subsume the particularities of these other definitions of identity; instead it creates an opportunity to call into question the systems of categorization that have served to define sexuality. There is already something "queer" about categories such as lesbian or gay, "inclusive disjunctures" that simultaneously employ speech and silences on sexual practice, desire, identification, anatomy, gender, community, and dare I say love.

In *Bodies That Matter*, Judith Butler analyzes the critical uses of "queer" and the implications raised by its deployment. She argues that while "it is necessary to assert political demands through recourse to identity categories, and to lay claim to the power to name oneself and determine the conditions under which that name is used, it is also impossible to sustain that kind of mastery over the trajectory of those categories within discourse" (*Bodies* 227). We may deploy language and categories but we can never fully possess them.

> If the term "queer" is to be a site of collective contestation, the point of departure for a set of historical reflections and futural imaginings, it will have to remain that which is, in the present, never fully owned, but always and only redeployed, twisted, queered from a prior usage and in the direction of urgent and expanding political purposes. (*Bodies* 228)

The deployment of language as an identity practice only becomes accentuated when it steps across linguistic and cultural boundaries. Butler questions how "'queer' plays—or fails to play—within non-white communities" (*Bodies* 228). Yet, for most Latinas/os living in the United States, the appropriation of language for our own uses forms part of the rituals of survival. Like "queer," the words Chicano, Pocho, and Nuyorican entered the vernacular with decidedly negative connotations, which were then appropriated and transformed within these communities. Queer becomes but one more in a series of terms we can employ to define ourselves. There are others, each ripe with possibilities. *Entender*, literally "to understand," has long served as a code word to define those who are "in the know." In their introduction to *¿Entiendes? Queer Readings, Hispanic Texts*, Bergmann and Smith write of the term,

> "Understanding" is clearly a cultural, not a natural category: it cannot take place outside of defined social structures. It is also a matter of knowing, rather than being: a woman or a man can be married and straight identified, but still be "wise" to same-sex culture. Finally, it is not an identity but an activity, requiring at least two partners in order to take place.
>
> Hence, both in the written texts of queer activism and in the oral tradition of lesbian and gay slang, Spanish speakers may have anticipated the critique of identity and community implicit in much recent Anglo-American queer theory. (12)

The idea that understanding "requires at least two" suggests the relation-ality and relativity of sexually nuanced cultural knowledge as a practice that informs the interactions between the self and the other. *Entender* is a queer social practice of translating and interpreting sexual codes.

De ambiente is another term popular among Latinas/os within and outside the United States. Literally "of an ambiance or environment," it is a term that speaks to a larger sense of community and belonging, not of a specific sexual practice or identification. Comparable to the popular African American term "in the life," it suggests participation in a subaltern space that is coded by cul-tural knowledge, and sexual and social practice within specific communities. In certain circles, however, the term *de ambiente* has taken on a certain bour-geois connotation, a social identity associated more with the milieu of dis-cotheques and discrete private gatherings than with a politicized and visible street presence. This instability in meaning represents another instance of the ambiguous nuances of naming as a marker of political and individual identity.

Nevertheless, naming as an identity practice has a broad range of expres-sion in Spanish; the many words we call ourselves reflect an acquired ease with the manipulation and transformation of language. The highly gendered nature of Spanish also creates the possibility of code switching between mas-culine and feminine forms of address as a spontaneous critical and imagina-tive practice of queering language. Some particularly lyrical examples in-clude *tortillera*, from the image of making tortillas where a flipping is in-volved, as a metaphor for lesbian sixty-nine; *buchota*, a Spanglish version of butch; *marimacha*, from María and a feminization of *macho*, used for butch women or sometimes dykes in general; *mariquita*, ladybug, but also a diminu-tive form of *maricón*, faggot; *reina*, queen, but not necessarily a drag queen, as it is also used as a term of endearment within and outside queer contexts; *bollera*, from *bollo*, which means a bread roll in most of Latin America but in Cuba it also means vagina; the suffix "*era*" as in *tortillera* implies an agent and is used for practitioners of female-to-female sex, possibly also suggesting a meatless sandwich; *maricona*, dyke or faggot, a feminization of *maricón*, faggot; *vestida*, literally meaning "dressed," which is commonly used for drag queens; *papi*, daddy, which unlike its use in s/m communities, where it generally signals a specific sexual/social role, in Spanish is most often used as a term of endearment for a butch (male or female) lover or friend; the term *mami* is also a popular term of endearment applied without regard to biological sex in queer Latino communities, but similarly nuanced by gender. Latinas/os in the United States also make full use of English words such as butch, femme, dyke, faggot, drag queen, dramadiva, switch, top, daddy, leather mistress, do-me queen, and a plethora of other terms.

Political and social group names, past and present, also incorporate the playful and imaginative qualities of language. These include the now defunct transnational Latina lesbian magazine entitled *Esto No Tiene Nombre* (This Has No Name), but also meaning something fabulous or scandalous beyond words; El Closet de Sor Juana, a collective in Mexico City (The Closet of Sor Juana), a reference to the early Mexican feminist nun, Sor Juana Inéz de la Cruz, who is widely known for lesbian references in her work; Salpafuera, from *sal pa[ra] fuera* (come out, but also slang for a big to-do), a multigender collective in San Juan, Puerto Rico, which plays with Puerto Ricans' characteristic chopping off of final syllables or consonants; the name of an international Latina lesbian magazine, *conmoción*, means an emotional commotion, but also can be broken down to literally mean with motion; Brujas (witches) in Medellín, Colombia; Colectivo Gestación (Gestation Collective); the National Latina/o Lesbian and Gay Organization in Washington, DC, uses the acronym LLEGO, or "arrived"; *Musas de Metal* (Metal Muses), a women's radio program; the group Himen (Hymen) and its publication *LESVOZ* (pronounced Lesbos, which combines Les and *voz* [voice]), all in Mexico City and the now defunct CURAS: Comunidad Respondiendo a AIDS/SIDA (Community Responding to AIDS/SIDA) in San Francisco, the acronym drawing on the double meaning of the word *curas*, meaning healings and priests. These are conscious manipulations of oral and written language, which often reflect the specific cultural, ideological, and/or linguistic context in which they occur. For example, the Miami-based magazine *¡Perra!*

includes a definition of the word *perra* (literally a female dog or bitch) in its credits page:

> PERRA es . . . en nuestro español caribeño, una palabra de exaltación para todo aquello que sea fabulosamente atrevido. Puede ser perra alguien, una voz, un vestido, un peinado, una canción, un show, un logro o una expresión. Para leernos, ¡tienes que ser PERRA! (¡Perra! 2)
>
> (*PERRA is* . . . in our Caribbean Spanish, a word of exaltation for all that is fabulously daring. *Perra* can be a person, a voice, a dress, a hairdo, a song, a show, an act, or an expression. To read us, you must be *Perra!*)

The oral quality of the word itself also benefits from the Cuban propensity for accentuating rolling r's. Many of the groups also add a form of translation or subtitle to their names. For example, the magazine *¡Perra!* includes the descriptive phrase "Vida y cultura gay latina de Miami" (gay Latin life and culture of Miami). Not all names are as playful; for contrast let me also mention the group Seminario Marxista Leninista Lésbico Feminista de Guadalajara (Marxist Leninist Lesbian Feminist Seminar of Guadalajara).

Yet most group names employ imaginative linguistic play, creative gender twistings, and the subversive appropriations of previously negatively intoned words. They also demonstrate the narrative elements of naming and vividly illustrate naming as an identity practice. There are no easy equivalents, direct translations, or clear definitions for any of these terms, and in fact they reveal very little about the complexities of sexual desires and practices or the political postures of the groups they name. These words can only be read and understood in relation to the context in which they are articulated, and even then only partially. Samuel Delany writes, "Gay Identity . . . is an object of the context, not of the self—which means, like the rest of the context, it requires analysis, understanding, interrogation, even sympathy, but never an easy and uncritical acceptance" (32). That identity is "of the context [and] not of the self" highlights the interrelationality between sub-

ject position and the "situated contemporaneous horizon of meanings"—
bodies and sites.

Within this conceptualization of language, identity becomes an act of storytelling constructed through memory, naming, and shifting language practices. Lisa Kahaleole Chang Hall suggests,

> Gay men and lesbians are the people of drama. I have a theory that gay
> identity is really founded on storytelling and gossip, not sex, that in fact
> people often have sex so that they can talk about it. From the moment of
> that first entry into "the community" or "the life," we're embedded in a
> legendary network of gossip, tale-telling, and multiple interpretations of
> the same events. . . . Identity becomes an art form at times, a pastiche of
> meanings, affiliations, and self-parody that can be baroque. (229)

And identity as an "art form" always remains open to reinscription and rein-
terpretation.

Within the emerging field of queer Latino studies, critics of various disciplinary persuasions have been dutifully engaged in our own sets of identity
practices through our acts of interpretation, inscription, and naming. Institutional spaces, such as universities and publishing houses, are also discursive spaces where articulations of academic identity are framed within parameters that simultaneously demand both innovation and adherence to established norms. As academics, working within the liberal or limiting
confines of our specific departmental and disciplinary mandates, often we
have had to have our critical projects positioned within recognizable (and
tenurable) taxonomies of scholarship. Generally these investigations have
been received as discipline-specific: literature (Foster, Yarbro-Bejarano,) theater (Muñoz, Román), history (Chávez-Leyva, D. J. González).[25] Yet most of
these texts invariably bleed into other disciplinary contexts. In José Esteban
Muñoz's *Disidentifications*, performance is read through the texts of popular
culture, photography, and politics rather than solely through the scripts of
the theatrical stage. José Quiroga begins his text *Tropics of Desire* with Latin

American literature and deftly dances through readings of La Lupe and Ricky Martin to end on a discussion of local queer U.S. Latino politics. Whether in single-author texts or edited volumes on queer Latino sexuality and identity, traditional disciplinary boundaries become inadequate containers for subjects whose lives and utterances traverse the categories meant to contain them.[26]

This observation will surprise no one, and should not be misread as the result of a current academic trend toward dismantling traditional disciplines, but instead as an ongoing impulse toward a radical rethinking of taxonomies of knowledge. In years past, texts such as Moraga and Anzaldúa's *This Bridge Called My Back: Writings by Radical Women of Color* (1981) or Ramos's *Compañeras: Latina Lesbians (An Anthology)* (1987) were already rejecting established academic and literary precepts by combining personal essays, poetry, multilingual writing, history, and artwork that theorized the texts of lived experience. And much of the queer Latina scholarship that has responded to these creative intellectual movements has likewise been invested in the disruption of borders of genre, language, disciplinarity, and geography. Consider the 1984 article by Lourdes Arguelles and B. Ruby Rich, which critiqued the white gay media's accounts of the Mariel boatlift by analyzing émigré enclaves in the United States, Puerto Rico, México, and Spain, combining personal observation with Cuban cultural history and political and social analysis. Or more recently, Yarbro-Bejarano's essay "Crossing the Border with Chabela Vargas," which traverses geographies of Costa Rica, México, Spain, and the United States, combining close readings of visual images, lyrics, and musical history, to discuss the production and consumption of culturally gendered representations of the erotic. As an object of study, queer *latinidad* demands a practice that moves across geographic, linguistic, and imaginary borders, not simply because it is more provocative to do so, but because the very disciplines that divide Latin American from North American, music from literature, politics from performance, or queer studies from Latino studies have been based on paradigms constituted through our marginalization. My own text attempts to examine what happens when discourses of identity traverse these borders of inquiry. I consider disciplinary instability not as an inevitable consequence of queer Latina subjectivity, but as the underlying premise through which the complexities of identity can begin to be understood.

Bodies and Landscapes

The subjects presented in this text are all "subjects-in-process," yet my understanding and analysis can only be read as an attempt to assign meaning to subjectivity in practice, a moment that is frozen in a text and reemerges as a fluid substance through reading and interpretation. Like a series of photographs in a gallery, the chapters in this text bring bodies and landscapes together to explore how they work in unison to create the discursive effect of figures and shadows, stasis and movement, strategy and risk. Yet I also want to leave a space available for the insertion of that "something else" that eludes language, the spark-spirit-chi-soul that gives cadence to that which constitutes the excesses of subjectivity, the *mojo* that flavors rhizomatic intentions.[27] The effect of a complete picture is wholly illusionary. The configurations are intentional and self-serving; other combinations are present even through their omission. Each subsequent chapter approaches the task of naming spaces and practices differently. Each discursive space I depict carries with it a different opportunity to construct *latinidad* and queerness, to employ difference and contradiction "as tactical interventions in the other mobility that is power" (Sandoval 225 n. 25).

Like Quiroga, I find that

My interest is less in theorizing on the present state of gay studies than in moving about, creating a book that is a sort of traveling and movable object, one that shows and tells at the same time. I think this is the queer praxis that should animate gay and lesbian studies—the space where theory and practice meet in order to open new possibilities (8).

Yet this praxis also conditions a methodology that is grounded in an analysis of the demands each of these spaces places on the subject. Understanding how identity practices operate within these different sites requires a theory and practice that are both situated in a specific localized time-space framework and cognizant of the fact that each new combination of circumstances and readings will yield different interpretations. Each chapter functions as a case study of localized sites and practices—specific subjects engaged in negotiating a particular discursive space under a unique set of circumstances. The shift from one theoretical or disciplinary space to another "is not seamless; indeed, the interstice, the discontinuity, the gap is precisely a site of textual production: the historical and ideological moment in which the subject inscribes herself" (Alarcón, "Anzaldúa's" 44). In law, for example, subjects must conform to established rules that construct identity within a "single-axis analysis" that erases the "intersectionality" of mutually constructed discourses (Crenshaw 139–40). In the spastic spaces of the virtual world, imagination and language become the tools through which subjectivities are articulated. In the Internet chatrooms of cyberspace, if you can write it, you can be it, changing your ethnicity, gender, age, measurements, even species with a keystroke.

Within much postcolonial and poststructuralist criticism, space has replaced time as "the most important ordering concept of reality" (Ashcroft et al. 37). Questions of space and place are accentuated in the analysis of performance and agency. It is the time-space matrix that is most useful to an analysis of site-specific practices. Such an understanding requires an analysis of the relationships within and between different localized discursive sites, different disciplines, different sites of knowledge production. Thus capital, heteronormativity, (post)(neo)colonialism, the AIDS pandemic, patriarchy, and the postnuclear age must serve as the "contingent currents" of ideology or the ubiquitous frame that informs any localized practice.

In *Mapping the Subject*, Pile and Thrift chart the contemporary theoretical uses and definitions of space, location, the subject, and metaphors of movement and travel through the texts of British cultural studies. They also remind readers that the critical emphasis on routes and travel, nomads and exiles must be continually read against a landscape of economic, social, and political restraint and confinement. They argue that subjects are not preexisting but are derived in practice, a practice based on the specificities of place.

> [T]here is a major emphasis in theories of practice on the specificities of place. Particular contexts are crucial elements of the practical sense because dispositions have to be constantly tuned to the indeterminacy of each context, often in creative ways, so the "rule" never stays quite the same. In other words place is constitutive of the subject's understanding of the world. (29)

Their theorization of subjects derived in practice has resonance with Alarcón's "subject-in-process." They state that a subject's understanding comes from the "continuous flow of conduct through time and space constantly interpellating social structure" (3). Alarcón's analysis goes further, however, to claim that these interpellated social structures remain operative even if they fail to fully determine the boundaries of subjectivity or agency. She writes, "the very contingent currents through which the geopolitical subject-in-process is dislocated and forced into (im)migration will retain an irreducible difference that refuses to correspond neatly to the subject's account of herself and the theory we produce to account for her appearance" ("Conjugating" 138).

By focusing my study on discursive spaces (activism, law, and cyberspace), I complicate facile constructions of location, community, and positionality. These spaces have already been disciplined by the discourses that constitute them, and which create and cut off possibilities of identity practices. Each requires a different methodological practice for understanding the relationship between bodies and sites. Each chapter functions as a case study of a particular localized instance of subjects' engagement with a particular set of discursive and ideological (pre)conditions. The texts and sites I have selected are not meant to be either representative or exemplary. Instead, I have self-consciously chosen situations that illustrate the shifts, gaps, and fissures in discourses of identity. I begin with activism because most of the critical work on identity has focused on its political and strategic uses in the struggle to bring about social change. Political activism within queer Latina/o communities also provides insight into the larger social and historical context through which other articulations of identity can be read. Identity politics, for example, constitutes a body of knowledge with specific historical investments for marginalized groups in this country. I focus the chapter on activism on the work of Proyecto ContraSIDA por Vida (Project Against AIDS for Life), a Latina/o HIV prevention social service agency located in San Francisco's Mission District. Through an examination of its programming and cultural production, I reveal its seeming investment in both a deconstruction and a rearticulation of identity politics. I suggest that the agency is remapping identity as something that is "in-process" rather than knowable or definable through static categories.

The chapter on law forecloses the possibilities of playful crossings. Law is already set up as a rigid discursive site wherein performance and language practices are structured to create conclusions about identity. Here, the subject is continually being constrained by the mandates of legal discourses. The subject is obligated to perform, and performance exacts a price; the risk is carnal. The case under consideration involves a gay Brazilian living in San Francisco who seeks political asylum in the United States based on sexual persecution in his native country. The "real-life" significance of borders and nations is acted out in a courtroom drama while the narratives invoked resonate with other discourses of persecution and freedom, identity and practice, savagery and civilization.

The chapter on cyberspace explores the possibilities and implications offered by self-constructed online identities. Here identity is reduced and/or multiplied by the enactment of language practices. Cyberspace is assumed to be a place where identity is always under erasure; at the same time, it is a space that facilitates other formations and representations of identity. The fact that the virtual is by definition not the carnal is the limit that troubles both its possibilities and its limitations.

The space of place is itself a precarious ideological construction. Attempts to situate each of these chapters within specific localized sites require vastly different configurations of spatiality. In the chapter on activism, place is geographic: Proyecto ContraSIDA por Vida is located at a busy intersection in the heart of San Francisco's Mission District. It also suggests how the spaces of community and neighborhood function as sites of ideological contestation. For the chapter on law, place is reduced to the space of a courtroom, the exact site where the text of the narrative, the court transcript, is produced. Yet what Tenório's narrative chronicles is precisely the interstitial space of the refugee, a place that is neither here nor there but is nevertheless mired in narratives of north and south, the United States and Brazil, San Francisco and Rio de Janeiro. The virtual space of the Internet is seemingly nowhere and everywhere simultaneously, yet it is accessed through the personal space of my home computer. The terms "queer" and "Latina/o" also shift in meaning as they move through these sites, from the multiethnic, multicultural, multigender site of Proyecto ContraSIDA por Vida, to the specifics of a gay Afro-Brazilian immigrant from Rio de Janeiro, to my own queer femme interactions with the multinational, multigender, multilingual virtual world that sits at my desk. Each of these spaces creates and forecloses distinct identity and narrative practices.

Discursive spaces are not autonomous; they are permeable and heteroglossic. They seep into one another, contaminating and enriching ideas and disciplines. There is a continual movement as individuals, texts, and ideas migrate across spaces, informing and transforming knowledge production. Although each of the spaces I present provides a unique set of conditions for the performance of identity practices, there is also an overarching relationship between these domains of knowledge. Repressive laws work to create the political conditions for grassroots activism; activists utilize the tools of literature, theory, and art to counteract dominant representations;

new technologies are employed by all sides to disseminate information and images; scholarship reinscribes all of these practices with old and new meanings. The languages of activism, law, academia, and technology are never fully contained; instead they tunnel into one another, remapping the disciplinary terrains they encounter. There is an extensive intertextuality between and among these spaces and their inhabitants, community activists who are also undocumented residents, filmmakers who are also students, administrators who are also DJs, academics who are also sexualized virtual beings and embodied social dreamers.

My thesis contends that language practices exist in relation to the discursive spaces in which they occur. Therefore, my own narrative practice attempts to enact these shifts as it moves through the chapters from one discursive and disciplinary field to another. Each discursive site under consideration, and each corresponding chapter, performs its own definition of queer *latinidad*. As I document and enact the limits and possibilities each of these three spaces provides for the articulation of subjectivity, there is also a fourth discursive dimension at play: the language of academia itself. While at times I may appear to be pushing at its seams, this text remains immured by its trappings, bound to a set of investments that can never fully escape the hold of the institutions that authorize me as an academic subject. Rather than the facile disavowal or deprecation of the academic project, I want to suggest that it too can exist as a site of co-optation, collusion, resistance, and transformation. While throughout these pages I may seem to be documenting how others maneuver the discursive spaces of activism, law, and cyberspace, this text is also the product of my own negotiation of the contours of academic discourse, my own modest attempt to reenvision the prickly practice of scholarly inquiry.

Activism and Identity in the Ruins of Representation

> Our scholarship on AIDS must be located at the crossroads of art and politics, life and art, and life and death.
>
> *Alberto Sandoval-Sánchez*

Activism is an engagement with the hauntings of history, a dialogue between the memories of the past and the imaginings of the future manifested through the acts of our own present yearnings. It is an encounter with the ghosts that reside within and inhabit the symbolic and geographic spaces that shape our worlds. There are the great-great-grandmother ghosts, the crazed slave spirit that Patricia Williams finds embodied through the contracts of law; the ghosts of "Grandma's Story" that Trinh T. Minh-ha uses to redefine the power of narrative and storytelling, the *abuelitas* of *memoria* that link back to *bohíos* and *revolución*. In the tracks on the native woman, we carry her bundles in language: the myths and metaphors that circulate in our breath. We live with the shadow of a man.[1] There are ghosts without names: the sea ghosts of the Middle Passage and the island *balseros* who die in the coral graveyards of their ancestors; the ghost children of diseased colonial ventures that brought us smallpox, automatic weapons, and crack cocaine; the marked targets of the holocausts of ethnic cleansing, moral crusades, and national warfare; the poets, perverts, and dispossessed who leave the traces of their stories in the transcripts of state institutions: boarding schools, hospital wards, asylums, and execution chambers.

AIDS has surrounded us with the living memory of familiar ghosts, faces that haunt our intimate realities of being infected/not yet infected, sick/not yet sick, alive but not yet dead. As we wait for passage to the other side, we plan our revenge and chart strategies of resistance to head off the silence.

There have been a total of 23,176 persons diagnosed with AIDS in San Francisco from July 1981 through June 30, 1996. . . . Of all persons diagnosed with AIDS in San Francisco, 31%, or 7,104, are still living. (San Francisco HIV Prevention 95)

I do the math and conclude that there are at least 16,072 ghosts in San Francisco that inspire the current manifestations of AIDS-related activism, a convention of spirits that inhabit the spaces of resistance and survival. And the numbers continue to climb. (These are not the only ghosts that haunt us.) We have been summoned to the halls of death and charged with the ominous mission of bearing witness. The late Melvin Dixon, echoing the sentiments of others who came before and will leave after him, has entrusted us with the responsibility of memory and vision: "You, then, are charged by the possibility of your good health, by the broadness of your vision, to remember us" (46). Activism implies *coraje y corazón*, a willingness to listen to the voices and interpret their traces within new worlds of meaning. Yet ghosts are unruly subjects, unreliable informants. We cannot act or speak in their name because their intentions are a dimension away from our own; the words they whisper are colored with our own yearnings and knowing. This chapter is not about death and dying, it is about vision and remembrance, about being alive and kicking, *vivito y coleando*. Mortality simply serves to remind us of the work we must do. A new Christian millennium is here and as we turn the pages of someone else's calendar of history and watch with wonder as our own corporeal vessels transport us through the pages of another more private calendar, every moment is an opportunity, a trace in the making, until we too cross into the dimension of dead voices.

Cartographies of Queer *Latinidad*

Getting to the work of changing the world is not without its own hauntings. The paths of insurrection are well-trodden ground; the dusty layers of still visible tracks push through the surface of our political imaginations. Leaders, living and dead, have left us cartographies of insurgency. The comfort of a map is its tangibility, its promise of reaching the end of the journey. Maps are useful guides, but they are site-specific ideological constructions and are quickly dated by the earthquakes of history. The postmodern turn has called into question the objective clarity with which maps are drawn, courses charted, flora and fauna categorized. The excesses of structuralism have shaken the grounds of base and superstructure, static hierarchies of power, and absolute truths. In its wake is a wild sea of possibilities and interpretations, the murky waters of ambiguity and uncertainty, the shifting tectonics of a spastic world.

Identity politics, as an organizing tool and political ideology, has historically had specific investments for marginalized groups in this country.[2] The civil rights movement, the women's movement, and gay and lesbian liberation movements have all depended on organizing around categories of identity as a way to link the personal with the political, a way to give voices to our shared ghosts and enact their vengeance. Likewise, most of the activism in gay and lesbian Latino/a communities in the United States has been organized around issues of identity, as a means to counter both the Eurocentrism of the mainstream gay and lesbian movement and the heteronormative mandates and queer effacement of most Latino political coalitions. Identity politics has contributed to the transformation of legal statutes and the establishment of a multicultural agenda, and has brought questions of visibility and representation to the fore.[3] A politics grounded in identity has forced a reconceptualization of how social categories have been constructed

39

and deployed as vehicles of control and domination. Oppositional strategies have driven us to seek out others whose struggles and experiences mirror our own political concerns and have galvanized the resolve to work collectively to bring about social transformation.

In her essay "Irigaray's Female Symbolic in the Making of Chicana Lesbian *Sitios y Lenguas* (Sites and Discourses)," Emma Pérez defends the need for "strategic essentialism" in order to practice "resistance against dominant ideologies that silence and/or model marginalized groups" (105). She argues that "as 'marginalized others,' essentializing ourselves within countersites thwarts cultural and political suicide. We must separate into decolonized third world spaces of our own making" (105). But are such spaces ever possible? Will we be able to recognize these decolonized spaces once we arrive? Or perhaps, more importantly, will we be able to recognize our newly conceived decolonized selves? Pérez uses ethnographic material drawn from sessions of a group of Chicana/Mexicana lesbians to suggest the possibility of a Chicana lesbian imaginary. She states that "the discussions could not have been as open, as free, or as nurturing if 'outsiders,' e.g., non-Latina lesbians, had attended" (114). Curiously, in this section of her essay her own language slips from "Chicana/Mexicana" to "Latina" lesbians. My own experience in groups labeled Latina lesbian collectives suggests that these slips resonate with differences. In fact, the differences that set us apart from the dominant society—culture, color, language, class, legal status, religion, and sexual practices—remain operative within these newly formed Chicana, Latina, and/or third world lesbian spaces. Pérez seems to acknowledge these differences, yet argues, "[t]he process is not permanent or fixed but instead somewhat dialectical, acknowledging irreducible differences within separate *sitios y lenguas* where the resolution of differences is neither desirable nor necessary" (105). The question that remains, however, is how are these maps of insider/outsider employed, negotiated, or contested within these *sitios y lenguas*? Pérez's project is concerned with a specifically Chicana lesbian identity and imaginary, my own treatise is further complicated by the larger category of queer *latinidad*, yet the question of how categories are constructed and the assumptions embedded in their deployment continue to have relevance. Ironically, the question of who "qualifies" as an "insider" emerges precisely in those sites posited by Pérez where cultural affinity, free from "outsiders," is demanded.

Political groupings based on these categories have in fact become highly contested sites, splintering ever further into more specialized and discrete social and political units, based on more precise, yet still problematic, categories of identification and concomitant modes of definition. Identity politics' seeming desire to cling to explicative postures, unified subjecthood, or facile social identifications has often resulted in repression, self-censorship, and exclusionary practices that continue to trouble organizing efforts and work against the interests of full human rights, creative individual expression, and meaningful social transformation. The incidents I record below illustrate the process of negotiation and rupture involved in the inner workings of groups based on sexual and cultural identification.

1986. The group SalsaSoul Sisters, founded in 1974 in New York City, composed of Latina and African American lesbians, splits into two separate groups, one for Latinas, Las Buenas Amigas (Good Friends), and another for African-diaspora lesbians, African Ancestral Lesbians United for Societal Change, as a result of debates around the presence of "white" Latinas, issues of language, and diverging political agendas.

October 1987. The first Encuentro de Lesbianas Feministas de América Latina y del Caribe (Gathering of Lesbian Feminists of Latin America and the Caribbean) is held in Cuernavaca, México. Many Chicanas are present and ask that the name be changed to include Aztlán. This proposal is rejected, and the subsequent debate remains absent from published proceedings. As the Encuentros move to Costa Rica, Puerto Rico, and Argentina, the presence and participation of Chicanas decrease.

October 1989. The first annual Mujerío gathering for Latina lesbians is held in the San Francisco Bay Area.[4] A Chicana proposes that due to the cultural affinities between Native Americans and Latinas, Native American lesbians be allowed to join Mujerío. After discussions that highlight the cultural affinities also shared between Latinas and others of African and Asian diasporas, the group decides that they can participate only if their identification includes the category Latina.

March 1992. The Puerto Rico–based organizing collective of the third Encuentro de Lesbianas Feministas de América Latina y del Caribe requests that Latinas living outside Latin America pay an additional U.S. $50 in registration fees. As in previous Encuentros, all the promotional and reference materials are published only in Spanish. Although there is a large contingent from the Dominican Republic, Haitians and other Caribbean women from Francophone and Anglophone islands were never formally contacted. In the closing ceremonies, organizers list all the countries represented. Latinas living in the United States and Europe are counted as representing these countries rather than their countries of origin, ancestry, or affiliation.

Spring 1992. The Latina lesbian magazine *Esto No Tiene Nombre*, which originally began as the newsletter of the Miami-based group Salamandras de Ambiente, separates from the group over issues of sexual language and imagery, specifically tatiana de la tierra's film review of lesbian sex videos. One Salamandra, Mari Castellanos, who is also a Christian minister, wrote a letter to *Esto*'s editors, stating in part:

> Lo que me confunde de la revista es que a veces no sé si estoy leyendo *off our backs* (revista feminista nacional) u *On Our Backs* (revista lesbiana pornográfica nacional). . . . No creo que sea representativo de los valores del grupo en general. . . . Para impactar a la sociedad hacen falta ideas tajantes y posiciones valientes, no groserías. (Castellanos 4)

(What confuses me is that at times I'm not sure if I'm reading *off our backs* [national feminist magazine] or *On Our Backs* [national lesbian pornography magazine]. . . . I don't think it is representative of the values of the group in general. . . . To impact society what are needed are specific ideas and valiant positions, not vulgarities.)

June 1992. A bisexual artist from Barcelona living and working with the Latino queer community in San Francisco joins the organizing committee for the Annual Latina/o Gay, Lesbian and Bisexual Visual Arts Exhibit. After heated debate, much vocalized resentment over the presence and participation of a "Spaniard" in a Latino space, and gossip about the last time she had actually slept with a woman, she participates as both a member of the organizing collective and an exhibiting artist in subsequent exhibits in 1993 and 1994.[5]

1993. Ellas en Acción (Those in Action): A Latina Lesbian and Bisexual Community Action Group becomes one of the first Latina women's groups in the United States to include the word "bisexual" in its name.

Spring 1995. A piece submitted for the erotica issue of *conmoción*, an international Latina lesbian magazine, is rejected due to the presence of a dick in the story. The coeditors print both the author's response to her rejection and their reply, which states,

> [S]ome of the writings we've chosen have dicks, but the "dicks" in question are "lesbian" ones. [T]he dick in "Gutting Dreams" is a real male dick, and for that reason, we won't publish it in *conmoción*. [I]t's a strong, well written, grabbing and potent piece, but we feel that it's inappropriate in this latina lesbian space.[6] (tatiana and Amy 7)

May 1995. At the Tercer Encuentro of LLEGO, the National Latino/a Lesbian and Gay Organization, held in Washington, DC, several Jewish members and others protest the presence of an altar with a large cross mounted next to the reception area. The altar and the cross remain in place during the length of the conference.

Spring 1997. An FTM member of the women's soccer team Las Diablitas is asked to leave after members of the team and the league complained that his newly emerging, hormone-enhanced, transmale body disqualified him from playing in a women's league.

These incidents are culled from my own experience and stories others have shared with me, and reveal my own participation and investment in cultural spaces defined as queer Latina/o.[7] They also present the contradictions that circulate within this text, describing the "different spaces of dissension." I recount these stories because they explicate the routine negotiations and implications involved in the formation of identity-based cultural spaces and suggest a means of gaining insight from within the site of contradiction. As a lived practice, the strategic essentialism posited by Pérez and others can become a messy and contentious organizing strategy that ultimately reveals the limits and problematic assumptions of identity politics.

Identity politics formed in resistance to state power thus remains implicated in the perpetuation of the narratives upon which it is founded, specifically the conflation of identity, ideology, and political practices and the lived ramifications of the constructed and problematic duality of insider/outsider. Furthermore, on a political level, recounting individual narratives within the private confines of identity-based groups is simply no longer sufficient as a means of effectively transforming the social conditions of our lives if we do not also reclaim a vocal public presence. Judith Butler suggests that what is required is "a double movement: the insistence on identity and the subjection of identity-terms to a contestation in which the exclusionary procedures by which those identity-terms are produced are called into question" ("Discussion" 129). Furthermore, when we look beyond the matrix of race, gender, class, and sexuality in order to understand how identity is deployed within diverse institutional, organizational, and aesthetic contexts, we can begin to grasp how these psychic excesses transform the meanings of structuralist categories of difference.

Postmodernism, with its deconstruction of definitive social categories of identity, has often been attacked as a means of dismantling political projects of community visibility, collective action, and organized resistance. It is feared that the postmodern turn will result in a nihilistic attitude of surrender to existing power relations, devoid of vision and political commitment. For many, it becomes impossible to conceive of political organizing without explicative narratives or definitive social positions. In her oft-cited essay "Foucault on Power," Nancy Hartsock writes, "Why is it that just at the moment when so many of us who have been silenced begin to demand the right to name ourselves, to act as subjects rather than objects of history, that just then the concept of subjecthood becomes problematic?" (163).[8] I suggest that for queers of color, and all of us who have multiple and contradictory identifications, affiliations, and political desires, the "right to name ourselves" in a manner that encompasses the complex dimensions of difference and identification has not been served by the structuralist categories offered by Hartsock and others. In fact, this "right to name ourselves," however partial and circumvented, can take place only outside the tyranny of binary categories. More to the point, however, is Alarcón's claim that

> To be oppressed means to be disenabled not only from grasping an "identity," but also from reclaiming it. In this culture, to grasp or reclaim an identity means always already to have become a subject of consciousness. The theory of the subject of consciousness as a unitary and synthesizing agent of knowledge is always already a posture of domination. ("Theoretical Subject" 364)

Rather than a nostalgic yearning for a unified and transparent historical subject evidenced in Hartsock's posture, or the search for a position of innocence in relation to domination, I am interested in a different set of questions in order to begin to imagine a postmodern activist practice: What possibilities for political and social intervention are opened up within the new language of postmodernism? How can we deploy power creatively and consciously in the service of radical justice? And how effective are these strategies for bringing about individual and social change?

Projecting Life

Understanding the discourse of queer Latina/o activism in San Francisco in the waning years of the millennium requires a necessary foray into that realm of discourse where gender, sexuality, ethnicity, capital, bodies, and geographies intersect: demographic statistics. The current AIDS crisis has produced a mountain of investigative research, behavioral studies, and statistical data organized variously around issues of identity and practices. Statistical information on incarceration rates, high school dropout rates, poverty, per capita income, and AIDS infection rates assures us that the socially constructed categories of race, class, gender, and sexuality continue to have material relevance; what it fails to account for are "the social dimensions of gender and ethnicity" (Krieger and Fee 16).[9] In their 1994 essay "Man-Made Medicine and Women's Health," Krieger and Fee write,

> The usual listing of behavioral and demographic risk factors, however, fails to capture the social context in which the AIDS epidemic has unfolded. Most of the epidemiological accounts are silent about the blight of inner cities, the decay of urban infrastructure under the Reagan-Bush administrations, unemployment, the drug trade, prostitution, and the harsh realities of everyday racism. We cannot gain an adequate understanding of risk absent a real understanding of people's lives. (21)

Understanding the relationship between social context and social agents, socially constructed categories and lived realities, is crucial if we want to impact society and its (non)citizens. Overarching categories such as gender tell us very little about the differences between women; even categories that combine gender and ethnicity reveal very little about the vast cultural and social forces at work.[10] In San Francisco, only 4 percent of recent AIDS cases are among women (San Francisco HIV Prevention 100); in Puerto Rico, as of 1994, 19.5 percent were among women (Alegría et al. 86); as of the end of 2000 it is estimated that "47%, or 16.4 million of the 34.7 million adults living with HIV or AIDS worldwide are women" ("Basic Statistics" 4).[11] Among Latinos in the United States, Puerto Ricans in the Northeast have the highest rates of HIV infection and those born in Mexico have the lowest rates (Ortiz-Torres 108). And according to the CDC, while "fifty-seven percent of Hispanics reported with AIDS in 1999 were born in the U.S.; of those 43% were born in Puerto Rico" ("HIV/AIDS among Hispanics" 1). Yet these statistics may be misleading. The relatively high rates of infection among Puerto Ricans seem directly related to the relatively high rates of infection among Puerto Rican women, and the seemingly lower overall infection rates of Mexicans living in the United States may in fact be related to the relatively low infection rates among Mexican-born women. How do national identity, city politics, migration patterns, and local drug culture impact risk factors and prevention strategies? How do these variables inform and transform our understanding of social categories of ethnicity, gender, and sexuality? How does AIDS itself redefine our understanding of the categories of race, gender, and sexuality? Alberto Sandoval-Sánchez writes,

> If AIDS identity is understood as an ongoing process of identification and subjectivities-in-process, there will be a chance for transformation, social and political change. . . . Ultimately, AIDS will be a fundamental component in the development of a new politics of difference, a new politics of affinity, and a better understanding of democracy and the possibility of transforming power relations. (183–84)

This chapter uses the example of one social service agency in San Francisco, Proyecto ContraSIDA por Vida, founded in August 1993, to analyze how it has negotiated and reimagined the discursive terrain of identity politics to respond to the social crisis that surrounds the AIDS pandemic.[12] Its name indicates both what it is working against, ContraSIDA (against AIDS), and what it is working for, por Vida (for life). Through an examination of the agency's programming and cultural production, I document how it employs various creative strategies of organizing and intervention to enrich the cultural and political climate in the service of radical social change. Rather than relying on personal interviews of clients, volunteers, or staff to document the work being conducted at the agency, I have chosen to examine the existing representations of Proyecto that have already made their way into the public sphere through flyers, brochures, promotional materials, public speaking engagements, and published accounts. This methodological decision stems from my interest in bringing into focus the ways these subjects are continually involved in speaking back to contest and reimagine subjectivity through individual and collective self-representation. Furthermore, by using archival materials generated by the individuals and groups I seek to present, I demonstrate in practice a methodological shift that foregrounds previously marginalized cultural production.[13] The focus of this chapter is on analyzing the ways Proyecto represents and names itself and the communities it serves in the public arena, and how these practices of self-representation circumvent some of the pitfalls and limitations of identity politics. I argue that Proyecto is involved in forging a new type of identity project based on ideas, affiliation, and alignment rather than on static categories of race, gender, culture, or sexuality. Its organizing and outreach strategies speak to the creative, transformative powers of reading and writing language and images as symbolic codes. Its texts engage the possibilities of refusing explication, without abandoning the political significance of inscribing subjectivity. In the process, it is challenging cultural, social, and state apparatus conceptualizations of sexuality and culture. The dynamism of its organizing practices continually seeks to respond to the state of emergency that constitutes survival and resistance in the postmodern wreckage of a metropolis crumbling under the weight of capitalist gentrification, racialized dis-ease, and social inequity.

San Francisco has been an epicenter of queer Latina/o organizing and resistance since the 1960s, as well as a focal point of the AIDS pandemic.[14]
Proyecto ContraSIDA por Vida (PCPV) emerged through the threads of the
many groups that preceded its existence: the United Farm Workers (UFW),
the Gay Latino Alliance (GALA), the Mission Cultural Center, Community
United in Responding to AIDS/SIDA (CURAS), Mujerío, the National Task
Force on AIDS Prevention, La Familia at UC Berkeley, and the strands of other
groups and influences as numerous and diverse as the individual personal
and political histories of its founders.[15] The texture of its political and social
ideology has been shaped through the traces of Black and Chicano nationalism, third world feminism, queer liberation, AIDS activism, immigrant rights
movements, the third world peoples' strike at San Francisco State University
and at Berkeley, Freirian models of consciousness raising and education, and
the Birmingham school of social education and organizing.[16] Individuals,
texts, and ideas from Ciudad de México, Los Angeles, La Habana, New York,
Miami, the California Central Valley, and elsewhere have traversed the social
and political landscape of San Francisco, creating established lines of motion
that have facilitated and informed local organizing efforts.

Proyecto is not the only queer Latina/o organization in San Francisco;
many other groups and agencies also serve and represent the diverse config-
uration known as the San Francisco queer Latino community.[17] The combined force of three ideological components differentiates Proyecto from
other Latina/o community organizing projects: its commitment to multigender organizing, its declared posture of providing sex-positive programming, and its commitment to harm reduction as a model for prevention and
treatment.[18] Proyecto ContraSIDA por Vida is neither representative of other
organizing efforts nor a unique exception; however, its strategies for effective
resistance and creative survival offer a window into the possibilities of local
organizing in the ruins of representation.

Proyecto ContraSIDA Por Vida is located at Sixteenth and Mission, a busy
intersection in the heart of San Francisco's Mission District, an area generally
figured as a Latino neighborhood. This street corner and its vectors have a

long history as a magnet for queer Latinos, having been the site of two gay Latino bars, Esta Noche and La India Bonita, and a short-lived Latina lesbian bar, Sofia's.[19] Yet the multiethnic, multicultural Latina/o majority of the Mission shares this geographic space with Arabs, Asians, Anglos, African Americans, and others, as well as a thriving criminalized drug culture and prostitution trade, elements that all come into play in Proyecto's self-representation. Proyecto's offices are street-level; there are couches and magazines; music plays in the background. Its walls are papered with flyers and art produced by students, volunteers, and supporters; a basket of condoms sits at the reception desk, generally staffed by one of Proyecto's many volunteers. Sex workers come in to pick up free condoms before running off to work, newly arrived immigrants come to find out about the intricacies of creating green cards and social security numbers, multihued transgenders and intravenous drug users stop by for information on needle exchanges for drugs and hormones, the queer neighborhood homeboys and girls come by to flirt or hang out with familiar faces. Sandra Ruiz, Proyecto's youth health educator, comments, "All kinds of people stop and look in our windows, including grandmothers, cops and kids. . . . They ask, 'What is this place?' Well, this is a place where I can be everything I am" (Ferriss A12). Proyecto's target audiences are gay, lesbian, bisexual, transgender, and questioning Latinas/os, yet those who walk through its doors and avail themselves of its many services reflect the ethnic and sexual diversity of the neighborhood and the complexities of social and biological families.[20]

Proyecto's mission statement combines the elements of a radical social analysis and visionary political conviction with a poetic urgency that demands our attention and merits its full citation.

Proyecto ContraSIDA Por Vida is coming to you—you joto, you macha, you vestida, you queer, you femme, you girls and boys and boygirls and girlboys de ambiente, con la fé and fearlessness that we can combat AIDS, determine our own destinos and love ourselves and each other con dignidad, humor y lujuria. Nos llamamos "a multigender, sex-positive, neighborhood-based Latina/o lesbian, gay, bisexual and transgender HIV service agency." *Multigender* because we believe as the gay poet Carl Morse states, " . . . I want at least 121 different words to describe gender. Because there are at least that many ways of having, practicing, or experiencing gender." Different nombres, different cuerpos, different deseos, different culturas coming together to form a community dedicated to living, to fighting the spread of HIV disease and the other unnatural disasters of racism, sexism, homophobia, xenophobia and poverty.[21] *Sex-positive* quiere decir positively sexual and shameless, profoundly perverse and proud. Queremos romper el silencio y represión among our pueblos who for 500 years have been colonized/catholicized/de-eroticized. In the tradition of lesbian and gay liberation creemos en our gente's right to desire as we please, to buscar placer when, how and with whom we choose. We believe that deseo transformará el mundo. We also understand that in order to examine our sexualities we must first participate in groundbreaking discussions of diverse sexual practices: butch y femme, leather, bisexuality, etc. *Neighborhood-based* means we work within the barrio most identified with Latina lesbianas, gays, bisexuales y vestidas—the Mission as it is bordered by the Castro. Our current location at 18th and Dolores and street-front offices allow for easy access, for off-the-street-clientele and keeps our programming en el pulso of our target population.[22] All of the programming we provide here at PCPV attempts to continue to expand these notions and develop new ones. Our definitions are not rigid but rasquachi, our position playful, our efforts at empowering done with grace in the face of so much dolor. (PCPV, calendar 1994)

This mission statement, which is also referred to by its title "Asi somos" (This is how we are), begins with the deconstruction of binary sexual and gender terms, a direct address to a multiply constituted constituency. It articulates these multiple enactments of identities through naming: "you joto, you macha, you vestida, you queer, you femme, you girls and boys and boy-girls and girlboys de ambiente." The piece is published without indicating an originating author; however, Ricardo Bracho, the Chicano poet and play-wright and Proyecto's health education coordinator, is responsible for its composition, which grew out of a group writing exercise he developed for his coworkers at Proyecto.[23] In a memo to this author, Bracho records how in this piece he intended to use the process of interpellation to effect hailing from a "non-dominant dialogic voicing." He writes,

> the althusserian model of interpellation posits the hegemonic hailing of the subject—the cop who screams "hey you" thus giving the you a you to be—a state-derived identity, the subject for the (dominant) other in hegelian terms. I wanted to hail without such dominance. hence you joto macha which not only reads the reader into the text but asks the reader to read the author(ity) within such signs of degradation.

Asking the reader to read both the author and the authority of hailing calls into focus the constitutive context in which discursive resignification oper-ates. Through the process of interpellation, the text validates the existence of a subject that had previously been constituted through degradation. Bracho's statements echo Butler's reworking of Althusser to suggest the way interpel-lation presents the paradox of offering both a promise of an already consti-tuted identity (submission to the law and language) and mastery through re-signification or the claim to misrecognition. "Submission and mastery take place simultaneously, and this paradoxical simultaneity constitutes the am-bivalence of subjection" (Butler, *Psychic* 116). Butler writes,

> Called by an injurious name, I come into social being, and because I have a certain inevitable attachment to my existence, because a certain nar-cissism takes hold of any term that confers existence, I am led to embrace the terms that injure me because they constitute me socially. The self-col-onizing trajectory of certain forms of identity politics are symptomatic of this paradoxical embrace of the injurious term. As a further paradox, then, only by occupying—being occupied by—that injurious term can I

resist and oppose it, recasting the power that constitutes me as the power I oppose. (*Psychic* 104)

In the context of a promotional text for a social service agency, this hailing offers "jotos and machas" not only a linguistic space to occupy, but a physical site as well: the space of Proyecto. Yet these words bring with them the haunted histories of these names and the memories of their previous enunciation. The narrative shadows of *joto, macha,* and queer carry with them traces of violence, familiar rejection, and cultural alienation even as they confer social existence and oppositional validation. As troubling as this discursive resignification is to some, for others it becomes a rallying point for a discursive autonomy, which while fictive, becomes a tool through which narratives of shame, violence, and alienation are verbalized and countered.

Shifting the pronoun from the "you" in "you joto, you macha" to the "we" in "We believe" recontextualizes these linguistic memories by situating them in a framework of a shared philosophy of sexual liberation: "deseo transformará el mundo" (desire will transform the world). Yet it also maps the contested grounds of community: "Different nombres, different cuerpos, different deseos, different culturas coming together to form a community dedicated to living" (Different names, different bodies, different desires, different cultures . . .). Cindy Patton suggests that "[t]he term 'community' has political valency in the United States, but fails as an analytic concept; for it cannot illuminate the shifting personal or network allegiances lived by individuals in face-to-face relations" (7). Bracho's text reaches for the political valency of the term without imposing an adherence to preexisting identity categories; instead identity and community are constituted through political commitment and action. It asserts desire and the expression of desire as a basic human right and advocates dialogue on sexual practices as a necessary strategy in order to counter silence and repression. The focus is on sexual liberation, rather than gaining "equal rights" under the existing regimes of state power. Furthermore, the text and the mission of Proyecto remain open, playful, continually in-process.

Neither the Spanish nor the English is italicized or visually marked as "different" in the text, creating a visual seamlessness as it moves from one language to another. The insistence on code switching from English to Spanish, as well as from street vernacular to political theory, blurs the boundaries of these discourses. Words such as "xenophobia" or "rasquachi" may not be equally accessible to all readers, yet the aim is not to create a text based on the lowest common denominator of language, but rather one that provides a diversely literate audience a point of entry into the text.

Proyecto's Spanglish poem–manifesto–mission statement reflects a disinvestment in static concepts of language, culture, and gender and mirrors the agency's irreverent style of community organizing and education. Rather than focusing on AIDS as a discrete disease or as a single and primary health priority, Proyecto focuses on understanding and addressing the multiple social, economic, cultural, and spiritual dimensions that contribute to individual and collective health and well-being. Proyecto's approach to HIV prevention and service affirms its belief that as we near the fourth decade of the AIDS pandemic, handing out condoms and brochures is simply not enough. Instead, its work addresses the underlying issues of sexual and cultural shame and alienation, gendered and racialized social and sexual repression, and the historical consequences of colonialism and political disenfranchisement. Underlying Proyecto's prevention agenda is the belief that giving people a reason to want to live, survive, and resist erasure is imperative if we are to combat the spread of HIV and promote health in our diverse communities. Its work challenges basic assumptions that have guided much of mainstream AIDS prevention, namely, that all people want to live, that all of us are equally capable of negotiating sexual contracts, and that all of us benefit equally from health maintenance.

Gladys Jiménez-Muñoz points directly to the ways these assumptions have ignored the social, cultural and sexual realities of Puerto Rican women. In her essay "¡Arrancame la Vida! Masculinidad, Poder y los Obstáculos al Sexo Seguro" (Rip Out My Life: Masculinity, Power and the Obstacles to Safe Sex), she documents the obstacles to female sexual agency within patriarchal culture and delineates how cultural discourses of sacrifice, self-abnegation, and maternalism have impacted the ability of Puerto Rican women to negotiate sexual contracts. In contrast, Proyecto's prevention programming directly tackles the ways health, disease, social and sexual power relations, and individual agency are socially and culturally constructed and the contradictions between sexual identity and sexual practices. In addition to more traditional prevention and support services, such as street-level outreach, treatment and prevention counseling, and in-service training to schools and other social service agencies, Proyecto has also incorporated several innovative features into its prevention programming. These include a community forum series entitled "Escándalo" (Scandal), a multicultural transgender support group, diverse multilingual rap groups, organized retreats, career guidance workshops, a soccer team for young women called Las Diablitas (The Little Devils), and an ever changing offering of creative educational courses organized as part of Colegio ContraSIDA. These activities directly target the conditions necessary for social health and well-being: self-esteem, meaningful social bonds, individual and collective consciousness through dialogue and education, personal and political empowerment skills, and the tools of critical inquiry.

Las Diablitas, for example, began as a Colegio class and later became established independently under the economic sponsorship of the bar Colors, although it still relied on Proyecto for resources, a meeting space, and a source of enthusiastic community–based support.[24] Initially, under Proyecto, it was geared toward *jotas* twenty-five years of age and under; since then the parameters of membership have been expanded, and have included players ages sixteen to thirty, lesbian, bisexual, questioning women, an FTM transgender, and players of diverse ethnic backgrounds. It is one of the youngest and most inexperienced teams in the Golden Gate Women's Soccer League. The vast majority of its members had never played soccer before joining and it is the only team in the league made up exclusively of women of color. The emphasis of the team is on "promoting young women's physical and mental health." One team member, Lisa Arellanes, writes,

I think the most unique thing about us is that, unlike most women's sports teams who are (for instance) a bunch of soccer players who happen to be dykes, we're a bunch of queer women of color who happen to now all be soccer players. We sort of use the sport to promote our identity and pride in ourselves. It's also been a great way to reach out to younger questioning women, since there's no stress around talking about identity and sexuality. Rather than sitting in a support group, having to "check in," introduce yourself, or worry about being put on the spot, all we do is play soccer, hang out, and build familia. If they need support later, they have seventeen fellow soccer players to turn to. (Arellanes)

Some of these events are configured around gender, age, language, HIV status, or culturally specific audiences; others are not. Some are organized exclusively by Proyecto; others are presented in collaboration with other community organizations.[25] Proyecto has a groundswell of community support, and receives donations and free services from several neighborhood and community businesses as well as from individual contributors and local residents, ensuring that at almost every major Proyecto event there is an abundance of food and beverages. The diversity of the food itself is also worth mentioning. The many dishes I have savored at Proyecto have included *lechón asado, arroz con gandules, yuca con mojo,* Mexican, Salvadorian, and Nicaraguan *tamales,* collard greens, macaroni and cheese, jerk chicken, *lumpias,* sushi, chow fun, and bagels. At these events, not only are participants and guests invited to eat, anyone who walks in the door is invited to grab a plate and help themselves, including those individuals who call that particular piece of sidewalk home. Proyecto has not abandoned the idea of creating identity-specific spaces as a means to interrogate the complexities of subjectivity; most of its programming is still designed by and for various configurations of queer Latinos. By continually shifting the terms around which these spaces are conceptualized, however, and by also creating spaces constructed only by a common interest or political agenda, its programs and events creatively circumvent some of the limits and exclusionary practices of other identity projects.

Proyecto's monthly informal community dialogues, "Escándalo," are open to anyone interested in the topic and draw very different crowds from one event to the next.[26] These have included "¿Y Tu Abuela Donde Está?" (And Where Is Your Grandmother?) in celebration of Black History Month, an event that brought together a panel of participants to talk about the legacy and lived realities of African culture, history, and identity in the Américas.[27] Another discussion, "Sex: What's Age Got to Do with It? A Discussion on Relationships between the Ages," tackled the relationship between age, agency, desire, and power, a highly charged and controversial issue in most queer communities. This flyer used an image of the Mexican comedian Cantinflas with the U.S. comedian Buster Keaton, with the heading "What's Too Young? Too Old? Jail Bait or Chicken Hawk."[28] Queer and questioning youth form one of Proyecto's primary target audiences; these are individuals whose sexual agency is currently criminalized by existing age of consent laws.[29]

One of the most controversial and well-attended roundtables was entitled "Cracking On! A Roundtable and Community Dialogue on Amphetamine (Crystal) Use and Misuse." The flyer depicted an image of a superhero cartoon figure surrounded with the phrases "Trick or Treat? partying hard? super stud? feeling powerful and alert? what's the date? coming down? need some sleep? did you eat? safer sex? what a tweak." Under the agency's address and contact information are the words "Confidentiality Assured." This particular roundtable attracted one of the largest and most diverse audiences, illustrating the lack of information and nonjudgmental dialogue on drug "use and misuse." It also raised considerable opposition from several drug treatment providers in attendance because its premise, that not all forms of drug use are equivalent to abuse and that harm reduction is an effective and necessary model for addressing risk, directly challenged the established biomedical discourse on drug use and treatment.[30]

Flyer produced by Proyecto por Vida, 1995.
Design by Joel Reyna.

The images used to advertise these events are as intellectually sophisti-
cated and visually complex as the ideas they represent. As part of Proyecto's
outreach to transgenders, another flyer reads, "¡Reina! CuidaTe-Ta: Infórmate
sobre Hormonas, tu Salud y tu Poder" (Inform yourself about hormones,
your health and your power). The language combines the word *reina*, an endearment meaning "queen," and *CuidaTe-Ta*, a word play that combines *cui-
date* (take care of yourself) with *teta*, or tit. It lists a series of three workshops
that present a glimpse of the range of services directed toward transgenders:
Hormonas, el Uso y Efectos Secundarios" (Hormones, Their Use and Sec-
ondary Effects); Las Relaciones entre Parejas, el Abuso, y el Autoestimo" (Relationships, Abuse and Self-Esteem) and "Televestida ContraSIDA: Un Talk-

show muy a tu estilo con panelistas Latinas Transexuales" (Televestida ContraSIDA: A talkshow, very much your style, with Latina Transsexual panelists). *Televestida* plays on the word *tele* from television, and *vestida*, a popular word for drag queens. The three different events in the series reflect the multiple strategies of intervention offered by Proyecto: providing concrete information about health and risk factors; addressing the underlying issues of sexual power and agency in relationships necessary to negotiate sexual and emotional contracts; and providing a public forum in which to perform, celebrate, and discuss lived experiences and theories of living.

The accompanying image is of a naked male-to-female transsexual standing in front of a portrait of herself, in which her hair, makeup, and dress are exaggerated. The image plays on a kind of doubling, where the "real" and the "representation" are set side by side. By providing a forum where the contradictions, implications, exaggerations, and lived consequences of identity, behavior, and affiliation can be explored, Proyecto creates a social, aesthetic, and critical context where questions of difference and divergence advance, rather than stifle, collective dialogue. The images and language used in these flyers are as thought-provoking as the events they advertise. In fact, their dissemination and visual presence in various citywide venues serve the function of providing a common cultural text that sparks interrogation and dialogue as it furthers the cause of propagating self-defined representations.

One of the most innovative and vibrant features of Proyecto's programming has been its Colegio ContraSIDA offerings. These are free multiweek classes taught by local artists, activists, and community residents. They have included makeup, sewing, and drama classes for Latina drag queens called "AtreDivas," a neologism that plays with the words *atrevida* (daring one) and *diva*; Tai Chi classes; "girl-colored," a photo-sculpture class for lesbian and bisexual women of color under twenty-five; various writing classes organized along and across language and gender; a multigender photography class entitled "Jotografía," a combination of *joto* (faggot) and *fotografía* (photography); and a video production workshop for young Latinas entitled "Shoot This."[31]

Inspired by both Freirian models of popular education and the Freedom Schools of Birmingham, the classes offered through Colegio ContraSIDA incorporate various interpenetrating levels of teaching and learning. The distinctions between students, clients, volunteers, and staff blur as students from one class take on the challenge of teaching another, as a longtime volunteer becomes a paid staff member. Diane Felix, Proyecto's program director, for example, is just as likely to be seen as a student in a writing class, leading a workshop on negotiating nonmonogamy, or cheering on the soccer team, as behind her desk preparing summary reports for funding sources. This constant shifting breaks down the entrenched categories of "victims, volunteers and experts" evident in many AIDS service organizations (Patton 5). But the movement is not linear or progressive. Past employees now attend classes; paid Colegio teachers become unpaid volunteers. There is a continual exchange, movement, and circulation of money, knowledge, and resources.[32]

¡Imagínate!

Many of these courses have been focused on or resulted in creative manifestations of self-representation through autobiography and self-portraiture. By not focusing exclusively on previously conceived categories of identity, these classes create the conditions where self-determined representations of "subjects-in-process" can emerge. In creative expression, engagements with identity may traverse the field of established categories but ultimately destabilize them through a depiction of their excesses. In the essay "Revenge of a Snow Queen," the photographer Lyle Ashton Harris writes,

> Self-portraiture allowed me a way to claim a metaphoric space for myself. From the beginning I had an interest in visually exploring racial and sexual ambiguity. Through autobiography I explored the many facets of my identity: my pleasure, fears, inhibitions and desires. This metaphorical space allowed me to unveil different identities. I could choose how I

wanted to be seen. Through play, I could visually address my vulnerability, and the frustration that I experienced. (10)

Whether it is within the intimacy of these small classes or through the public persona of Proyecto's promotional materials, Proyecto is continually engaged in the process of creative individual and collective representation. Its programming is directly involved in addressing the themes of desire, pleasure, fear, and humanity to remap the theoretical and aesthetic terrains of sexuality and culture. These themes constitute the psychic excesses of structuralist categories of identity that often elude, or are excluded from, mainstream discourses on HIV infection and AIDS.

The course offerings through Colegio ContraSIDA have also valued the role spirituality plays in healing and cultural activism. As Cherríe Moraga has stated, "if the spirit and sex have been linked in our oppression, then they must also be linked in the strategy toward our liberation" (*Loving* 132). One such class, "Retablos del Retrovirus," appropriates a culturally specific art form to meet the needs of gay Latinos living with "the heartbreak that is the AIDS epidemic." Drawn through folk renditions of Catholicism, *retablos* have been used in different geographies in the Southwest, México, and Latin America to represent conceptualizations of spirituality. In México *retablos*, or *ex-votos*, have historically been used as a form of visual prayer, painted on tin, and often combining both a visual representation of the spiritual or physical crisis and a textual accompaniment asking or giving thanks for divine intervention. This class, taught by the Chicana artist Celia Herrera Rodríguez, combined a culturally specific art therapy with self-determined spiritual expression as a means of coping with the loss, alienation, grief, and spiritual anxiety associated with AIDS.[33] The flyer advertising the class used an established *retablo* image and situated it within a new interpretive context that complicates the form's relationship to Catholicism and culture. It is the image of a man turning away from the priests at the hour of his death, facing instead the image of his desire in the hands of the devil. The accompanying text from the flyer reads,

Retablos have been used for centuries by Latinos to speak of faith, suffering and miracles. PCPV's Retablos del Retrovirus continues this tradition within the Latino Gay and Vestida communities and our heroic response to the heartbreak that is the AIDS epidemic. This series of visual art workshops will allow participants to discuss and draw the losses and grief they have experienced in the AIDS crisis, as well as illuminate moments of divinity and outrage.

The following three images are examples of the *retablos* produced in the class that were reproduced in Proyecto's first promotional calendar (PCPV 1994).

Daniel Genara, *retablo*, 1993.

In the first, the artist, Daniel Genara, writes, "Le pido al Sagrado Corazón de Jesús que oiga mis ruegos y me ayude en mi pelea contra este vicio" (I ask the Sacred Heart of Jesus to hear my pleas and help me in my fight against this vice). The solitary figure facing us sits with three bottles of beer and a lit cigarette. The bar slopes down onto the figure, as the Sacred Heart rests on a separate horizon flanked by Grecian columns, suggesting a heavenly plane. The bar depicted conforms to the visual layout of La India Bonita and is reminiscent of many Latino nightclubs. It appears as a kind of altar, complete with an image of the Virgin, flowers, and a picture nestled between bottles, glasses, and packages of chips. The "vice" in question is never named, yet the image allegorizes the alienation associated with the bar culture prevalent in many queer and Latino communities. In their paper "An Introduction: The Context of the Mexican Retablo," Armella de Aspe and Meade quote Justino Fernández, the nineteenth- and twentieth-century art historian, on the role of *retablos* in depicting popular culture: "In the *ex-votos*, the village bursts into the painting in a dramatic way, as much by the circumstances depicted as by the religious faith infused in it" (78). The village depicted in Genara's *retablo* becomes the physical boundaries of the bar, as a new site of cultural and spiritual geography.

In the second image, the artist, Juan Rodríguez, writes, "Sto. Niño de Atocha que me has protegido y cuidado desde el día que nací, te pido por mi

Juan Rodríguez, *retablo*, 1993.

salud en mi lucha contra el SIDA" (Santo Niño de Atocha who has protected and cared for me from the day I was born, I ask you for my health in my struggle against AIDS).[34] Floating above the horizon are two seemingly celestial images connected along a curved path. At one end is a church marked "Plateros" and at the other the smiling figure of El Santo Niño de Atocha encased in a white and gold aura. Plateros is the site of the sanctuary dedicated to El Santo Niño de Atocha, a small village in the area of Fresnillo, the artist's birthplace. At a reception for the artists, Juan recalled his childhood memories of making the pilgrimage on foot with his family to Plateros to visit the shrine of El Santo Niño. The image is marked by three dates, two incorporated into the image, and the other, in red, marking the date of signature. The first, Sept. 1964, appears next to a man and a woman carrying a child almost midway along the path, and suggests birth. The July 1989 date is situated below the path next to two images, one turned away from us with the letters HIV, and the other crying figure facing the viewer, with the initials VIH emblazoned across his chest. Here the artist uses both the Spanish and English initials for human immunodeficiency virus to denote a possible date of diagnosis, although it is noteworthy that the image marked in Spanish, VIH, is the one facing us. These red letters physically mark the body, in the same way that an HIV diagnosis marks one physically, socially, and spiritually.

In the third image, the artist, Angel Borrero, rather than relying on the words that usually accompany *retablos*, uses a combination of symbols to construct his prayer. These eclectic icons—yin and yang, the Sacred Heart, the Bible, the moon, an ankh, the symbol of infinity, a butterfly, and others—hover above a weeping naked red figure. Borrero redraws the precolonial ideographic codices to produce a new postcolonial, transcultural imaginary landscape. To his right an image of a *conquistador* stands above two dark statues spewing yellow and white liquids, possibly urine and semen. These seem to be creeping into the blue water-like surface below the reclined figure as sources of contamination. The "bodily fluids" depicted in this *retablo* also include the tears of the figure and the red blood-like color of the body.[35] The

64

Angel Borrero, *retablo*, 1993.

recessed window peering out into a dark blue sky, situated in the center of the image, suggests the infinity of an afterlife, as the figure lies in a space between life and death.

This workshop and the images produced attempt to address the question posed by Alberto Sandoval-Sánchez, "What is the question of identity for a person with AIDS? After the diagnosis and continuous symptoms and diseases, how is a new speaking-subject constituted, articulated, and configured?" (183). These artists are "speaking" their subjectivity through a visual language, but the medium and the context in which these articulations are produced respect both the process and singularity of individual subjectivity. This workshop and others like it reach toward an understanding of difference and affinity, of individual inscriptions of subjectivity within a larger political context of collective action and resistance.

de(a)dicated to the one i love, a flyer advertising a reading from Bracho's Chicano gay writing workshop "(t)he (w)rites of mourning," transforms the

Design by Ricardo Bracho and Willy b. Chavarria, 1993.

lyrics of the oldies classic and juxtaposes it with an image of a fallen revolutionary hero, who lies bleeding, wrapped in the mantle of the Mexican flag.
The image/text plays with and against romanticized visions of Mexican nationalism and heterosexual romantic martyrdom, by situating them in a
queer Latino context. In this refiguration of nationalism, "dying for the nation" also becomes intermingled with "dying for love" in the age of the AIDS
pandemic (Bracho, Presentation). It is the text, "de(a)dicated to the one i
love," that calibrates the image within this new appropriated context.
Barthes contends that it is through the "linguistic message" that the
reader/viewer is able "to *fix* the floating chain of signifieds in such a way as
to counter the terror of uncertain signs. . . . At the level of the literal message,

the text replies—in a more or less direct, more or less partial manner—to the question: *what is it?" (Image* 39). The "more or less partial manner" is dependent on a particular kind of "diasporic literacy," access to other preexisting bodies of knowledge, or in this case the iconography of Mexican independence and the relevance of sixties pop music to urban Chicano culture.[36]

Similarly, the flyer for a sex-positive women's retreat employs a 1927 photograph by the Peruvian Alberto Chambia entitled *La Señorita Torera* to draw in the imagination of its audience. The use of an image from the twenties with a sexually ambiguous figure serves to situate the Latina butch as part of a historical cultural iconography, to reclaim a queer Latina past. Again the framing text attempts to answer *"what is it?"* with the words "Tetatúd" and "el deseo es la fuerza" (the desire is the power), responding to questions about both the image and the idea of a sex-positive retreat. The term "sex-positive" inverts the negative connotations of being "positive" in a queer context, and resignifies it as a statement of resistance against the imposed sexual abnegation evidenced in much mainstream AIDS prevention.

The word *tetatúd*, assembled from the phrase *actitud con tetas* (attitude with tits), was coined by Marcia Ochoa and Nancy Mirabal.[37] It is one of several neologisms employed in Proyecto's promotional materials and resonates with power and sexuality.[38] Equally important, it was a catchy phrase, the significance of which traveled quickly throughout the communities it was intended to reach and beyond. Initially, the word *tetatúd* functioned as an intentionally imprecise translation for sex-positive, evidencing the need to recreate or "trans-create" a sexual language in Spanish. Since then, it has been used in multiple sites to name a specifically Latina attitude regarding female sexuality.[39] Much of the retreat itself centered around the role of language. One workshop, led by Jacqueline Martinez, invited women to write their responses to the words *puta, Virgen, Malinche,* and *lesbiana* in order to explore the role these categories of womanhood have played in defining us, and to create a space wherein these words can be redefined, appropriated, and transformed. Loana Valencia, a "Tetatúd" participant, a longtime volunteer at Proyecto, and a safer-sex performance artist, redefines the word *puta* (whore)

Flyer produced by Proyecto ContraSIDA por Vida, 1994.
Design by Marcia Ochoa.

in her essay "Wanna Be a Puta?" She writes, "puta quiere decir Porque Usted
Tiene Animo. For those of you who don't know, a *puta* is a sinvergüenzaventurera—a woman who loves sex and is *never* ashamed to admit it. . . . It's time
we claim that word on our own terms because *nothing* we *proudly* call ourselves can *ever* be used against us to hurt us" (38–39).[40] Redefining the words
that have been used to silence or shame us, reinterpreting them within a new
queer cultural context that values sexual expression and sexual self-determi-

nation, subverts the hegemony of linguistic and cultural codes and uses language itself as an expression of agency.

¿Y Qué?

Recently, Proyecto has produced several new bilingual promotional brochures targeting specific audiences as part of its social marketing campaign.[41] The idea behind social marketing is to use traditional marketing tools "to 'sell' healthy behaviors to target audiences" (San Francisco HIV Prevention 402). Proyecto's reconceptualization of social marketing extends this concept to confront community norms and values. Rather than simply using advertising to advocate condom use or promote its services, Proyecto's promotional materials invite the audience to challenge ideas about sexuality, culture, representation, and communities. One such brochure, entitled *What's the T?* is geared toward transgenders. It is small, bright, colorful, and seductive. The opening text reads,

> Pues, tú sabes, we the T. Transgenders, that is. Oh, so who exactly are transgenders? Well, that's anyone experimenting with their biological sex. This includes a whole lot of folks, so it's safe to say anyone who calls themself a transgender is one.

"What's the T?" is San Francisco queer barrio-speak for what's up? new? hot? happening?[42] The text directly engages the reader and responds to a question, "What's the T?" but shifts it into a new context of meaning. Inside appear the words Props, *Respeto*, *Riesgo*, Risk, Presence, *Presencia*, Rhythm, *Ritmo*, Magic, and *Magia*. Though these words include the repetition of translation, there is no attempt to make them equivalent or even parallel. The word *Respeto*, for example, is translated as Props, borrowing from an intersecting queer and urban lexicon.

The front image is of a papaya, already charged as a visual and linguistic female sexual signifier for many Latinos/as, sliced both vertically and

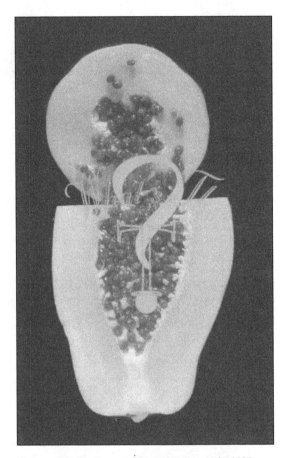

Flyer produced by Proyecto ContraSIDA por Vida, 1997.
Design by Jill Bressler, Pail of Water Design. Photograph by
Patrick "Pato" Hebert. Text by spikxildren kolectiv.

horizontally and situated so the pieces fit together to suggest a female sex.[43]
Inverted, it becomes a small penis and the circular hole dripping with shiny
black seeds becomes an anus, suggesting the rich complexity of organic
forms, magic, and incisions as a metaphor for transgender realities. A group
picture included in the flyer depicts a diverse set of individuals consciously
posing for a camera. A frequent stated or unstated response to this photo-

graph is the question, "Are they all transgenders?" An equally charged question might also be, "Are they all Latinos?" It is the question rather than the answer that produces the moment of critical intervention, forcing a confrontation with assumptions about transgender identities and communities. Rather than relying on authorial strategies of representation or explicative narratives, the image draws in the viewers' faculties of interpretation.

From flyer produced by Proyecto ContraSIDA por Vida, 1997. Design by Jill Bressler, Pail of Water Design. Photograph by Patrick "Pato" Hebert. Text by spikxildren kolectiv.

From flyer produced by Proyecto ContraSIDA por Vida, 1997.
Design by Jill Bressler, Pail of Water Design. Photograph by
Patrick "Pato" Hebert. Text by spikxildren kolectiv.

In the flyer geared at youth *¡Y QUE! Young, Queer and Under Emergency*,
photographs, images, and text work together to lure and entice, to make action, *vida*, and learning desirable and even sexy. It is a message of exploring
options, of figuring it out together, of doing something for yourself and for
others. The language is sweet and *picante* at once, layers of barrio youth Spanish and English rub and play together. As in the flyer *What's the T?* the text

appears in both English (heavily spiked with Spanglish) and a more standard but still colloquial Spanish. The opening "English" text reads,

> Wassup mujer? Qué onda homeboy? What's up with your young, fine Latina/o lesbian, gay, transgender, bisexual or just curious self? If you got questions about coming out, dealing con tu familia, friends and your sweet thang, and how you can help stop the spread of HIV en tu barrio y entre tu gente. . . . Pues, then you gots to come check out ¡Y Q.U.E.!

Inside it offers youth a whole range of opportunities for self-discovery and self-expression from résumé writing and participation in one of Colegio ContraSIDA's many youth-specific classes or rap groups, to learning street outreach and tabling. It also tells them that Proyecto is a place where you can come by and just "kick it on the couch with your friends."

¿Y qué? (so what? or literally, and what?) functions as a response to the hailing of the subject, a response to the names *jota, macha, vestida*. It is a statement against the totalizing implications of interpellation. By responding to the injurious name with a question, rather than an explanation, a counterattack, or a claim to misrecognition, it shifts the focus back onto the author and the authority that hails. *¿Y qué?* forces an interrogation of the constructed significance of those names. It deflects the power of naming away from the singularity of the hailed subject and restates it as an indictment of heteronormative authority to name and thus define.

Included in the brochure are two panels that echo the words of what other youth think about ¡Y QUE! Some of the quotes read, "Me siento en casa" (I feel at home); "Me di cuenta de mi misma y mi comunidad" (I became aware of myself and my community);[44] and "I'm going to become an advocate for lesbian safe sex." These responses in many ways capture the multiple levels of empowerment and discovery available through Proyecto's programming and presence. To "feel at home" suggests the most basic need for safety and support, a home in the world being a rare and precious commodity for youth and for all of us. "Becoming aware" of self and community reflects a process of conscious and critical learning about ourselves and our relationship to the world. "I'm going to be an advocate . . ." takes it to the level where consciousness and support create the conditions for action. In fact, many of the queer youth affiliated with Proyecto as either volunteers, clients, or staff have gone on to gain employment in other community-based service and arts organizations, testifying to the material benefits of the formal and informal job skills (public speaking, teaching, community outreach, public relations, computer skills, and direct service) gained through their association with Proyecto.

The prevalence of Spanglish in Proyecto's textual self-representation suggests its dynamism as a powerful language of *activismo*. In the essay "Living Borders/*Buscando América*: Languages of Latino Self-Formation," Juan Flores and George Yúdice appropriate the marketing term "trans-creation" as both a means to speak about the excesses of translation and as a metaphor for Latino self-formation. They suggest that Spanglish, or what they term "interlingual speech," as a "trope of border culture," emerges from "the ways in which Latinos *deploy* their language in everyday life. It corresponds to an ethos under formation; it is *practice* rather than *representation* of Latino identity" (203). Equally as important, language itself is revealed as an organizing principle of identity:

> Interlingual puns, multi-directional mixing and switching, and the seemingly limitless stock of borrowings and adaptations attest to a delight not only in excluding and eluding the dominant and exclusionary, but in the very act of inclusion within a newly constituted expressive terrain. (220)

The ability to make sense of linguistic codes, whether constructed by age, geography, culture, institutions, or experience, also constitutes another vector of analysis in social mappings of insider/outsider. Linguistic and cultural codes, however, create permeable borders that can be traversed through knowledge and affiliation. Understanding how these borders are constructed and mediated also gives us another way to understand and appreciate the cultural phenomenon of U.S. African American *santeros*, Filipina artists constructing altars for El Día de los Muertos, or barrio-bred Anglo *cholos* cruising the Mission in their low-riding Impalas. A shared cultural and spiritual heritage, a mutual colonial religion, or a common city block creates the organic conditions for the expression of these cultural affinities to emerge. This is not to say that learning Spanish, taking salsa lessons, traveling through México, or a new Latin lover amounts to understanding the "Latino experience" or provides instant membership into cultural communities. In fact, conscious attempts to learn about a culture only serve to reveal the intricacies, complexities, and depth of cultural codes. The process of cultural affiliation, appropriation, and transformation occurs interethnically, but it also takes place within ethnic groups. Particularly for Spanish speakers, participation in the multiethnic, multicultural, multinational, multigenerational Latino community of San Francisco necessitates a willingness to learn and adapt to new cultural idioms, regional synonyms, and local vernacular. This is particularly evident in sexual language. Words such as *chocha*, *cuca*, or *concha* may serve as synonyms for female sexual anatomy in one cultural context, and as personal nicknames in another.

The movement is neither linear nor unidirectional; we all have the potential to be transformed through our involvement in the political struggles and cultural practices of others. The process is never easy or without its own problematic implications; however, it does suggest that social positioning within community constellations implies more than biology or ancestry. On a political and collective level, this multilingualism becomes an acquired skill used to navigate different discursive spaces in order to achieve specific goals: to reach and inspire different constituents; to get and maintain funding; to learn about viral counts, double blind studies, and the language of pharmacology; to manipulate the intricacies of the legal system; or to access the resources of the social service sector. Understanding the ways communities are structured linguistically assumes paramount importance in creating promotional materials that speak the languages of their target audiences. Part of Proyecto's success has been its ability to speak and respond in multiple registers of language in order to reach different constituents. In addition to the interlingual mission statement cited earlier, Proyecto also has a more "traditional" monolingual mission statement directed toward its various funding sources, and has recently produced Spanish and English versions of a newly conceived mission statement directed at a more general audience.

The life histories of Proyecto staff members reflect the range of personal and political trajectories, language skills, and identifications that have informed the growth and direction of this organization. Space and shifting personnel prevent me from providing personal histories of the many staff and volunteers who have contributed to Proyecto over the years, yet the following three individuals illustrate the diverse activist backgrounds that make up Proyecto. Diane Felix, often referred to by the Spanglicized version of her name, Diana, or her DJ name, Chili D, has been one of the most dedicated and influential figures in San Francisco's queer Latina communities for over twenty-five years. Her political involvement began with the Chicano Power Movement in her native Stockton, and led her to become one of the founding members of GALA in 1975. At the onset of the AIDS crisis she worked with CURAS and when that organization dissolved in a fury of gossip, internal fighting, and political controversy, she helped to organize Proyecto in 1993 and became program director in 1996. Her work as a DJ and club organizer, who produces the club Colors and more recently Back Street, also forms part of the invaluable service she has provided to Latinas, dykes of color, and Latin music devotees in the San Francisco Bay Area. She has been honored for her many years of service by several community organizations, including a lifetime achievement award by Ellas en Acción and an award recognizing her twenty-five years of community service by the San Francisco Gay and Lesbian Historical Society.

Adela Vázquez, Proyecto's outreach worker, is also known by her stage name, or as she describes it, her "*puta* name," Adela Holyday. During a panel discussion on "HIV in Our Communities" as part of the "Boca Abierta" conference at UC Berkeley, she stated, "I was a hairdresser before I was an activist." Born male in Cuba in 1958, Vázquez was part of the Mariel boatlift.

Her association with Proyecto and the activist community began when she won the Ms. Gay Latina beauty pageant sponsored by the Instituto de la Raza at Esta Noche, a neighborhood bar. This title catapulted her into the local public arena, inspiring her to advocate in various public forums on behalf of transgender Latinas. After working as a volunteer member of Proyecto's Advisory Program Committee, she became a paid staff member in 1996 (A. Vázquez).

Hector León, who initiated Proyecto's outreach into the transgender community through his AtreDivas collective, was also known by his female persona, La Condonera (The Condom Woman), who distributed condoms, lubricants, and safe-sex information in local Latino gay and straight bars. He worked at Proyecto since its inception to 1997. In his native Mexico City, he was a member of the Frente Homosexual de Acción Revolucionario, and with that organization participated in the first gay pride march in México in 1978. He was also one of the original founders of Colectivo Sol, a queer multigender sociocultural collective in Mexico City involved in street theater projects and cultural activism, and in founding several publications, including *Del Otro Lado* and *Las Amantes de La Luna*. The organization and these two publications continue to this day. After arriving in San Francisco in 1989, he worked as a volunteer with several AIDS organizations, including the San Francisco AIDS Project, the Latino AIDS Project, and Shanti, and also with the groups GELAAM and AGUILAS. In 1987 he formed part of the original staff of CURAS, where he worked until joining the staff of Proyecto as a coordinator of outreach. It seems more than curious that many of Proyecto's past and present employees also employ context-specific aliases or stage names. On an individual level, the multiplicity of naming reflects our individual complexity and creativity.[45]

The final text for consideration is the three-minute public service announcement for Proyecto entitled *Sabrosura* (Tastiness), directed by a young Puerto Rican filmmaker, Janelle Rodríguez.[46] This fast-paced, colorful collage of moving images is set to the sizzling sounds of salsa and relies almost exclusively on visual language to promote its message. In her comments following

Photograph by Patrick "Pato" Hebert, from *Sabrosura*, directed by Janelle Rodriguez, 1996.

the film's screening, Rodríguez noted that the film involved twenty-three separate location shoots and the collaborative work of eighty individuals (Rodríguez). Most of the film is shot in the bright light of day and draws heavily on the local color of the urban geography. It intercuts scenes depicting young *cholos* and *cholas* flirting against a backdrop of one of San Francisco's many vibrant murals, wrestling in grass, dancing on the steps of Mission High School, masturbating in the dim light of a bedroom, marching down Market Street, kissing on street corners, hanging out in Dolores Park, and cruising through *el barrio*.

Advocating and eroticizing safer sex forms part of the message. In one scene a fierce femme blots her lipsticks through a dental dam; in another a young *cholo* flashes a rainbow collection of condoms, in still another a lounging Diane Felix, Proyecto's program director, slowly slides a condom down a banana. *Cultura* is everywhere, but it is the cultural hybridity of San Francisco's Latino community that is evident rather than any specific national or regional culture. Loana Valencia, wearing a traditional multilayered Mexican dress, spins her skirt to the soundtrack of a Caribbean salsa beat; another shot captures a zoot suiter flashing the twists and turns of a veteran *salsero*. In one scene, reminiscent of a gang jumping in ceremony, a topless Ruben Carillo, Proyecto's intake specialist, is held down and sprayed with a hose in slow motion as he playfully resists. Proyecto is about *familia*, but it is also about a new gang of urban warriors "fighting the spread of HIV disease and the other unnatural disasters of racism, sexism, homophobia, xenophobia and poverty." The message of the film is that belonging to a community is life-affirming, that safer sex is sexy, that activism is about reclaiming the streets where you live and play. The film is meant to turn you on; the rhythm and energy of the music and images are contagious, they make you want to join the party, join the gang, join the movement. The film is not about explaining or translating experiences or culture. It is representation without explication. The individuals who appear in the footage may not all be Latina/o or queer, some of them may be sex workers or academics, some of them may shoot drugs and others may be celibate; there is no attempt to make representation and identity equivalent. Yet in the final scene they all come together under the banner of Proyecto ContraSIDA por Vida: "a community dedicated to living."

Proyecto's willingness to address the issues of desire and difference, fear and power, evidenced in representations of subjectivity, respects and fosters the deployment of agency as a tool for individual and collective empowerment. Its programming, cultural production, and critical practices function as missiles of resistance against the hegemonic structures that demand our conformity or erasure. Proyecto's strategies for survival and resistance creatively engage and transform ideas of visibility, identity, representation, community, and activism within the ruins of postmodern representation. In the process, Proyecto has also succeeded in impacting the lived realities of some of the most disenfranchised members of queer Latina/o communities: immigrants, youth, IV drug users, sex workers, transgenders, and people living with HIV and AIDS. Toward that end, Proyecto has trained and supported a new generation of artists, activists, thinkers, and community workers to respond to the state of emergency that constitutes queer life *en el barrio* and in the world.

Initially, the connection between these neologisms, multilingual wordplay, eclectic programming, appropriated images, and HIV prevention may not seem obvious. Yet these practices all serve to help dismantle external definitions of language, gender, sexuality, and culture and create the conditions where self-determined representations of "subjects-in-process" can emerge. Proyecto creates spaces where not only individual "subjects-in-process" emerge, but where the collective subject of "community-in-process" is also given an open venue for expression, self-representation, and self-discovery.

States of Resistance

Proyecto has used the meager financial resources made available through AIDS-related funding to respond to a panoply of issues that surround the immediacy and history of the pandemic and the social dimensions that contribute to community health. The broad-reaching objectives of Proyecto have also had to directly contend with the limits and objectives imposed by these various funding sources. Finding and maintaining funding to provide services to women, for example, has been consistently difficult because queer women are not viewed as a high-risk population for HIV transmission.[47] Dedicated to multigender organizing and to addressing the multiple health and empowerment issues of all its constituents, Proyecto's programming geared toward women has been in large part supported by volunteer efforts, private donations, and the creative use of existing resources. The advent of protease inhibitors and other medical interventions offers the false promise of the "medical management" of AIDS and threatens to shift already inadequate economic resources away from community empowerment and HIV prevention projects. The economic, social, and psychic consequences of poverty, social injustice, and sexual repression remind us that these medical interventions will not benefit all of us equally; we need to continue to demand strategies of remembrance and vision.

In San Francisco and elsewhere, queer Latinos have long banded together to argue for government monies and programs that specifically target the particular social, cultural, and linguistic needs of our diverse communities. Despite its revolutionary politics, Proyecto remains a state-funded entity. Now, Proyecto and other groups like it are forced into opposing one another for access to those funds that have been targeted to meet those needs. Required to compete with other Latino HIV service organizations for funding, the strategically essentialized identity categories asserted in opposition to the state have now become a centralized feature of the workings of the state.

At a roundtable discussion sponsored by Proyecto, entitled "Latinos, The State, and the State of AID$," these issues emerged as the central challenges Proyecto and other community organizations must contend with as the politics of funding and resource allocation shift away from prevention.[48] Community activists present were acutely cognizant of the ways state forces work to pit Latino organizations against one another, yet paychecks and programs are at stake, and being aware of the rivalries fostered by the state does not erase the anxieties they generate. Caught in a web of social categories that have been predetermined by state forces whose objective is the control and domination of the subject, we are made complicitous in replicating the totalizing power of social categories even as we attempt to assert them in opposition to those forces.

While Proyecto's work may seem to unsettle categories of identity operative in individual and community representation, part of its public role has been to make queer Latinos a political constituency to be reckoned with. Butler, in her work on Foucault, illustrates how identity categories collude with the liberal state by reifying a juridical subject, "which presume[s] that the assertion of rights and claims to entitlement can only be made on the basis of a singular and injured identity." She continues, "The more specific identities become, the more totalized an identity becomes by that very specificity. Indeed, we might understand this contemporary phenomenon as the movement by which a juridical apparatus produces the field of possible political subjects" (*Psychic* 100). Rather than seeking out an ethical posture that will extricate us from the insidious web that is power, Butler poses the question, "Will this, paradoxically, become a time in which we reflect upon the more pervasive dimensions of complicity and what might be derived from such a vexed relation to power?" (*Psychic* 65). Her question suggests that identity politics, formed in resistance to state power, must also reflect on the implications of its own power to construct political subjects. Born out of identity politics, Proyecto's work is involved in creating conditions where the complexities of social and political consciousness and subjectivity can be manifested. But simultaneously as a social service agency dependent on state funds, it remains enmeshed in producing juridical subjects demanding entitlements. It is this paradoxical and contradictory relationship to the state that continues to haunt organizing efforts by marginalized communities as they struggle to survive in a political landscape where funding is primarily allocated to target groups formed from categorical models. The same contested strategies for resistance deployed by these various groups become manipulated by the state as a means of maintaining divisiveness and subverting unified efforts for more radical structural changes. The state does not only agglutinate populations in terms of organizing against its noxious effects, it creates divisions within those same groups that in turn divide them and diminish their potential to effect change.

More recently the financial challenges faced by Proyecto and other social service and arts organizations have been exacerbated by skyrocketing rents in San Francisco, fueled by the proliferation of dot-com and other technology-based industries. These economic currents have resulted in the unrestrained gentrification of the Mission District and the resulting displacement and poverty faced by the lower-income sectors of the city. Against such a backdrop, gossip, *chisme*, infighting, and personal attacks among diverse groups advocating for social change flourish as they are required by the state to compete for available resources and with wealthy business sectors invested in sanitizing the Mission District for limited real estate space.

Unlike other plagues and pandemics, the nightmare of AIDS has been used by activists as an attempt to bring diverse sectors together to talk about the ways death and sex are represented in our diverse communities, to begin to understand how our fears and desires unite us. AIDS itself creates a community of ghosts, linked through transmission. Bracho writes, "Given that it takes one to infect one, in aids heaven there is a relationality, a collectivity that undoes the individuated singularity of Western morbidity" (Memo). Perhaps the ironic collectivity that we share in death will serve as the occasion for our collective will to creatively circumvent the systematized divisiveness that haunts our organizing efforts, a homage to our shared ghosts enacted through our daily practices of survivance and resistance.

3 The Subject on Trial

Reading *In re Tenorio* as Transnational Narrative

> It is my deep belief that theoretical legal understanding and social trans-
> formation need not be oxymoronic.
>
> Patricia Williams, *The Alchemy of Race and Rights*

> I wanted to live my life with freedom.
>
> Marcelo Tenório

Enter now the space of a U.S. Immigration Court House, blocks away in downtown San Francisco. Walk past the metal detectors and armed guards and through the cool dry open hallway bustling with lawyers carrying thick black bags. Wait for the elevator that will transport you to the echoing corridor and leave you facing the heavy doors of the designated courtroom where a trial is about to begin. Here the deployment of identity takes a different turn. Here the city of San Francisco serves as the seemingly arbitrary site for a federal court of law. Now detailed descriptions of space become pure speculation and the only text under analysis becomes a hefty stack of loose-leaf sheets entitled *In re Tenorio*, no. A72 093 558.

This is the story of an immigration ruling involving a thirty-year-old gay Brazilian man, Marcelo Tenório, who was granted political asylum on the basis of sexual persecution in his country of origin. After suffering a severe beating at the hands of "gay bashers" in Rio de Janeiro and being repeatedly denied a visa to the United States, Tenório traveled to México and entered the United States illegally before his arrest by INS agents in San Francisco where he was subsequently granted political asylum in 1993. The INS appealed the decision but six years later the Board of Immigration Appeals dismissed the case. The characters presented in the text are few: Marcelo Tenório, the Brazilian national seeking political asylum; Tania Alvarez, his lawyer; Allen Lee, the trial attorney for the INS, presiding judge Philip Leadbetter; and Dr. Luiz Mott, the Brazilian academic and activist who serves as the only witness in the case. These are the competing and intermingled voices that author(ize) this text. Unlike the activist practices of Proyecto ContraSIDA, here playful linguistic expression is replaced by the precise rules that govern legal discourse. Instead of flyers, spaces, and events, what is selected for examination is a singular document, a court transcript. The dictates of law require that what is presented is the detailed explication of facts that constitute the identity of the juridical subject.

While this case may serve as Marcelo Tenório's *testimonio*, it is a testament written within the confines of a very precise and politicized discursive space, a U.S. immigration courtroom. Like other *testimonios*, Tenório's requires an understanding of the material conditions in which it was produced and the politics of location in which it was received (Kaplan 123–25). The United States justice system creates a space where subjects can give testimony about their lives and have that testimony recorded, scripted, and preserved for future study. While it provides a space for speaking subjects to be heard, it also continually seeks to limit and restrain the kinds of speech acts that are entered into the official record. Rather than court transcripts, what are generally made available to the public are judges' final summary decisions. Thus while the full process of a legal proceeding is scripted and archived, public accounts tend to erase the polyvocality of the actual events of the trial and are instead authored individually by the presiding judge. My own access to the transcripts of this case was facilitated through a chance meeting with Tenório's lawyer in a neighborhood bar shortly after the ruling. I asked her for a copy of the available documentation of the proceedings, and she generously complied. Using the original court transcripts of the case as a primary text enables me to probe how identity is represented within legal discourse, and how subjects negotiate the imposed discursive confines of the court to speak the space of resistance and desire.

The voice of the legal subject is always mediated by an interwoven layering of translations, interpretations, and inscriptions, transposed from one context to another. In this text, Portuguese, the original language of much of the testimony, is erased, undocumented like Tenório himself, and is instead represented through the linguistic filter of the court-authorized interpreter. The official transcript changes Tenório's name, by removing the accent, already effecting an Americanizing process. The accent, like the original Portuguese, is deemed an excess that constricts the efficacy of the legal process. The court transcript also does away with intonations of voice, facial expressions, body posture, and setting. A court reporter transforms the spectacle of oral testimony to a legally coded shorthand and ultimately creates a written transcript that is then stamped with the state's official seal of approval. The text itself is the remaining vestige of the speech acts that transpired, a series of questions and answers set off like the dialogue of a play, precisely transcribed to reproduce every utterance. It is this transcript that is read and recorded by my own analysis and received by a reading public that enacts new sets of linguistic translations.

Using narrative analysis and contemporary critical legal theory, I examine how competing legal constructions of sexual and national identity shape strategies of political intervention and the implications raised by their deployment. Through close textual readings, I examine the ways Latin America and the United States, Rio de Janeiro and San Francisco, and the ideological deployments of freedom and persecution are depicted in the court documents. The connection between narrative and legal theory has been well established by two decades of critical legal scholarship that draws on the analytical tools of contemporary literary criticism and cultural studies as strategies for legal interventions and examinations. Themes of law and justice are well-established tropes of both literature and literary criticism, particularly in writings that focus on marginalized communities.[1] Conversely, legal scholars have made particularly effective use of the tools of cultural studies to bring together feminism, ethnic studies, sexuality, and the law.[2] In the process, our understanding of narrative and its connection to cultural history, philosophy, and psychoanalytic theory has been transformed. In her groundbreaking text, *The Alchemy of Race and Rights*, Williams describes how this interdisciplinarity reshapes her own production of legal discourse. She states,

> I want to look at legal issues within a framework inscribed not just within the four corners of a document—be it contract or the Constitution—but by the disciplines of psychology, sociology, history, criticism, and philosophy. The advantage of this approach is that it highlights factors that would otherwise go unremarked. . . . I would like to write in a way that reveals the intersubjectivity of legal constructions, that forces the reader both to participate in the construction of meaning and to be conscious of that process. (7–8)

Both law and literature are intrinsically concerned with language, interpretation, and reception; and in recent years lawyers and literary scholars have begun to reach beyond the traditional limits of the text as sources of insight and analysis and have found dynamic ways to articulate their interrelatedness. Put succinctly, literary criticism and legal treatises are both involved with constructing credible subjects, narratives, and readings. Yet law is discourse with a difference; the stories and characters are real and the interpretations have long-lasting consequences. *In re Tenorio* combines the intersection of complex narratives, intriguing characters, competing theories of identity, multiply coded geographies, and a very distinct set of legal challenges for the Board of Immigration Appeals (BIA), the consequence of which has been to open a precarious window of opportunity for other gays and lesbians seeking to emigrate to the United States. It is both a compelling text and an important legal precedent. The stories behind *In re Tenorio*, however, like those presented in literary works, exceed the limits of the written records that contain them.

In the United States, immigration policies have always existed in relation to political and socioeconomic governmental demands and have functioned as a means to regulate, classify, enfranchise, or disenfranchise inhabitants of the nation-state (Higginbotham; Takaki; Montejano; Barrera). In turn, the language of these policies has served as a discursive medium for the legal and imaginary construction of citizenship and the nation. The politicized nature of these policies is nowhere more evident than in the political construction of refugee status.

Since the adoption of the Refugee Act of 1980, the policies of the United States have been guided by the United Nations Protocol Relating to the Status of Refugees, which the United States formally endorsed in 1968. This protocol defines a refugee as one who,

> owing to a well-founded fear of being persecuted for reasons of race, religion, nationality, membership of a particular social group or political opinion, is outside the country of his nationality and is unable or, owing to such fear, is unwilling to avail himself of the protection of that country; or who, not having a nationality and being outside the country of his former habitual residence as a result of such events, is unable or, owing to such fear, unwilling to return to it.[3]

Yet historically, in the United States the category has been selectively applied to admit those individuals emigrating from countries with whom the United States has had a hostile relationship (Cuba, Vietnam, Cambodia, and the former Soviet Union), and to deny entry to those who, while claiming persecution on similar grounds, are seeking to emigrate from countries whose governments are supported politically, economically, or militarily by the United States (Haiti, El Salvador, South Korea, or Brazil, for example).[4] Such pro- and anti-immigration policies serve as the politicized landscape, the "contemporaneous horizon of meanings," for the case of *In re Tenorio*.

THE SUBJECT ON TRIAL

Sexual Testimony

In May 1993 Tania Alvarez, Marcelo Tenório's attorney, filed a claim preventing his deportation from the United States on the grounds that homosexuals are systematically persecuted in Brazil and that a homosexual identity constitutes membership in a particular social group, a designation that was created precisely to deal with categories of persecution that existed outside the recognized parameters of race, religion, and nationality (McGoldrick 209). Yet in order to satisfy the BIA's criteria for "social group," Alvarez also had to establish homosexual identity as "an immutable characteristic." The BIA defines this as "a characteristic that either is beyond the power of an individual to change or is so fundamental to individual identity or conscience that it ought not be required to be changed" (quoted in McGoldrick 213).

The type of language summoned by the BIA speaks to the inextricable linkages between psychiatric and legal discourses. As Foucault has argued, psychology establishes definitions of the normative and the law regulates its enforcement. The discursive coupling of criminality and deviance has never been deployed as masterfully as it is in the psycho-legal construction of the homosexual.[5] Add to this a history in this country of legal, psychosocial, and media depictions that continually criminalize the image of the man of color, and Marcelo Tenório, poor, Black, immigrant, illegal, queer, and male, is inextricably cast as criminal. In fact, during the proceedings he was asked three times whether he had any history of criminal activity. Not surprisingly, he was also asked whether he had HIV or AIDS, a negative status being another condition of entry.[6]

Rather than directly addressing a racist and homophobic judicial tradition, establishing the "normalcy" of homosexuality, or attempting to establish why this characteristic "ought not be changed," Tenório's lawyer instead relied on the psychological discourse of the last twenty years and an assumed liberalism of a San Francisco–based court to construct a theoretical definition of identity that complicates its legal deployment while expanding the possibility for its application. Using a combination of sociological, psychological, and legal documentation to support its argument, the Lambda Legal Defense and Education Fund, which filed an *amicus curiae* brief in support of the respondent, succeeded in constructing sexual orientation not as an essential biological category, but as a complex interplay of sexual practice, desire, identity, and affiliation. Its definition echoes Deleuze's rhizomatic dimensionality to stress "and" over "or" to account for the intersecting and contradictory vectors of sexual subjectivity. Suzanne B. Goldberg, the staff attorney for the Lambda Legal Defense and Education Fund, writes,

> The term "sexual orientation" itself encompasses several aspects of human identity and activity: 1) sexual conduct with partners of a particular gender; 2) enduring psychological attraction to partners of a particular gender; and 3) private identity based on sexual orientation (thinking of oneself as lesbian, gay, bisexual or heterosexual.) In addition, one may claim or be assigned a public identity based on sexual orientation and identify with a community based on sexual orientation. (10)

The final sentence of this definition speaks to one of the difficulties in supporting Tenório's claim, because rather than sexual practice, desire, or political or social affiliation, what was targeted for attack was his "perceived" identity as a homosexual. In the summary arguments after the testimony, Alvarez did refer to the La Jolla study on the male hypothalamus and another unidentified study on identical twins to suggest possible "biological" arguments that claim homosexuality as an immutable characteristic. Yet Alvarez seemed to rely more on the argument of "perceived" homosexuality, even suggesting a hypothetical situation wherein "an effeminate man who is not a homosexual could be attacked without ever having been a homosexual or engaged in sexual activities" (47).

Marcelo Tenório did not belong to any gay political groups, had not declared himself a homosexual in any recognized public forum, and was not engaged in any sexual act or other overt manifestations of homosexual desire at the time of the assault that prompted his emigration from Brazil. In fact, it was suggested that he was identified as a homosexual and targeted for attack because he was in a recognized gay ghetto and was wearing an earring (37). It is both the body and the space that are coded and read. Within the geography of the city, gay ghettos establish both a marginal physical space and an imaginary one, a space of deviance, unregulated desire, lawlessness— a zone of sexual otherness (Knopp). Tenório's experience in the gay ghetto of Rio de Janeiro of being identified and targeted for violence based on geography is echoed in San Francisco's Castro District, where the largest number of reported gay bashing incidents take place (CUAV).[7] Occupying the unregulated, marginal public space designated as queer reserves the heterosexual sanctity of the larger cultural space, while it eliminates the possibility of protecting a "private" sexual identity.

In his testimony, Tenório states he had been a practicing homosexual since the age of fourteen, and claims "everything in hiding" (17).[8] Yet, when asked by Allen Lee, the trial attorney for the INS, "Well, how would people know that you were gay?" Tenório responded, "Because I live among gays. I live with gays. My friends are gay, and I can't live in hiding. Sometimes when I talk in Brazil, just because of my voice, they'll say I'm gay" (20). Tenório's seemingly contradictory statements about hiding and visibility speak of the practice of hiding and secrecy, in order to spare oneself the violence and stigma fueled by the hegemony of homophobia. They speak of the inability to hide, because the body itself can betray the codes that mark one as gay; and most important, they speak to the anger of having to hide, a conscious resistance to the societal mandate for queer erasure. Tenório is therefore punished for occupying the only geographic space available to him, for performing a "private" identity in "public." In his essay "Sexuality Injustice," a persuasive critical legal analysis of the tradition of legal arguments used to both protect and condemn gays and lesbians, Cheshire Calhoun argues,

> Sexuality injustice is not best understood as a matter of confining persons who are gay or lesbian to subordinate, disadvantaging, exploitable places within sexuality-structured public and private hierarchies. . . . Instead,

sexuality injustice is better understood as a matter of displacing gay and lesbian identities to the "outside" of civil society, and thus denying a place for gay and lesbian identities within both public and private spheres. . . . Displacing gay and lesbian identities from the public sphere in this way amounts to reserving the public sphere for heterosexuals only. (274)

Standing outside the club Encontro forced to occupy a space outside civil society, outside law, Tenório's presence in public destabilizes ideologies that situate sexuality solely within the realm of the private. It is this challenge to the normativity of an assumed heterosexual geography that precipitates the attack, as those whose hegemony establishes the margins of queer spaces seek to exercise their control over those who inhabit it.

In an exchange with Judge Leadbetter to determine the specific details of the incident, Tenório recounts the homophobic violence he was subjected to in Brazil, not surprisingly, it converges with racist notions of male sexuality:

Q. Now, Mr. Tenorio, tell me a little bit more about what happened at the club. Were you in the club?

A. I was dancing in the club. I like to dance.

Q. And you left at about 3 o'clock in the morning?

A. Yes. I left at 3 a.m., and stayed at the bus stop waiting for the bus.

Q. Now, the people who made remarks to you, they called you faggot, what have you, were they hanging outside the club or were they just by the bus stop?

A. No. They stopped their car in front of me. They began to yell. They got out the car, and they grabbed me and hurt me.

Q. Well, they had a car and they got out of the car and they came, and they stabbed you after they got out of the car?

A. After they out the car and after they swore at me, they said, what are you doing here? A strong black man like you. What are you doing here in a . . . a place of faggots? (22–23)

The episode ends with Tenório being beaten, stabbed repeatedly, and left unconscious in the street.

Here in the courtroom, Tenório is taken back in time, forced to both hear and repeat the epitaphs hurled against him. Only now it is a U.S. immigration judge who utters the word "faggot." His account of the assault is repeated three times in the court testimony, forcing him to performatively relive the violence of the attack. Yet it is only in this third retelling, in response to Judge Leadbetter's persistent request for the details of the assault, that Tenório mentions the way he was also racialized in the assault, suggesting an uneasiness with the categorization of himself as a "strong black man." To say *negro* in Brazil, while not seen as a racial insult in and of itself, is continually dependent on context and other nonverbal categories of language to establish meaning and intent, subtleties erased in the official court version of the narrative. Recalling the scene in which Frantz Fanon heard, "Look, a negro," the enunciation constitutes an enforced naming that marks Tenório racially.

Naming Tenório "a strong black man" reinscribes the colonial imaginary of the sexualized, Black male subject, a demand that Tenório disrupts. The moment of interpellation by his attackers also serves to establish the difference between Brazilian and Black Brazilian, between man and faggot.[9] Nowhere else in the document does Tenório himself claim African ancestry, an Afro-Brazilian or Black Brazilian identity, suggesting that like sexuality, racial identities can be inscribed on willing or unwilling subjects. The way Tenório imagines himself is never allowed. The imposed structure of judicial question and answer is intended to limit his testimony to only those details that are germane to the case.

During the courtroom exchange, he does finds subtle ways of reinserting his self-imagined identity to recast the interpellations of others. "I like to dance" is both an affirmation of pleasure and a metaphor of desire. "I can't live in hiding" is a statement of resistance and a forceful reclaiming of the boundaries of his tolerance. Though testimony is supposed to be a retelling of the past, both of these statements are claims to present longings and limits. These insertions within the formal, precise language of the legal system disrupt the demands of the court, forcing it to contend with the underlying passions behind Tenório's claim for asylum—desire and resistance. These momentary glimpses are all that are available in the text about how Marcelo Tenório imagined himself. Although he is the central character in this court-room drama, he has very few actual lines in the court transcript. The law, while supposedly creating a space where the defendant can "speak for himself," uses the structure and rhetorical impositions of the court to contain and define the speaking subject, a containment that is resisted by Tenório.

In contrast to the ways Tenório's racial identity is simultaneously invoked and unclaimed, Tenório's class identity is repeated in the text by both himself and others. The court is told that he was orphaned at age eight, after both his parents died in an accident. His life spent in Rio consisted of menial jobs, homophobic harassment on the street, limited opportunities, and overt employment discrimination. His testimony reveals that in the six months following the attack, Tenório, who was working as a kitchen aide at the Copacabana Palace, applied for a visa to the United States four separate times. Each time he was denied entry because he lacked the required income level. In response to the judge's suggestion that robbery might have been the motive for the attack, Tenório responded, "They would have just asked for the money, and I would have given them the money. And they knew I was poor. I don't have money to well dress . . . to well dress in Rio" (23–24). So like sexuality and race, Tenório's class status marks his body and his testimony.

The law, however, mandates an erasure of color and class and requires legal arguments that construct Tenório's claim for asylum solely on the grounds of persecution based on sexual orientation. The formal exchange between Alvarez and Judge Leadbetter that begins the hearing establishes the singularity of the legal mandate.

A. He seeks to file asylum, political asylum, Your Honor.

Q. And he's from Brazil. Your basis of asylum.

A. The basis is that he is a homosexual, Your Honor, and that they persecute homosexuals there. (2)

The dictates of the law require an erasure of the way Tenório's life is impacted by the enmeshed particularities of nationality, color, class, age, voice, and positionality, or what the legal critic Kimberlé Crenshaw terms "multiple intersectionality."[10] Considering the ongoing disparities in employment, education, health care, and political power between white and nonwhite Brazilians (Hasenbalg; Valle Silva; Hanchard), viewing Tenório's petition solely based on sexual persecution may fit the court's desire for a singular claim for asylum, but it does not reflect Tenório's reality in Rio de Janeiro.

Using Crenshaw, Elvia Arriola posits a new model for understanding the ways these categories work in concert to impact the legal subject:

The holistic/irrelevancy model recognizes the role of unconscious attitudes and the ways that interrelated factors create unique, compounded patterns of discrimination and affect special social identities. In doing so, it rejects the idea of arbitrarily separating out categories to address discrimination in our society. Instead, this model understands discrimination as a problem that arises when multiple traits and the stereotypes constructed around them converge in a specific harmful act. (141)

It is precisely the multidimensionality of Tenório's position in Brazilian society that informs his request for political asylum. His decision to enter the United States illegally is predicated in part on his condition of poverty, a status that can be grasped only within a larger framework of Brazil's racialized social policies. Tenório's assault is more fully understood as an instance of racially gendered homophobia: "A strong black man like you. What are you doing here in a . . . a place of faggots?" The language used by Alvarez clearly reinforces an ideology that situates persecution as "there" and not "here," something "they" do, from which "we" are separate. Furthermore, "they persecute homosexuals there" assumes a recognizable "they" and "there." Tenório is from "there," Brazil, yet the "they" who have displaced him from "there" to "here" remain unclear. Are "they" Brazilians, heterosexuals, the government? Ironically, just as the singularity of his claim works to his advantage in the court, the reference to this vague omnipresent "they" who persecute gays actually serves as an effective legal strategy to establish the hegemony of homophobic violence that makes his request for asylum all the more compelling. Yet Tenório is simultaneously a part of and apart from the "they" that are invoked. His national identity as a gay Brazilian complicates an easy division of "us" and "them," while his political status as a refugee challenges binaries of "here" and "there." Tenório exists in the shadow space of competing nationalisms. The undocumented refugee seeking asylum, trapped between legal constructions of citizenship, rights, and nations, speaking publicly against a "home" that has excluded him, embodies the excesses of nationalism. This carnal excess is witnessed as Tenório lifts his shirt in the court to show the physical scars left by his attackers, evidence of his testimony written on the body.

Having articulated the ways Tenório is marked by both his body and an enforced geographic positionality within the cityscape, Alvarez succeeds in both legally claiming and theoretically problematizing a fixed homosexual identity as an "immutable characteristic" that constitutes "membership in a social group." The next legal condition to be satisfied was providing proof that homosexuals were systematically persecuted in Brazil. Dr. Luiz Mott, a Brazilian university professor, a well-known homosexual activist, and the outspoken founder and leader of Grupo Gai de Bahia, is Alvarez's only other witness. He provides the expert testimony and supporting documentation that establish the systematic persecution of homosexuals in Brazil, forming the cornerstone of the case. In his testimony, Mott recounts a litany of chilling narratives of "deer hunters" (31), groups organized with the specific goal of murdering homosexuals; death squads aimed at eliminating gays, lesbians, and transgendered people; police harassment of known or perceived queers; state apathy toward and collaboration with homophobic violence; media accounts depicting homosexuals as stereotyped caricatures, AIDS carriers, or deviant criminals; and judicial rulings that absolve homophobic murderers.[11]

Mott also uses his own autobiographical accounts of discrimination and harassment to delineate how race and class inform sexuality in a Brazilian context. In responding to the question about why the doctor has never been arrested, he states, "I am a Ph.D. And because I'm white, and I am from a higher class. And I have good connections with the authorities. For that reason I've never been arrested" (38). Interestingly, Mott, also Brazilian, claims a racial identity as white and thus privileged, unsettling U.S. constructions of Latin America in general and Brazil specifically as a space of *mestizaje, mulatismo*, and racial harmony. Later in his testimony, he states, "But those case that are poor and of color, in other words black, they are more vulnerable to police intolerance" (45). Unlike Tenório, Mott is readily able to assert and insert a "self" in the courtroom. Whereas Tenório's role is to state the facts, Mott's role is to explain the facts, about both himself and others. Mott can embellish and distance; his elevated status in the court affords a geographic spatial privileging of difference. Tenório's racialized poverty does not; his fate is to be sealed in this U.S. courtroom.

Mott's previous testimony of the difference class and race make in experiences of sexual persecution seems to suggest an understanding of the layered significance of racialized class in relation to sexual persecution. Yet he ultimately uses the "difference" between himself and Tenório to suggest that there are more worthy applicants for asylum, and recasts Tenório as a victim of his color, class, and sexuality rather than as a social agent of change. When asked by Lee whether he would like to add anything to his statement, Mott replies, "Honestly I would prefer to be defending a gay of the . . . of the gay movement in Brazil, but Marcelo Tenorio is a person of a poor . . . poor origin" (41). In Mott's analysis, the ideal subject, a "gay of the gay movement," claims a homosexual norm that is "white," educated, economically privileged, and politically involved, much like Mott himself. Mott uses his own class and color to separate himself from Tenório, using a "gay of the gay movement" as a code for a gay man of a certain educational and class background.[12]

As the expert witness, Mott is cognizant of the need to assert his privileged identity in Judge Leadbetter's court and thus establish his authority to provide informed testimony. He begins his testimony in English, and delineates his credentials, including his position as a university professor, an M.A. from the Sorbonne in Paris, a Ph.D. in anthropology, a published book of 750 pages on the Inquisition and the history of sexual repression in Brazil, and membership on the National AIDS Control Commission in Brazil. Curiously, Mott specifies "a Master Degree in Paris at Sorbonne," claiming both the prestige of the Sorbonne and its European location, and then simply mentions a "Ph.D. in anthropology in Brazil" (27). Through self-aggrandizement—"I am the most famous gay in Bahia" (43)—and his association with a European center, he establishes himself as a successful gay Brazilian professional in contrast to Tenório, the subaltern subject seeking imperialist protection. Mott, wishing to position himself as a welcomed inhabitant of the center, seeks to define and explain Tenório to the authorities of the center who will determine whether he is eligible for entry, an entry that Mott subtly resists by privileging "a gay of the gay movement."

Mott's self-claimed racial, class, and educational status, however, is undercut in the U.S. courtroom, and shortly after his lengthy introduction, the transcripts reveal an uneasy halt in the testimony. At this point, Mott is still responding to Alvarez's questions regarding his history with the Bahian gay rights movement and the violent incident that prompted his activism:

A. It was . . . it wa . . . first time my life that was victim of a physical violence, and I was so . . . so worried about that that I said we need organ . . . organize org . . . a group to fight homophobia.

Q. Okay. And . . .

A. What about my English?

Ms. Alvarez to Judge

Q. I . . . I . . . he's . . . you understand, Your Honor, his English?

A. I understand.

Judge to Mr. Lee

    Q. You have any difficulty, Mr. Lee?

    A. I . . . I'm not sure if the transcriber will be able to pick it up.

Judge to Ms. Alvarez

    Q. We may have to get the interpreter then.

    A. I see. (28)

Here, during the description of his own experience of homophobic violence, the conversation momentarily excludes Mott from the dialogue and the subsequent switch from English to Portuguese mediated by a court-authorized interpreter recasts him not as expert witness, but as native informant. A residual politeness continues to operate, however, as each member of the court asks the other to name Mott's failure to conform to the center's standards of language. In the end, the INS attorney resolves the matter by placing the concern on the court transcriber, the only member of the court who has no voice within the text. Mott is thus repositioned as another Latino, like Tenório himself, who requires the assistance of an interpreter, and unlike Alvarez, the Cuban-born lawyer, who questions them both in English.[13] This enforced translation subverts Mott's intent to assert his privileged identity and instead repositions him as a visitor, an immigrant into the "English-only" space of the U.S. justice system.

Additionally, Mott's testimony as a homosexual in Brazil reestablishes his connection to Tenório, in the process forcing him to recognize the tenuous safety afforded him by his color and class. He cites the case of another "famous gay" Brazilian, Reinaldo Jose de Santos. While gruesome, the details of the case merit full citation.

He was the first Brazilian politician to declare himself as a homosexual publically. He lived in a small town in Northeastern Brazil. And population rebelled because one of the . . . one of the councilman declared himself a homosexual.[14] This statement really hit hard machismo in the region. That's why he was threatened with death by the mayor and the family of the mayor. He asked the state authorities to protect his life. Bahia's Gay group asked for a coun . . . Canadian consulate for political asylum for him. And a week later he was actually kidnapped and was found tortured. His eyes were poked, the ears, nose and tongue cut off. The fingers of a hand cut off. And castrated. And his head was cut off. His body was burned. The head was found in a river. And never in the history of Brazil have I heard of such torture as that one . . . as bad as that one. And the people responsible for the murder were arrested, but released a week later. So Bahia's Gay group is protesting internationally against this worst impunity against the first homosexual politician. He was 32–years–old, and he received a salary of $70 a month. (40–41)

Several factors seem to be operating in this retelling. For the second time during his testimony, Mott invokes the image of the "macho" to account for homosexual violence, a word choice with specific racialized gender implications for a U.S. audience. In the transcript the word *macho* remains untranslated, having already entered into the American English lexicon, as if no English equivalent were available, suggesting misogyny and its specific manifestation within homophobia as a particularly Latino phenomenon. Second, he describes the torture and murder of de Santos as the "worst" case of torture in the history of Brazil, a country with a long and brutal history of massacres of Indigenous people, forced enslavement, systematic rape, and the subsequent mutilations, murders, and atrocities documented in the history of colonialism (Degler; Mattoso). In unpacking the implications of this paragraph, we see that the first statement, wherein the residents "rebel" for the cause of "machismo," reinscribes Latin America as a site of violence spurred by misogyny and ignorance, while the second statement, which claims this as the "worst case," serves to selectively erase a history of racialized torture and genocide, a history that Brazil shares intrinsically with the United States, well-known for its own history of sexual mutilation, brutalizing violations, and systematic murder of non-Europeans and others categorized as threat-ening to the nation-state's security and interests (Higginbotham). A contex-tualized reading of this event, however, does not diminish the atrocity of the crime committed against Reinaldo Jose de Santos; rather, it suggests a con-tinuum of violence across spatial and temporal divisions. Throughout the trial it is this continuum of violence, this shared history of racialized and ho-mophobic violence and persecution, that haunts depictions of both the United States and Brazil.[15]

Looking for the Site of Justice

The reality is that the fatal consequences of homophobic violence evidenced in Brazil have distressing parallels in the United States. Information gathered by a coalition of twenty-two local lesbian and gay victim service and antivi-olence programs in the United States clearly establishes the connection. The New York City Gay and Lesbian Anti-Violence Project reported 151 murder victims in gay/lesbian-related homicides between January 1992 and Decem-ber 1994, the period covering the events of this trial ("Gay/Lesbian-Related Homicides"). Like the case of de Santos, the statistics culled from this report suggest that the intent was not simply to murder the victim, but to annihi-late their presence. Close to 60 percent of these murders were marked by an extraordinary degree of violence or "overkill." "Overkill" refers to dismem-berment, genital mutilation, bodily mutilation, and "an extraordinarily high level of gratuitous violence." According to the coalition, "Report after report recites that the victim's head was mutilated beyond recognition in the fatal attack." Two trends worth noting in the findings establish the intersections between anti-queer violence and racially gendered homophobia in a U.S. context: "African American and Latino/a victims were more likely to be 'overkilled' than white victims."[16] Second, "if the victim was a person of color, it was less likely that the case was solved" (4–5).[17] These incidents have no place in the official record of the case. It simply does not serve Tenório's interests in the courtroom to depict how sexuality, torture, race, and justice converge in the United States—it is Brazil's history of persecution that is on trial in the court, not the United States'.

Yet at times, Mott also seems to consciously resist situating Brazil as the savage counterpart to the civilized image of the United States. In fact, he makes certain that the court recognizes that in its search for asylum for de Santos, his group sought out the aid of a Canadian consulate, not one from the United States, in a sense disavowing the myth of the United States as "great protectorate of the world." Later in his testimony, he makes mention of three other cases of gay Brazilians seeking political asylum, two in Canada and one in Australia (43). Mott manipulates the discourse of the "savage, unenlightened" third world versus the "liberal and tolerant" first world to issue a challenge to the U.S. court, namely, which of the three countries mentioned will "prove their civility" by agreeing to grant asylum to victims of Latin American "machismo," ignorance, and intolerance. Nowhere is the challenge more evident than in his response to Lee's questions regarding his own homosexuality:

Q. Now you know that Mr. Tenorio is claiming political asylum because he's gay.
A. Yes, I know.
Q. Now, did you state that you're also gay?
A. Yes, I'm a homosexual.
Q. Now, you're in the United States as a visitor?
A. Yes.
Q. Are you going to claim political asylum?
A. No. Only if I'm a victim of a specific violence. I would prefer to go to Denmark that recognizes weddings . . . marriages of homosexuals.
Q. Well are you known in Brazil as . . . as being actively gay? What I mean is not actively . . . actively so much sexually, as actively in the . . . in the gay cause. (43)

Lee's rhetorical fumbling, using the word "actively" four times, reveals his uneasiness with his own fantasized image of "active" homosexual sex. His line of questioning reasserts Mott's connection to Tenório, as both an "active" homosexual and a "visitor." Lee manipulates the murder of de Santos and the attempted kidnapping of Mott to suggest that if gay persecution were in fact a real threat, then Mott, who has the means, by virtue of his color, class, and education, would have left Brazil. Furthermore, he assumes U.S. desirability as a site of immigration for gays, and reinforces the fear in the court's mind that if Tenório's claim is granted, a great mass of asylum-seeking queers will be knocking on the doors of the INS.

Mott, however, resists being cast as the marginal subject seeking entry into the center. His coy reply makes clear that what passes as tolerance in certain parts of the United States does not meet his higher standard of homosexual equality. In effect, by displacing the centrality of the United States as a site of queer liberation, he succeeds in momentarily challenging the rhetoric of center and margin, suggesting that centers and margins are multiply positioned within differently imagined geographies. It is relevant to note that at the time of the case, Canada, Germany, the Netherlands, and Australia had already granted asylum to gays from other countries (Tuller, "Gay Request").

As his testimony proceeds, Mott again attempts to resist a discourse of Brazilian savagery or a desire to gain access to the "center." Instead, he claims the rights of the nation for its queer inhabitants.

> [M]any friends advised me to move. Not out of the country, but at least move out of the city. But I have no vocation for being a martyr. But I hope that I will never have to abandon my country, for defending the citizenship rights of this minority group. (44)

At this point, rather than using the space of Canada, Australia, or Denmark as a site of refuge, Mott claims the discourse of citizen and minority rights, international human rights language whose legal currency strikes at the heart of U.S. liberal constructions of citizenship and democracy. Mott claims this language and these rights to speak about Brazil, suggesting that Brazil, like the United States, has both the opportunity and the ethical mandate to provide and protect the human rights of its inhabitants.[18] Mott's strategy proved effective. In Judge Leadbetter's summary decision, he looked at international refugee law and made use of a Canadian decision that granted asylum based on homosexual persecution to support Tenório's petition.[19]

The specific mythologized geography of Rio de Janeiro is also operative in the courtroom drama. The popularized image of Rio as a North American and European sexual playground, a space where sexual excess is the norm, is destabilized through Mott's testimony and his exchange with Lee:

Q. At least in this country, Rio has a reputation of being a very liberated city where everything goes on. . . . To state the question again.[20] Rio has the reputation of being a very sexually liberated and free city or area. Are you saying that's not true?

A. This image of Rio as a paradise, unfortunately, does not correspond with reality any more. Nowadays Rio de Janeiro is the city with the most murders in Brazil. The death squads are the most violent. (38)

Murder, violence, and death squads disturb idyllic commercialized notions of an exotic, yet tamed, vacation paradise where "everything goes." It was this contradiction between the imagined and the real Rio that the media sensationalized. In the *New York Times* the headline read, "In Live-and-Let-Live Land, Gay People Are Slain." While they echoed the instances of violence and homophobia presented in the court, they also used the case to perpetuate an image of Rio as a carefree, liberated zone for international tourism. The *Times* reporter James Brooke writes,

But Brazil is also renowned for its tolerance of gay life. Transvestite shows, where many of the performers are gay, are considered family entertainment, and transvestites play an integral part of Rio's Carnival. . . . Rio's gay bars and gay Carnival balls have long attracted tourists from Europe, the United States and Brazil's more conservative South American neighbors. (Brooke)

Meanwhile, in Brazil's largest-selling news weekly, *Veja*, the headline read, "Judge Tricked: Gay Win Aslum with Lie about Brazil." The *New York Times* quoted *Veja* as writing, "There is no conspiracy or evidence that could indicate an organized practice. In the hands of the noisy American pink lobby, Tenorio's cause became a festival of demagoguery—and of Brazil-bashing" (Brooke). The neocolonialist demand for tourist dollars necessitates a disavowal of the violence and rewrites the event as a "trick" in which a Brazilian with the help of the "noisy American pink lobby" outfoxes a U.S. judge.

Ironically, during the court proceedings San Francisco, like Rio de Janeiro, is depicted as a site of sexual freedom. Tenório states, "I wanted to come to the United States. I knew that in San Francisco I could live my gay life" (15). Tenório's imaginary ideological construction of San Francisco functions in the same role as Brooke's depiction of Rio de Janeiro: both create an illusionary seductiveness that obfuscates material realities. The same seductiveness that propels Tenório to San Francisco lures thousands of American gay male tourists to Rio every year to revel in the perceived "anything goes" attitude toward sexuality. In a huge cosmopolitan city, with a thriving tourist trade and ten times the number of inhabitants as San Francisco, the "carefree" attitude of a tropical paradise rarely extends to encompass the impoverished realities of queers living on the margins of the chic commercial tourist centers of Rio de Janeiro.

Likewise, despite the image of San Francisco as a "queer mecca," most of its queer residents live and work outside recognized gay and lesbian geographic communities. Tim Davis writes,

[A]ttempts to create a safe space or "liberated zone" in San Francisco and other cities have not come to fruition. Instead of safety, these areas, because of their visibility, have become the focus for many gay-bashings, and AIDS has had a profound impact upon the social structure of the gay scene and the life of these neighborhoods. The dream of the liberated zone has been undermined, as other neighborhoods and suburbs are considered viable destinations for many gay men and lesbians. In moving from a liberated zone to a gay ghetto, gay territories have lost their sheen. (285)

The viability of "other neighborhoods and suburbs," however, is restricted by color and class. Gay economic and political clout in San Francisco is rarely extended to immigrant queers of color. Tenório's day-to-day life in San Francisco consisted of sharing an apartment with three other men, working as a lab assistant, and trying to complete his high school diploma.[21] In fact, what happened to Marcelo Tenório in Rio de Janeiro could have just as easily taken place in San Francisco or in any other city or town in the United States. Furthermore, these liberated zones exist within a larger national terrain that does not recognize the rights of its queer citizens, and the few "liberated zones" that do exist are continually under attack.

The underlying implication veiled in both the proceedings and the news coverage that followed is that while these events could happen in the United States, our government would act to protect its citizens. The Tenório case relies on a subjectivity constructed through the liberal, humanistic discourse on judicial "freedom of expression" to suggest that political asylum in this country offers the privilege of this "freedom" unconditionally. While the arguments employed in the Tenório case may exemplify bourgeois legal reasoning and the implied moral superiority of the north as a strategy for a temporary reprieve from the immediacy of violence in Brazil, they also reveal a complex set of legal contradictions operating within the United States.

Legal (Un)Reasoning

Ironically, Brazil decriminalized most homosexual acts in 1823 (Brooke). In the United States, sodomy laws remain on the books in over a dozen states

(Duncan and Young 93). In fact, the 1986 Supreme Court decision *Bowers v. Hardwick* upheld the constitutionality of a state's right to make certain sexual acts illegal, including sodomy between consenting adults. The Supreme Court justices who argued against the constitutionality of sodomy laws relied heavily on arguments based on the constitutional right to privacy. Calhoun outlines how arguments based on privacy or the sanctity of the "private" space sustain heteronormative narratives. He writes,

> The Court's rhetoric served to legitimize what is arguably the central feature of sexuality injustice, namely the reservation of the public sphere for heterosexuals only. This is not to say that securing a right of privacy with respect to gay and lesbian sexual activities is unimportant. It is, however, to say that the rhetoric of privacy arguments can do as much to sustain sexuality injustice as to intervene in it. (253)

Furthermore, the Supreme Court presiding over *Bowers v. Hardwick* focused specifically on sodomy as a "private" sexual practice, not homosexuality as a public identity. Yet the relationship between acts and identities, crimes and criminals, public and private is embedded in the legal discourse. Put more succinctly, in Georgia, to declare oneself a practicing homosexual is to declare oneself a criminal. In his article "The Eclipse of Reason," Kendall Thomas echoes Calhoun to argue that what is really at stake is the regulative power of heterosexuality:

> The most promising target for a deconstruction of the metaphysical infrastructure that subtends both the distinction between sexual acts and sexual identities, and a more nuanced understanding which sees the two as relational and dependent, is neither the act of "homosexual sodomy," nor "homosexual" identity. Instead, we must begin to take rigorous and relentless critical aim at the ideology and institution of normative heterosexuality. (1806)

In his psychosexual analysis, Thomas goes further to state that the Supreme Court's repeated invocations of the patriarchal "Founding Fathers" imply that sodomy (whether in a homosexual or heterosexual context) destabilizes heterosexual male identification and that it was precisely this destabilization that the Court needed to contain (1822). It is this same destabilizing anxiety that prompts the INS attorney Lee's repeated fumbling over the image and language of "active" homosexuality.

The ideology and institution of normative heterosexuality is what extends property rights, health benefits, life insurance, power of attorney, inheritance, child custody, adoption rights, tax incentives, and a host of other benefits to those who publicly declare heterosexuality through state-sanctioned marriage, including the right to extend U.S. citizenship to one's spouse.[22] For queer couples whose love transcends borders, marrying one's undocumented partner simply does not exist as a legal option. And despite the Tenório ruling, for queer asylum applicants seeking similar protection from the United States today, the rules have changed drastically.

Nevertheless, *In re Tenorio* and other similar cases did have both subtle and overt impact on subsequent U.S. immigration policies. In 1994 attorney general Janet Reno "issued an order that would allow homosexuals from other countries to seek political asylum in the United States if they could prove that they were victims of government persecution solely because of their sexual preference" (Johnston par. 1). Of course, while stressing the singularity of a claim works directly to disadvantage queers whose lives have also been harshly impacted by other forms of state-sanctioned injustices based on religion, color, gender, and poverty, Reno's comments did provide a new avenue of legal recourse for many. However, in 1997 Congress stepped in to make the conditions for asylum and other forms of immigration even more stringent with the Illegal Immigrant and Immigrant Responsibility Act. The act now requires that all asylum seekers be routinely detained before a first interview. If they pass this initial interrogation, they are maintained in detention months or even years as they await an asylum hearing. Other elements of the statute include expedited removal; the immediate deportation of asylum applicants who have been convicted of a crime, no matter how minor, here or abroad; and a requirement that applicants file within a year of entry into the United States. The act also impacts those wishing to sponsor an immigrant. Now sponsors must meet an income test of 125 percent above the poverty level. And until immigrants become naturalized citizens, they are ineligible for most forms of government assistance, including Supplemental Social Security Income, food stamps, and Medicaid. The most insidious provision of the act, however, is that it drastically restricts, and in some cases eliminates, the process through which immigrants and refugees can appeal their decisions.[23]

In light of *Bowers v. Hardwick* and the Illegal Immigrant and Immigrant Responsibility Act, the case of Tenório raises the question of how the United States can offer refuge from persecution based on sexual orientation when the rights of its own queer citizens are not federally guaranteed and the rights of due process are denied those seeking entry. These are the underlying paradoxes that need to be explored if the Tenório case is to be viewed as a site of political intervention. Uncovering the roots of these internal contradictions could then be used as a tool to refigure the politics of citizenship, the regulatory power of heterosexuality, and the "intersubjectivity of legal constructions." And still the daily drama of lives and intersecting geographies continues to unfold, demanding new interpolations.

Outside the Courtroom

Inside the courtroom, Tenório is represented by his lawyer. Outside the courtroom, his case is represented by a series of individuals and organizations that seek to rewrite his petition for asylum as part of their own political agendas, including the Lambda Legal Defense and Education Fund, the International Gay and Lesbian Human Rights Commission, the largely white gay media, and queer Latinas/os in both the United States and Latin America. Yet neither the legal proceeding itself nor the flurry of media attention it garnered ever gave Marcelo Tenório much of an opportunity to speak for himself. In

Marcelo Tenório and Tania Alvarez, press conference, 1993. Reproduced by permission of Copyright Archive Photos.

law, individual subjectivity can only serve as a case in point. The face behind the petition is almost interchangeable with the host of others seeking similar legal interventions. Tenório's case attracted public and media attention because it was the first of its kind, a landmark ruling, and Marcelo, the gay *carioca* who likes to dance, has not been heard from since.[24] Yet in that fleeting moment following the trial, Marcelo Tenório enjoyed fifteen minutes of fame, an uneasy glory where everyone else found something to say about him.

The *New York Times* reported that after the ruling in which Tenório was granted asylum, queer activists in Brazil used the decision to rally international attention and demand investigation into the unprosecuted murders of homosexuals and transvestites in their country, while the gay and lesbian activists in the United States unanimously applauded the ruling (Brooke). As the issue became a "gay" issue, Tenório's realities as a poor Black Brazilian, orphaned at the age of eight, working a series of menial jobs for menial pay, began to slip away. Reuters news service circulated a photograph of Marcelo Tenório, dark skin and serious eyes, wearing an earring and dressed in a crisp white tee shirt imprinted with a photograph of two small boys hugging, one black and one white, around his neck a chain of rainbow rings and a small crucifix, symbols that bring together the racial, cultural, and sexual markers of his identity. In the background is the banner of the International Gay and Lesbian Human Rights Commission, at his side Tania Alvarez. His hands are stretched apart in a gesture that suggests he is trying to make clear a point, and in his eyes there is uneasiness about occupying the interstitial space of dark, queer refugee.

Outside the pages of the news media, many queer Latinas/os on both sides of the U.S. border voiced their concern and opposition to the strategies of demonizing and exoticizing Latin America that were employed in the trial and promulgated in the media. In a speech made at the closing plenary of the Tercer Encuentro Nacional de LLEGO, a U.S.-based Latina/o gay, lesbian, bisexual organization, Jorge Ignacio Cortiñas delivered an eloquent speech on the need to establish meaningful dialogue between Latinos/as in the United States and Latinas/os in Latin America, and argued that these bonds across borders need to directly inform our strategies for political intervention and analysis:

We are fond of saying that "*Nuestra lucha esta aquí*," but there is no *aquí* that does not include *allá*. The over there that is here to stay. When we fail to insist on these links, our amnesia becomes disastrous. . . . Such amnesia allows our silence while the gay movements in this country establish asylum rights based on sexual orientation through use of what they call the most effective strategies they have: regurgitation of neo-colonial narratives of the barbarity of the south, juxtaposed with a just barely unstated belief in the liberty and development of the metropolitan North.

Cortiñas ended his speech by challenging his audience to reconceptualize the daily work of our lives as we struggle to change the conditions of our existence both within and outside the very institutions and structures we are compelled to resist, both *aquí* and *allá*.

By moon light, inaugurating with passions we only dimly understand, sovereign nations of leaderless hearts driving us forward as we write our biographies in ink and a lover's saliva. And in the broad day light of the noon sun, insisting outside impenetrable government buildings, and later inside once impenetrable buildings, leaving the writing of manifestos behind while we write laws. Laws we will write as Latinos and Latin Americans, open laws that will be partisan, on the side of the dispossessed and the poor, which is where we came from and will return.

Even today, hosts of other asylum seekers rub their hands together and wait, hoping they will be able to follow in Tenório's footsteps, through the promised gates of legalized residency in the United States. I, too, am implicated in this elusive and convoluted search for temporary local solutions to seemingly overwhelming global problems. I have been the official translator, the advocate, the friend who squeezes the asylum seeker's hand and wishes them well.

If *In re Tenorio* should not be read as evidence of a demonized south, it should also not be read as merely another example of U.S. imperialist discourse that imposes an imagined brutality that does not exist. To do either erases the pain and the passion of Marcelo Tenório's desire and will to resist, Luiz Mott's commitment to ending the homophobic violence in his country, and Tania Alvarez's attempts to use the law "on the side of the poor and dispossessed." Tenório states as his reason for leaving Brazil: "I wanted to live my life with freedom" (15). This case is Tenório's *testimonio*—his act of bearing witness to the contradictions of his life—always incomplete, always written through and against other narratives. Marcelo Tenório and Luiz Mott are both inescapably inscribed by the circulating discourses of deviance, desire, nation, and law—the naturalized narratives that have constituted their lives. Still, at times these men resist and speak against the totalizing implications of the discourses that surround them, the language and laws that threaten to engulf will and agency. Tenório's desire "to live with freedom" is at the center of the trial, a desire that cannot be simply explained away by (post)(neo)colonial constructions of subjectivity, even as it is informed and constituted through these discourses. Yet we cannot be content with fugacious victories without interrogating the consequences of the discourses we employ to achieve our ends, because after the fleeting moment of reprieve has passed, the bitter taste of remembered narratives lingers in the imagination. We must use *In re Tenorio* as an opportunity for international dialogue on human rights that examines the ethical responsibility of all the players in the transnational drama of desire, persecution, exile, immigration, and resistance, a drama that must always seek to account for the subject caught in the interstitial shadow space between nations.

4 "Welcome to the Global Stage"

Confessions of a Latina Cyber-Slut

> There is no pronoun by which we can refer to the lurker. . . . This one is
> pure potential. That's why the words that describe lurking are ominous,
> filled with threat. This silent one might speak; this reader might sud-
> denly become a writer. And if that one doesn't care anymore to stay hid-
> den, what might spring forth? . . . . opinions of all kinds, facts and em-
> barrassing revelations. Here's where the body lies.
>
> Ellen Zweig, *"The Lurker: Outline for a Murder Mystery"*

> Language is a skin: I rub my language against the other. It is as if I had
> words instead of fingers, or fingers at the tip of my words. My language
> trembles with desire.
>
> Roland Barthes, *A Lover's Discourse*

Una vez, y dos son tres. Once upon a time I entered a volcanic space in an online world, quietly, without expectation, to polish my Spanish and to amuse
myself after hours of study. I lingered in silence for a while, lurking, discon-
certed by the banter of men who seemed to know one another, frustrated by
the myriad of regional colloquialisms, at times bored and at other times en-
vious of a camaraderie of which I was not a part.[1] Like a stranger in a gay bar
encountered on a foreign adventure, I was intrigued but not yet enchanted.
On occasion, I would see the traces of a woman, with a soft and feminine
name. From her e-mail address I surmised that she posted from Spain, and
on several occasions she mentioned that her account was made possible by
an oppressive Catholic university operated by the Opus Dei.[2] She continually worried that her messages, written in a computer lab bustling with students, would be intercepted, and her e-mail account and educational career
terminated. She studied biochemistry, and spent hours peering into micro-
scopes, cultivating cells, watching viruses grow. One day rather than chatting publicly, I sent a private e-mail to her personal account. It was not well

received. I had asked what I thought were conversational questions: Do you have a girlfriend? How long have you been a lesbian? What is the gay scene like in Spain? In her response she stated that she was not a lesbian, she had never been with women. She also told me she had recently joined an all-male group of militant *marikas* in Euskal Herria, and she was *gallega*, not *española*.

She had found this queer Spanish-language listserve where we met through a series of links on the World Wide Web, a virtual accident of sorts. Exploring the diverse spaces of alt.soc., she eventually stumbled onto Queer Planet, and without knowing the meaning of the word "queer," entered and discovered a discursive realm that spoke to her in a foreign language about her own uneasy relationship with gender and sexuality. From there, she was invited into this interactive Spanish-language listserve, where our digital paths would meet. Thus confusion, misidentification, and curiosity created the catalyst for a cyber-cellular romance that spanned two continents, six cities, innumerable phone calls, telegrams, faxes, and 1,067 e-mail exchanges. Sex, love, quarrels, and reunions mediated through technology.

As I read the traces of these exchanges now, it remains unclear at times who is writing. The voices melt behind jettisoning markers of authorship. A lovers' discourse, enacted through technology:

>si, mi amor, me gusta cuando me haces preguntas
>>ya vez, te hice muchas en mi última carta. no tienes preguntas para mí?
>mi santiña, es como si estuviera navegando tu cuerpo, descubriendo la fuente de tus ríos, explorando las fronteras de tu ser.
>>mi ombligo es ondo, vaya no creo que sea muy feo
>y ahí me gustaría poner mi lengua y empujar contra la piel que separa lo de adentro de lo de afuera[3]

(>yes, my love, I like when you ask me questions
>>you see, I asked a lot in my last letter. don't you have any questions for me?

>my saint, it is as if I was navigating your body, discovering the source of
   your rivers, exploring the borders of your being
>>my bellybutton is deep, well, I don't think it's too ugly
>and there I would like to put my tongue and push against the skin that sep-
   arates the inside from the outside)

The exchange is as much sensed as read, questions asked and not answered, unsolicited responses, sudden changes in tone. Language is disjointed, fragments of thoughts brought together to create a mood and meaning understood only by the two participants, the white spaces of personal history and emotion haunting the lines of text. The traces of accents and regional colloquialisms observed in phrases hint at ownership, yet even these instances of linguistic differences began to be copied, erased, transformed through months of online textual interaction. Voices blurred in romantic union.

At the beginning of a romantic adventure, it is never clear how the narrative will develop, how the story will unravel. Endings and new beginnings are continually imagined, scripted, abandoned, and rewritten. Who could have imagined that the fragments of these exchanges would end up here, in this alien academic text?

But he who utters this discourse and shapes its episodes does not know
that . . . as a good cultural subject he should neither repeat nor contradict himself, nor take the whole for the part; all he knows is that what
passes through his mind at a certain moment is *marked*, like the printout
of a code. (Barthes, *Lover's* 4)

In the discourse of e-romance, lovers produce a textual history of their involvement, written archives of their amatory electronic encounters, 1,067 declarations of desire whizzing across space.

"Like desire, the love letter waits for an answer" (Barthes, *Lover's* 158). Obsessed with my virtual object of affection, I would wait for an answer, checking and rechecking my e-mail several times a day, waiting for her reply, waiting for the return of desire. Each post received became a confirmation of mutual longing, an invitation and enticement to continue, another episode in the unfolding drama of virtual desire. Through the course of these early electronic exchanges, details of bodies and worlds were described, depicted, exchanged, transformed. I wondered about the curve of her neck, the view from her bedroom window, the rhythm of her stride, the scent of her hair. Over time we exchanged photographs, xeroxes of our hands, letters with wildflowers pressed between the pages. Slowly we became more embodied— a face, a voice, handwriting, a scented handkerchief, the visual imprint of a kiss. One day we meet face to face (F2F) at an airport in Los Angeles. Over the months that followed we would meet again at a railroad station in Pamplona, say good-bye in San Francisco, exchange embraces in New York. As the harshness of the material world seeped into our relationship, we had to deal with mounting phone bills, visas, and immigration offices, the demands of career and employment, the emotional turbulence of a shared commitment to nonmonogamy. Real-world realities and differences ended up dismantling our idealized virtual union.

La Máquina Seductora

Technology can be a sensuous seductress or a cruel dominatrix. It requires conquest and mastery and in return it offers the rewards of thrills and experiences as yet unknown. Its enchantment lies in the allure of possibilities, new ways to imagine the sensations of a seemingly familiar world. The powers and the privileges technology offers are always inscribed by other circuits of power and privilege. Cyberspace is not the final frontier; it is not a space of liberation; it is not a decolonized zone where gender, nation, and the constraints of culture lose meaning. Existing "in the machine" does not assuage the social, economic, or political conditions that construct both ourselves and our new mechanical habitats. Joseba Gabilondo writes, "By emphasizing its interiority rather than the geopolitical and cultural interfaces that form it, the ideology of cyberspace is enforced instead of being critically thought

117

out. The interpellation of the individual as a consumerist cyborg is determined by the specific modern, colonial, or non-Western cultural structures that interface with cyberspace and consumerism" (429). Designed as another tool of the expanding war machine, it was not created with me in mind. Yet, as Shannon McRae has noted, "Demonstrating an adaptability admirably in keeping with the seemingly endless evolutionary permutations of capitalism, human beings have turned the machinery of power that surrounds them into sources of play and pleasure" (244). I am one such human being, a cyborg who has found pleasure in a machine.

The stories you are about to read are virtual: they exceed the boundaries of narrative even as they are recounted through them.[4] They require readers to imagine another context through which the world can be experienced, an interactive world that is perceived through pixels on a screen and is made possible by the hidden intricacies of microchips, phone lines, and cybernetics. As an escort into this virtual terrain, I am an untrustworthy guide. My journey has traversed the terrains of newsgroups and listserves, the World Wide Web and Internet Relay Chat. There are many stories to tell, stories that come to me through the quiet hum of my computer. There are love stories about transatlantic encounters, violent stories about massacres and mutilations in places I have and have never visited; there is the endless stream of news, events, protests, denunciations; there are gossip and friendship; there is sex.

Digital discourses, those virtual exchanges we glimpse on the Net, are textual performances: fleeting, transient, ephemeral, already past. Like the text of a play, they leave a trace to which meaning can be assigned, but these traces are haunted by the absence that was the performance itself, its reception, and its emotive power. To write about these online performances already alters their significance; a shift in temporal and spatial context produces a shift in meaning. Instead of submission to the impossibility of representing presence, Peggy Phelan has used performance as a means to redefine writing itself.

To attempt to write about the undocumentable event of performance is to invoke the rules of the written document and thereby alter the event itself. . . . The challenge raised by the ontological claims of performance for writing is to re-mark again the performative possibilities of writing itself. (148)

Cyberspace, like the theatrical stage, implicates the real outside the machine, as it produces its own real inside the machine. Both serve as a catalyst for the radical reconceptualization of reality, its representation, and its reproduction. Taking up the challenge set out by Phelan, this chapter is an exercise in performative writing.[5] These virtual stories, these cryptic pieces of my own engagement with queer *latinidad* that I have composed for your consumption, are both confessional and allegorical. They have been rescripted through transcription, through narrative, through translation, through nostalgia, and through the filtering veneer of academic writing. If you look for traces of my stories in the virtual world, you may or may not find them. Perhaps our electronic paths have already crossed and you may think you have found a piece of yourself within these pages. The only evidence of my travels is the stories I am able or willing to recount.

As I begin this virtual journey, where space, place, and time begin to shift in meaning, it seems only fitting that I first situate myself IRL (in real life). I am writing in the shelter of a studio apartment on Hyde Street between Eddy and Ellis in the Tenderloin District of San Francisco. It is morning and the view promises a sunny day. I don't live there anymore.[6] But for now it forms an integral part of my life in this city. There are other queers, immigrants, students, cyborgs in my neighborhood. I have never been assaulted here, but I live surrounded by the many subtleties of violence. I have kissed women on the steps of my apartment building. I have been asked "how much?" on the street. I have seen undocumented residents sitting handcuffed outside the door to my building and teenage dykes overdose before my eyes. As I have sat writing, the sounds of gunshots and sirens, bird calls and children's laughter have crept their way into the audioscape of the private world where I sit at my computer. Like an e-mail address, a street address is an address to a reader, an attempt to map myself onto the cityscape, legible only to those who are able to decipher the code. Have your travels taken you down my city block? Can you imagine what is outside my door? It will be different the next time you visit. The space outside the machine haunts the space inside. The inside is a window into other worlds, but the world outside my door continues to knock incessantly. The carnal reality I live in refuses to be ignored.

Cybernetic Rhizomes

The Internet was first used as a means of communication between members of the military's scientific digerati under the name ARPANET.[7] As it slowly made its way into wider circles of influence, it maintained its function as a medium for professional and personal exchange. One can imagine that even within its sheltered role among these earliest Internet users, the slippage from professional to personal to erotic may have already existed. And it is this act of online social communication that users, including myself, have continued to find most appealing. Rather than the barrage of news and information currently available online, it is the possibility of connecting with other human beings that may suggest how computers have managed to endear themselves to millions. tatiana de la tierra discusses her own infatuation with this new technology:

> There is nothing adorable about computers, not even the sleek black laptops; never are they anything beyond a machine. Yet I hear the ocean when my Mac chimes on, I anticipate the layered words that await me within, the people who are my electronic fantasies and family, the opportunity to play. (5)

This connectivity across vast spaces has transformed the practice of typing text onto a screen into a social act that can in fact resonate with interpersonal intimacy. We sit at a computer screen alone; it is perhaps the privacy of this solitude that encourages exchanges that are less guarded. Are we writing to ourselves? Ironically, the enigmatic aspects of words flying through space can often allow us to image a more intimate connection.

Like the grids of nation-states that lie across the lines of topographical maps, cyberspace is an imagined terrain. Cyberspace is never one. There is no there out there. There is no singular cyberculture, no singular language with which to speak of the ways identity is practiced and experienced online. The amiable e-mails we receive from friends are only distantly related to the anonymous sexual exchanges we may experience in real-time chatrooms. My own relationship to communication online has included mundane professional exchanges, a constant flow of international news and gossip, browsing the homepages of friends and strangers, exploring maps of real and imagined places and spaces, and unknowingly exploring the maps of my own psyche.

The architectural structure of the World Wide Web is rhizomatic; there is no center, no linear progression to guide users (Stivale). Architects of these sites use links to create entry to other spaces, which in turn provide entry into new sets of online linkages. Digital bits appear, disappear, and recombine to form and re-form information as digital systems compress, decompress, encode, and decode. Information, once digitized, is afloat in a ubiquitous network of nodes.[8] Through these multiple networks, users can construct their own avenues of engagement with these sites, entering and moving through various links to actively participate in their own production of knowledge. Sites emerge and disappear; linkages are assembled and dismantled. The unregulated nature of these sites dismantles authoritative versions of knowledge production, creating a multitude of problems and possibilities.[9]

On the Web, institutions, governments, businesses, groups, and individuals can create Web sites that serve to represent aspects of themselves they wish to make public. This technology has been used in innovative and practical ways by community activists to disseminate information, rally international support for local campaigns, issue press releases, and network with other community-based organizations. The most famous of these is the ¡Ya

Basta! homepage of the Zapatistas.[10] Like print media, these sources generally offer the "official" version of events, such as an organization's mission statement, political agenda, and news bulletins. Having a Web page creates instant access to a global audience, yet these sources, like any other, are limited to those who have access to the materials and technical skills necessary to produce, disseminate, and receive them. For example, Dr. Luiz Mott, mentioned in the previous chapter, has used the Internet very effectively to disseminate information internationally about his own group, Grupo Gai de Bahia. Yet very rarely does any information from the hundreds of other grassroots gay organizations in Brazil reach the United States except by word of mouth or through the importation of local print-based newsletters. Having an online presence means having the opportunity to reach a global audience, yet in countries where few queer groups have access to this technology, those groups that do are often viewed as the official national representatives. It is not that these groups who create Web sites for global consumption actually define themselves as being the official representatives of their countries; more often it is the erroneous assumption of Internet users who find it more convenient to accept the most easily accessible version of information available.

The Internet does not create the conditions of unequal access to media and their respective audiences, but it can compound the problem by rhetoric that emphasizes the democratic and multivocal nature of the World Wide Web and other online sources. Theoretically, any individual or group can create and maintain a homepage, but not everyone has equal access to a phone line, a computer, an Internet provider, or the technical resources required to have an online presence. As Gabilondo has so clearly stated, the exterior, the social and material conditions that inform local and national circumstances, continues to impact the interior, the textual representations of the world that reside inside the machine. The Web can create the sense that we have the world at our fingertips, that we have instant unmediated access to news, information, and viewpoints otherwise unavailable. But the World Wide Web, like the public library down the block, is an ideological artifact. It is important to note, however, that information received online also gets replicated and disseminated through other sorts of mediums, such as local news sources, community-based bulletins, or oral transmission, and this movement of information is multidirectional. Lesbianas a la Vista, a local group in Argentina, for example, posts excerpts of local meetings to Infogay, which I have used in U.S. classrooms. Information on oral-anal sex and hepatitis C that I posted to Arenal, a Spanish-language listserve for lesbians, gays, transgenders, bisexuals, and their friends, made its way into a local gay magazine in Uruguay. In addition to the many alternative news and information sources, subscription services such as Lexis-Nexis, Project Muse, and others have also begun to impact how other kinds of writing are researched and referenced.

The Internet, like television, newspapers, storytelling, gossip, and other means of communication, never presents the "whole" story; it is never a transparent and ideologically neutral discursive medium. The Internet does not allow us to do anything new. Activists have been networking, issuing press releases, disseminating information, and attempting to create a visible public presence before the popularization of online communication. Individuals and groups have been arguing politics and linguistics, making art, friends, allies, and enemies throughout recorded time. Lovers have been writing letters, confessing affections, and declaring passions for centuries. The Internet simply provides us a new tool, problematic and complicated in new ways, with which to enact social communication.

The Internet has also become famous for quickly spreading inaccurate news and gossip. For example on the newsgroup soc.culture.cuba,[11] the entire list mourned the death of Celia Cruz for close to twenty-six hours, before it was realized that the reports of her death were false.[12] soc.culture.cuba was the first electronic community in which I participated, a newsgroup where Cubans (mostly in the United States), scholars, and aficionados of Cuban culture would discuss politics, recipes, music, and *cubanismos*. It was a fervently bilingual community, and one of the few spaces where Cubans of divergent political convictions actually communicated. There were the fervent *anti-castristas*, the committed, unwavering defenders of *la revolución*, and those of us, self-named *los sospechosos* (the suspicious ones), progressive leftists who nonetheless insisted on more nuanced and complicated readings of political events. While politics formed one of the never-ending threads of dialogue, other types of exchanges and interactions also flourished. After a massive system breakdown, members of the list staged a virtual *despojo*, or spiritual cleansing, complete with offerings of rum, cigar smoke, and songs to Elegua, to banish the evil spirits that had invaded our small corner of *ciberlandia*.[13] The following post, written by Daisann Mclane, a journalist and graduate student at Yale at the time, details a week in the life of soc.culture.cuba (s.c.c):

> Wow! me emociona todo eso. What a week! Consider the sequence of events . . . Leo comes out as a sospechoso. Juana Maria declares,definitivamente, y con mucho orgullo: "I am not Alf!" Then Sonia reveals her true identity as a mole for the Wellesley branch of the CANF . . . Alf admits his secret longings for Clark Gable. Ernesto slips into pre-revolutionary religiosity. Juana Maria—que tremenda ella—comes out!!!! What's come over s.c.c???? When I started reading it was a happy little electronic community of strictly enforced categories and permanently fixed positions. Now everything's fuzzy, in flux, indistinct, and up for grabs. It feels like this newsgroup is passing through a—excuse the terminology—revolutionary moment. What could possibly happen next???????? (Mclane)

Written as a tongue in cheek commentary on the nature of interactive community exchange, Mclane's post also details the routine revelations, inside jokes, and topics of conversation witnessed on these sites. Coming out, politically or otherwise, on soc.culture.cuba was a rite of passage, a declaration of political posture that in many ways served to structure further discursive interactions. As the first member of s.c.c. to come out as queer, I was also flooded with personal stories from everyone who had queer friends or family members, and repeatedly directed to check out the musical offerings of Albita, the butch Cuban singing sensation who at that time was just beginning to make her mark on the Miami music circuit.[14] Members of soc.culture.cuba have also met IRL on various occasions in different U.S. cities and many members have developed lasting social and professional relationships.

The other online community where I have found a more permanent home is Arenal.[15] Named after a volcano in the northeastern part of Costa Rica, it was begun by gay users who had previously belonged to a Costa Rican listserve, Irazu, named after another national volcano.[16] One of the original founders of the list, Daniel Soto-Mayorga, affectionately referred to as *el Papi* by *arenalin@s*, recounts the origins of the list:

Arenal nacio de la necesidad de crear un forum abierto para la expresion Lesbiana, Gay y Bisexual, despues de una larga discusion en la lista Irazu . . . con referencia a la tematica lesbigay, Anibal y yo decimos salir del closet con nuestros compatriotas y se armo la de San Quintin, hasta amenazas de muertes recibimos. Pero lo mas interesante es que Irazu nunca volvio a ser lo mismo, y fue alli que decidimos crear una lista para nosotr@s, primero eramos solo Costarricenses y poco a poco decidimos incluir otr@s. (Soto-Mayorga)

(Arenal was born out of the need to create an open forum for lesbian, gay, and bisexual expression. After a long discussion on the Irazu list referencing the topic of lesbigay, Anibal and I decided to come out of the closet with our compatriots, and a scandal *à la* San Quintin was formed, we even received death threats. But the most interesting thing was that Irazu was never the same after that, and we decided to create a list for ourselves, first we were just Costa Ricans, and then little by little we decided to include others.)

This post, under the subject line "Jornada Astrológica," was a response to a request for the natal details of the list for the purposes of charting its astrological coordinates. The technical origins of Arenal were jointly orchestrated in Indiana and Finland, and the list was officially inaugurated on November

9, 1992. The death threats described by Soto-Mayorga are also not uncommon in cyber-communities, where individuals roaming the World Wide Web stumble onto a site (or seek it out) and send hate messages or other sorts of threats to its owners.

Also evident in the original Spanish-language version of this post is the use of the *arroba* or @ sign in the words *nosotr@s* and *otr@s*. This is a creative linguistic intervention in the highly gendered structure of Spanish, and appears to have emerged in Spanish-language cyber-communities. Unlike the slash in words such as Latinos/as or *amigas/os*, which maintains a gender binary while attempting to be inclusive, the @, or "at sign," literally marks where an individual is "at" in terms of gender, a sign of positionality. The *arroba* functions as a diacritic intervention into a problem of language, yet as the language changes, all other indices for which language is used are also impacted. The orthographic @ impacts the semiotic, the metaphorical, the phonetic and categorizing function of a word such as Latin@ in productive and problematic ways. Its use was the subject of much debate on Arenal, where it has become increasingly popular, with certain members adamantly opposed to such a disregard for the purity of *castellano*, and others vehemently arguing for the need to transform language as part of a larger movement to transform gender relationships. Many *arenalin@s* enamored with this new linguistic option have tried in vain to find a way to pronounce the *arroba*. Of course, discussing verbal pronunciation over e-mail only accentuates the problem. The use of the *arroba* in queer Spanish-language texts has also crept into certain non–cyber-communities. However, current electronic bibliographic indexes and word searches where symbols are assigned specific functions are unable to make linguistic sense of such a term, providing evidence that despite popular attempts to transform language, the disciplinary functions of language as an institutional vehicle for categorization remain operative. Technology only serves to highlight the fact that language is a code.

In the virtual world, the human at the keyboard is continually engaged in reading and writing meaning, in decoding images and text, in representing physical and virtual worlds, often at lightning speeds. Allucquère Rosanne

Stone writes, "The older metaphor of reading undergoes a transformation in a textual space that is consensual, interactive, and haptic, and that is constituted through inscription practices—the production of microprocessor code" (121). In the process, the self and selves that emerge participate in a constant production of identification and signification, often with curious results. de la tierra writes,

> Who am I electronically? Well, I am not very different from who I am in person, but I am more of who I really am. Electronically I tend to be more honest, spontaneous, affectionate, wild, hip, desirous, poetic, and easygoing than I am in real life, where I tend to be moody, to put it politely. In fact, I'm a much more pleasant person to be around when I'm not really there. (3)

This disembodiment, this sense of being there and not there simultaneously, allows for other pieces of identity to develop and emerge. The body does not disappear; fingers, eyes, hands, arms, and more often a voice enable the immersion into the virtual realm, and may similarly suffer from a breakdown caused by repeated use. Once inside, however, the body is imagined liberated from the moors of physical reality. Likewise, the psyche is also allowed to come undone, to release the texts of identity continually under production. McRae writes, "In virtual reality, you are whoever you say you are. And, as some people who thought that virtual reality was a fun place to be somebody else for a while have discovered, it's often true that who you are is a lot more complicated than you ever imagined" (245). This connection between language, identity, and performance becomes repeated, imitated, and transformed through each encounter. As writers return time and again to enter the virtual worlds we discover and create, we leave behind cryptic markers of our subjectivities-in-process. Each time we log on, the scripting of identity starts anew.

Electronic communication can seem to provide an unfettered space in which to represent and explore subjectivity. Through text we are able to reveal aspects of ourselves that may be difficult to communicate in person, we may discover fantasies and fetishes we had never expressed in language or simply never imagined, we may find baring our souls to strangers easier than confiding in friends. It is not that a truer, more genuine or essential self emerges; instead the mere act of continually communicating the self generates a textuality of the self, a written record of interior ruminations, a constant coding and decoding of the self and the other. The liberatory potential of digital interaction, however, remains largely dependent on the social, cultural, and linguistic mandates of specific spaces where identity is performed, and the reception by other members of those online communities (O'Brien).[17]

Virtual Vices

Internet Relay Chat, or IRC, is real-time, multi-user online chat. Users log on to one of several available servers that connect them to everyone else logged on at that precise moment on that particular server, hosting anywhere from hundreds to thousands of users at any one time. The particular server I began frequenting in my earliest forays into the underground world of the IRC would greet me with the phrase "Welcome to the Global Stage," a self-conscious advertisement for the theatrical potential lurking behind the screen.[18] Once on a server, users elect a nick, or nickname, an online name that is unique to that server at that instance, and then choose from one of the many chatrooms or channels available. Most servers give users the option of changing their nicknames at will, allowing users to create, deploy, and often juggle separate and distinct online personas as they enter different channels, or even within the same channel. Selecting a nick, naming yourself, becomes the first conscious act of constructing an online identity.[19] These can be variations on given names, but more often reflect aspects or characteristics that the user wishes to make public, even if the meaning is encrypted and unreadable by other users. Nicks such as "LuckyStrike," "pelAme," "chupacabra," "Guardi@n," "POKER," "boyricua" may contain their own narrative histories, their own shadows, or they may simply be the nick *du jour*—a momentary and random decision of language. Some servers allow users to register their nicks, a form of staking a claim to an online identity through the ownership of a name.

The next step is to select a channel or room. Any one server can house hundreds of rooms, and users can employ search commands such as "gay," "Christian," or "sex" to search for rooms that match their interests. Rooms generally come with both a name and a description, although the description often changes from day to day, or even minute to minute. Some rooms are well-established spaces, others appear and disappear like shooting stars. Any user on a server can create a room. Some rooms are empty; others can include close to one hundred users at a time. These rooms can be structured around an interest, identity, or place, and the name generally provides some glimpse of the social grouping: #30+singles; #gayboys; #zoosex; #argentina; #x-files; #sexpañol. These are public spaces in the sense that the window of text is visible to everyone currently signed on to that channel. Within digital discourse, private spaces are those messages exchanged and viewed between two or more users, although the tacit assumption is that all information transported through the Net may in fact be monitored by anyone possessing the technical means and savvy. But the illusion of privacy remains an integral aspect of Internet communication, a necessary fiction that constitutes the premise of most online interactions. Thus, any user currently on the server can send you a private message that, at least theoretically, only you will receive. Often individuals meet in the public space and agree to "go private." Through the use of multiple windows of text, users can maintain various conversations in public and private simultaneously. Though many rooms exist for the purpose of social chatting, sharing information, hobbies, or interests, a vast number are designed, explicitly or implicitly, to create the possibility of online sexual encounters. And "sex on the Net" is one of the most noted and notorious uses of cybernetic connectivity.

Entering the world of online virtual erotic exchanges, I began with the assumption that my online desires would somehow align with my real-life sexual practices. As I began exploring the sexual spaces of Internet chatrooms,

I entered first into spaces coded as lesbian. Entry into these spaces presupposes a "female" identity. One such chatroom, #lesbians, provided this description: "no men, no flirting, no sex, no lurking." As I entered this chatroom, I was immediately sent a private message:

> webgrl: m/f?
> caridad: f
> webgrl: What is the difference between an ob and a tampax?
> caridad: Is this a joke?
> webgrl: No. Answer the question.
> caridad: an ob has no applicator.
> webgrl: What is a speculum?
> caridad: A cold metal snare that gyns torture women with.
> caridad: I get it now.
> webgrl: What size do pantyhose come in?
> caridad: That is a tough one, I know they have these funny charts on the
>   back. Is that right?
> webgrl: Great! Welcome to #lesbians and enjoy your stay.
> caridad: Why the questions?
> webgrl: We really want to keep this a woman-only space, and it's the only
>   way to keep out men.
> caridad: But these questions are by no means culturally neutral, don't you
>   see that as a problem?
> webgrl: Those are the rules the chanops have set up. Enjoy your visit.[20]

I had successfully managed to "pass" as a woman, fully aware of the way my
access to these cultural codes, the "right" answers, was marked by my partic-
ipation in U.S. consumer culture, and a certain classed position within it. The
Internet is touted as being a "global" space. Would women in Colombia or
Pakistan know what an *o.b.* was? Would biological men raised in the United
States know? If this is a space for "lesbians," how does the pantyhose ques-

tion exclude butch women who may have never bought a pair of pantyhose in their lives? How does a speculum impose an assumption of access or willingness to participate in a Western health care system? I certainly couldn't think of any set of questions that all women have access to that no man would be able to answer, and felt uneasy about the process of exclusion. Nonetheless, I felt a guilty pleasure at having been allowed entry. Once inside the public space of #lesbians I was greeted with several hellos from the other small group of chatters assembled, and I responded with "Hola chicas!" seeking to both assert my Latina identity and scope out any potential Spanish-speaking participants.[21] I also assumed that this rudimentary Spanish would be intelligible to most English speakers. I was quickly informed that #lesbians is an English-only space, that the use of other languages in public would make it impossible for channel operators to monitor whether or not women were being harassed. My level of uneasiness increased, but perhaps more important, I was quickly bored with the chatter on k. d. lang, Ellen, and the small clique of already established online friendships. After a few moments I politely asked what channels were appropriate for sex and flirting and was directed to #bifems.

#bifems also came with an exclusionary description: "women only!!!! no men, no lurking, no exceptions!!" but it at least offered the possibility of flirting and cyber-sex. I joined the channel. This time I was sent a public message: "m/f?" "Very female," I responded. This proved to be the end of the identity patrol, or so I thought. I entered the public space, intent on discovering the pleasures of cyber-sex.

> sugardoll: Hi caridad! Nice nick, How are you doing?
> caridad: I'm fine, not quite as fine as you, but I'm doing okay.

I was quickly informed that I had been kicked off the channel. I was incredulous. What had I done? I sent a private message to the channel operator, "barbisbi," demanding an explanation.

barbisbi: No men allowed!!

caridad: I'm female!!! Really!! Ask me a question!!

barbisbi: I don't think so. Like I said no men, no exceptions.

caridad: wait a minute, I've been a dyke all my life, what do you want? I can name lesbian bars in NY, SF, LA, Miami, what is the deal?

barbisbi: Anyone could know that, I can tell you're a guy by the way you write, why don't you just leave us alone and go play elsewhere.

caridad: I'm a lesbian!!! Do you want me to name lesbian writers? artists? just name it!!

barbisbi: lots of Women's Studies classes at Berkeley eh Juan???? No dice.

I realized she had done a "/whois" search and seen my "real name," which she interpreted as a feminized fictional one. I had in fact been interrogated, only this time it was without my knowledge. My own technical proficiency had not advanced to changing either my name or my online affiliation with Berkeley. In fact this exchange of private messages continued for some time, and I remained totally aghast that I was unable to prove my identity as either a female or a member of the lesbian community. My language, which I had meant as subtle flirting, had been "read" as male, my wealth of knowledge about dyke culture had been determined to be accessed through women's studies classes, which I was in fact teaching at the time. I was outraged, and wondered who "barbisbi" *really* was, this individual who was denying me access to a space I felt I had a "right" to occupy. Perhaps "barbisbi" was the cyber-girlfriend of "sugardoll"; perhaps the incident was racially motivated; or perhaps, as a friend later suggested, I was simply trying too hard.

Rather than being a space without borders, chatrooms such as #lesbians and #bifems strive to enforce the impossibility of rigidly defined gender categories. Of course, "barbisbi" could have been a man or boy off-line yet, if her online gender performance convinced other members of that particular cyber-community to grant her access to channel operator privileges, she would become the enforcer of the law, the gender police within that space. Or she might have been one of the original founders of the channel, allowing her not only channel operator privileges but the ability to extend those privileges to whomever she deemed fit. Rather than a kind of lawlessness, these chatrooms occasion the opportunity for each community to write and enforce its own rules about online conduct and self-elect its enforcers. Users can be "kicked," a programmed command that removes a user from a given chatroom for a specified period of time, or "banned," which permanently denies access to that user. Users who continually flood, spam, or otherwise disrupt the operations of a server can also be "K-lined," or "killed," permanently denied access to the entire server.[22] To further complicate the matter, channels are peopled with both real-life users and robots, or "bots," system programs that execute any number of commands. "Bots" can be programmed to welcome users, serve virtual drinks, dish out insults, deliver virtual flowers, censor language, or "kick" out offending users. New participants, or "newbies," may often spend considerable time chatting with a "bot" before realizing that they are interacting with the programmed responses of a nonhuman.

A chatroom entitled #lesbians must surely be bombarded with men posing as women in order to gain access to the exoticized fantasy of lesbian sex. Yet unlike traditional pornography, which frequently depicts men watching women having sex, in chatrooms such as this one, men are required to "perform" femaleness, to enact their fantasy of lesbian sex through language. At some point in the sexual exchange, some men might feel compelled to confess their "true" gender. This moment of confession in fact corresponds to the moment in cinematic pornography where the man joins the women and ends up fucking them both, thus reestablishing the primacy of heterosexuality (L. Williams 140). In cyberspace, however, the moment of true confessions may result in the revelation that his "lesbian" sexual partner is also male.[23]

Scripting Genders

While many authors writing on cyber-culture emphasize the possibilities of cross-gender performativity on the Internet, often it is discussed in terms of disguising "real" biological sex, thus reinscribing a unitary sex as gender norm. In contrast, what is often witnessed in these spaces is the creative production and transformation of genders and their signification.[24] Stone writes,

> In cyberspace the transgendered body is the natural body. The nets are spaces of transformation, identity factories in which bodies are meaning machines, and transgender—identity as performance, as play, as wrench in the smooth gears of the social apparatus of vision—is the ground state. (180–81)

My own experiences passing as a man were few. I found it taxing, particularly in Spanish, where every adjective, every description of self is gendered. Unlike many butches who routinely disrupt the dominant cultural and linguistic connections between gender and genitals to reconfigure their bodies, simulating sex with a body that is not my own required entering into what, for me, constituted a foreign body: I had never lived within the space of a male anatomy. As a lesbian femme, I had considerable experience with dicks and the verbal and sexual practices associated with them, but I had never "owned" a dick before.[25] Passing as a man, and owning a dick discursively, required entering into male interiority, a sexual sensibility that presented its own set of linguistic challenges.

gloria: *acariciame* [caress me]

galan: *tu piel es como seda* [your skin is like silk]

galan: *quiero bañarme en tu perfume* [I want to bathe in your perfume]

gloria: *mmmmm, me encanta como me tocas* [I love how you touch me]

gloria: *como me miras* [how you look at me]

galan: *tus pezones se hacen perlas en mi boca* [your nipples become pearls in my mouth]

gloria: *si amor, si, tomame* [yes, love, yes, take me]

galan: *tengo la polla tan dura* [my dick is so hard]

gloria: *eres tan hombre, tan fuerte* [you are so manly, so strong]
galan: *estoy tan mojado pensando en tu hoyo* [I am so wet thinking about
  your hole]

I had slipped. I had proclaimed wetness, a wetness typical of female excita-
tion—a momentary lapse into my own gendered body. Wetness, in a male
body, indicates a premature release of semen, not a desirable condition. I had
managed to maintain the male gendering using *mojado*, rather than *mojada*,
yet I instantly sensed that my performance had suddenly come undone. Did
Gloria notice? Was she so immersed in her own fantasy that this release of
female fluid onto the text of a heterosexual encounter was overlooked? In
fact it was overlooked, and throughout the exchange she repeatedly claimed
how masculine I was, how she loved the way I made love to her, how I epit-
omized everything she wanted in a man. Toward the end of the exchange,
she asked me to promise to seek her out again; she wanted me as her cyber-
lover.[26]

I never used that nick again.

On another occasion, in a Spanish-language lesbian space, I had gone private with a woman from México. Rather than sex, we were politely discussing our lives, our tastes, our material circumstances. In another slip of
language, I innocently wrote, "estoy cansado," using the masculine form of
the word "tired." She jumped all over me, convinced I was male, fed-up and
frustrated at the many men who attempted to pose as women in order to
gain access to lesbian spaces. In that instance, rather than argue, rather than
attempt to prove my femaleness, my dyke self, I simply admitted to maleness, apologized, and ended the conversation. Language had again failed me.

The repeated failures of language and identity only serve to highlight their
instability as transparent signifiers. Yet in chatrooms there is the possibility
for performing gendered identities that are understood and valued as performative, generally in those spaces marked as S/M. Although in some circles
S/M has become a kind of shorthand for all kinds of interactive sexual play
and performance, on the Internet, as in these communities themselves, these

spaces are highly codified and specific, with channel names such as #bondage, #gshowers, #leatherdykes, #gayCBT, #boy_daddy. It seems that every conceivable fetish and fantasy has established an online presence.[27] Within these chatrooms, often very little information needs to be exchanged in order for a scene to be established; many participants come to these channels with specific fantasy story lines they wish to enact. Based on her study of phone sex workers, Stone writes about the implications of narrowing the bandwidth of communication. She writes, "In enacting such fantasies, participants draw on a repertoire of cultural codes to construct a scenario that compresses large amounts of information into a very small space" (94). These cultural codes can be founded on narratives of submission and domination, age-play, a site-specific context, or an established set of characters—doctor/patient, priest/sinner, master/slave. A public posting in #familysex could be, "Any naughty mommies want to spank this bad boy's behind?" Any interested "naughty mommies" could then send a private message to the user and either begin immediately, "Did you forget to take the trash out again? You bad boy, Mommy is going to have to discipline you," or chat first to provide further information such as the character's name, age, situation, the desired degree of violence, the general mood of the scene, or any specific requests. Some players may also ask for real-life information either before or after the scene.

Although this sort of sexual play routinely occurs IRL, cyberspace provides a "safe" space for individuals to explore their fantasies. Writing in *conmoción*, Gina Violeta Anderson details her own experimentation with S/M in cyberspace.

> I've always had an interest in s/m but I'm too timid to go to our local s/m lair. I found a lesbian s/m room in an online service that I subscribe to and soon found myself happily submitting to online dominatrixes that bent me to their will. I discovered that although I enjoyed the online scenarios, in real life I am quite happy with "vanilla" sex. Cyberspace is

a safe place to play out my fantasies. And I learned that the real sex organ is my mind and I could explore my fantasies and go as far as I like, online. (10)

In addition to the relative safety of these exchanges, sustaining these fantasy roles textually draws directly on the possibilities offered by the absence of visual markers that could disrupt a scene. After I mentioned I was Latina to one online participant, she asked if I was "hairy," and indicated her proclivity for hirsute women; online it was easy to conform to her fetishized image in order to fulfill her erotic fantasy.

Gender in this context extends well beyond any recognizable binaries of male and female: rebellious white trash teenage boy, coquettish mom, innocent Catholic schoolgirl, gentle granddad, lecherous professor, submissive Latina femme, the list goes on and on. As C. Jacob Hale has suggested, "Instead of speaking of a person's gender status, we might do well to speak of a person's gendered status in a given cultural location, at a given time, and for a given purpose" (232). Some participants may form an attachment to a particular persona and develop the nuances of that characterization with an established partner or through exchanges with multiple partners. Yet these spaces also create the possibility to explore, play, or "try on" various forms of identification. In cyberspace the schoolgirl, the slave, the rapist has no body; there are no immediate corporeal consequences. These identifications and desires may be experienced through the body but are not lived through them; this (dis)association can function as part of the erotic charge. McRae writes, "The intensity of pleasure results from the kind of sustained dislocation required when your body is entirely real and entirely imagined at the same time" (261). This dislocation permits an abandonment or expansion of the usual limits of physicality. Pain, like pleasure, is sensed differently. Inhibitions, ethical considerations, and self-imposed taboos are more easily disregarded or dismissed. Guilt, shame, or a sense of culpability may form an accepted and integral part of the erotic encounter. For other users who have suddenly found themselves sexually aroused by acts they would normally find unconscionable, these emotions may continue to haunt them once they log off.

Wild experimentation with gender and sexual practices necessitates a certain desire, willingness, and imagination. If viewed as simply an exercise in "acting," it requires an incredible amount of work. The singular or occasional experience of performing "maleness" or "schoolgirl" online is not quite equivalent to gender performativity. Without an emotional attachment to gender, without a deeper sense of identification, these online performances can only be read as gender play. And in the realm of cyberspace, it is play that has little material or carnal consequences, unlike the ramifications for gender play and transgender performativity outside the machine. But through the repeated enactment of a gendered subjectivity, these new scripted identities may begin to acquire individual significance. Attachments and shifts in identification can and do occur as a result of online experimentation, and can seep into real-life sexual practices. My own attachment to gender remains quite ordinary; I like being a girl. But I love being *una mujer*.

Performing *Mujer*

#espanol, a Spanish-language chatroom where I found a temporary home, provided a space to expand and explore my own definition of *mujer*. Latin@ identity as such is intricately tied to language in cyberspace; although English-language Latin@ spaces exist, the emphasis on text makes the Spanish language itself a primary vehicle for expressing cultural identity and, more important, connecting with other Latin@s around the world. Unlike the other channels I visited, #espanol was much more populated, thus faster and initially more disorienting.[28] Conversations about *fútbol* and system programs, friendly chatter, and flirtatious exchanges whizzed by at lightning speed. Reading and decoding national accents became one of my favorite pastimes: the *vale* of the Spaniards, the *sale* of the Mexicans, the Argentinean *vos*, the Puerto Rican *chévere*. Of course accents and regionalisms, particularly those read through text, can be copied, borrowed, or imitated. Once inside #espanol, questions of "place" seemed to scroll down my screen every few minutes, directed at one user or another, usually in the form of "¿de dónde eres?" (Where are you from?) or "¿de dónde escribes?" (Where do you write from?). Reading the responses, I was struck with the many ways that place was described: B.A. (Buenos Aires), Sinaloa, Caguas, Minnesota, Valencia; others simply responded with country names, Uruguay, Colombia, Venezuela; still others would write, "at home," "at school," "at work." My own response always seemed more convoluted than simply naming a place: "Soy cubana, pero vivo en yankilandia."

The omnipresent question of "m/f?" became "h/m?" and caused a moment of initial confusion: was this *hombre/mujer* (man/woman) or *hembra/macho* (female/male)? "Mujer," I would answer. From my experiences in the public space of #espanol, I quickly discovered that those users with hyperfeminine names, "mamicaliente" (hot mama), "Sxygrl," or "tetona" (big tits), or who were actively advertising for sex, "busco un hombre ardiente para hacerme explotar, mandame un priv" (I'm looking for a hot man to make me explode, send me a priv [private message]), were generally perceived to be men "disguised" as women, and were often shunned by many of the male users. Others either didn't care or preferred to maintain the fantasy. Aside from homophobic anxiety, it also seemed that seducing *una mujer decente*, or at least one who performed "hard to get," posed more of a challenge and was therefore more desirable, mirroring the values in the outside world. C. Jacob Hale writes, "Gender performativity, just as any other form of performativity, must occur within social constraints to be intelligible; it must be intelligible if it is to be efficacious; and if it is not efficacious it cannot succeed as performative" (225). In #espanol, female gender had to conform to a regulated heteronormative performance: Latinas aren't supposed to advertise for sex, even when they want it. While certain male users would post subtle or overt public postings for cyber-sex, most users, male and female, preferred more subtle forms of seduction, often mirroring pickup lines in face-to-face encounters. In #espanol, these exchanges were often peppered with dialogue reminiscent of the *piropos* that men direct at women on the street.[29]

I soon discovered that heterosexual flirting in Spanish required a more attentive and playful use of language than anything I had experienced on English-language lesbian or heterosexual channels. In turn, it generated a heightened sense of excitement and intrigue. It allowed me to bask in the amorous discursive attentions of my many online suitors within the safety of my home in a language I had always associated with intimacy and sensuality. Wearing sweatpants and a tee shirt, I found it easy and intensely gratifying to relish the compliments and heterosexual advances of men I surely would have avoided had I encountered them in person. "Passing" as a heterosexual female opened up a new world of possibilities; single, heterosexual *cubana* enacted a set of performative gender expectations that I had never experienced as a "real-life" lesbian femme. My transgender performance was under way; a performance that I had once repudiated became a new kind of fascination.[30]

It has been frequently noted that users posting messages as women tend to generate a great deal more attention than those posting as men (McRae; Stone), a sexualized attention that may or may not be desired. Christina Elizabeth Sharpe extends that observation to account for the responses to racialized cyber-identities. She notes, "The Internet allows for the consensual as well as the nonconsensual acting out of racialized fantasies" (par. 12). Describing myself specifically as a Cuban female generally sparked a series of public or private messages, either addressing the political situation in Cuba or, more often, suggesting that I must be a fiery hot female.[31] "Dicen que las cubanas son muy calientes, es así?" (They say Cuban women are very hot, is that true?). Many times questions were directed at my racial makeup, that is, am I the hypersexualized *mulata* of their racialized dreams? Although at times I would consciously take pleasure in the stereotypes I constructed, at other times I was offended and alarmed by the pejorative and racist associations I encountered. Christina Elizabeth Sharpe's essay "Racialized Fantasies on the Internet" does not ask us to think about whether these online performances subvert or reinscribe real-life sexual dynamics; instead, she offers a more intriguing proposition. She asks, "But what if imaginatively occupying particular positions in cyberspace, rather than contesting those embodiments, helps us begin to address how we are constituted through these relations with racial and sexual others in RL as well?" (par. 14). As I began to frequent the virtual space of #espanol more regularly, I had no idea what I would encounter in myself or those I came across. In part, this uncertainty about what reflections, fantasies, or habits would emerge formed part of both the anxiety and the allure.

In general, public conversation on #espanol steered away from the controversial or inflammatory if sexual conquest was part of the desired goal. Most attempts at flirting were usually indirect; users would chat publicly for some time before suggesting we adjoin to a private space. Not all private exchanges ended in cyber-sex, and even those that did generally would touch on work, age, school, marital status, or private life before asking more intimate questions that marked the initiation of a sexual exchange, frequently beginning with "¿Cómo eres?" (What are you like?). This routine of describing the physical body I found initially disconcerting but eventually came to be one I enjoyed. It allowed me to alter or exaggerate details such as age, hair, and body type (for example, I would routinely "grow" my hair and clip ten years off my age). In these private exchanges, my own descriptions tended to be laced with self-exoticization, subtle invitations to fuel the amorous discursive exchange: "tengo los ojos el color del mar caribe, la piel clara, pelo oscuro y largo y un cuerpo firme y sensual de bailar rumba, salsa, y merengue. ¿Te gusta bailar?" (I have eyes the color of the Caribbean sea, light skin, long dark hair and a body firm and sensuous from dancing rumba, salsa, and merengue. Do you like to dance?) Thus we would begin, at times ending up on a beach in Cancún, fucking in the lapping waters under moonlit skies. On other occasions the exchanges were merely descriptive of what my sexual partner would like to do to me were we together: "ahora te estoy acariciando el pelo, dejando mis manos pasar por todo tu cuerpo. me encanta el olor de tu piel" (right now I am caressing your hair, letting my hands roam all over

141

your body. I love the smell of your skin). In these exchanges, rather than a discursive disembodiment, the body becomes a discursive fetish, continually described, adored, coveted precisely because it is absent. Elaborate descriptions of the senses—touch, sight, smell, taste, and hearing—become the medium through which arousal is cultivated and maintained. Here the bandwidth of language expands beyond the narrative to do the sensory work usually associated with the activities of the body. As Butler noted in *The Psychic Life of Power*, attempts to escape the body result in a reaffirmation of the body, just as an escape from consciousness implies a reassertion of consciousness (53). The body never disappears in cyberspace; it is continually reaffirmed, reimagined, reified—written and rewritten, over and over again.

Many times, toward the end of these exchanges, I would penetrate these men anally, often while virtually performing fellatio, my attempts to "queer" these heterosexual exchanges. Rarely did my partners object, and many cited it as incredibly exciting, something they would not dare do IRL, just as picking up anonymous men is something that falls outside the realm of my current carnal sexual practices. Thus, both of us would safely explore aspects of our gender and sexuality within the shelter of our real world habitats. Sometimes after sex, while smoking cigarettes and chatting about our lives outside the Net, I would "come out" as someone who only has sex with women in real-life, provoking lengthy discussions about gender, sexual practice, and queer realities. Many times, however, I did not reveal this fact until I had had several sexual exchanges with the same partner, preferring to keep my offline identity closeted within the public space of #espanol, my new electronic hangout.

In online sexual exchanges on the IRC, participants need to adapt to the high speed of electronic intercourse. In the virtual world a vivid imagination, fluidity with language, and fast typing skills come to be highly valued sexual traits. Rather than the pleasure attained from any particular set of sexual acts, the thrill and excitement become the description of those acts, the virtual language of sex.

Net.sex in text mode plays into an "ascii unconscious," the mutual spelling out of desires, commands, and positions; the fantasies that usually accompany any sex suddenly appear "real" and generated between you and your partner/s. What was implicit becomes explicit; what was thwarted becomes liberating. The result can be overwhelming. (Sondheim 10)

Having sex through language necessitates a literal "spelling out" of desire, the textual declaration of sexual intent. It requires participants to ask, perform or write what they want. While acceptance, cooperation or satisfaction is never guaranteed, the mere practice of articulating desire through language rather than through behavior, accentuates the process of the conscious and mutual negotiation of sexual acts. Accidents happen. One line of text [I sit on your face] can contradict the other's response [I push you against the wall]. The opportunity for discursive inconsistencies or physically impossible couplings is very likely in these rapid-fire exchanges, and only increases with the number of sexual participants. Referred to as trainwrecks, participants are usually able to quickly amend the narrative to recover a plausible story line, quickly sewing together the seams of verisimilitude that have been momentarily undone (White 854).

As exists between real-life lovers, over time cyber-lovers develop their own language, rhythm, and repertoire of expressing sexual pleasure and a routine for sexual exchanges. I came to expect a certain kind of interaction with the regular sexual partners I discovered on #espanol. And as IRL, some were much better lovers than others were. Juggling dozens of online lovers, many of whom routinely visited the same chatrooms, became an exercise in diplomacy and discretion. Romance, jealousy, and intimacy do not disappear, rather they become multiplied, spread out across the virtual bodies of numerous sexual partners, although online, nonmonogamy is the rule rather than the exception. Intimacy is maintained in part by remembering relevant details of each cyber-lover: "tojo" is twenty-six, from Mexico City, and works long hours, and we often talked about food before or after sex; "camilo" is married, from Buenos Aires, and a university professor who preferred political debate and depictions of sexy lingerie; "alb2u" is Catalán, engaged to a Dominican woman he met on #espanol, and he enjoyed three-ways, golden showers, and spankings; "jippy" is really named Juan, and we met each other on a lesbian channel. Conforming to the regulative gender expectations on #espanol, I tried to make each one feel special. Some, infatuated with the allure of respectability brought about by extended periods of courteous courtship, felt certain that they had somehow managed to seduce *una mujer decente*, the seduction of a decent woman being a much more valued conquest. Others enjoyed the *puta* in me.

The textuality of online sexual exchanges draws on the interpretive possibilities of reading and writing language, creating both an absence and an excess. The absence is the carnal, the fleshed out details of voice, intonation, gestures, and visual markers that in F2F interactions code romantic and/or sexual exchanges. Yet this absence also creates a phantasmatic excess, an imaginary space where participants can fill in the details of the encounter in such a way as to maintain the idealized image of the desired other. During the course of my online sexual adventures, many users would ask for pictures, or offer to send them. Many times this is seen as a way to confirm "femaleness," although a multitude of digital images are readily available online if desired. More than one very hot sexual moment was ruined once the image arrived and I had to reconcile my imaginary lover with the grainy details of a photograph. I learned to either not look at the pictures or claim ineptness at being able to view them. Other users would choose to send commercial Web-based photographs from established pornographic sites depicting various sexual acts as a means of attaching a visual image to the textual exchange under way—a fantasy image to match a fantasized act. Still others wanted to shift the exchange from text to voice, and asked for a phone number. Thus photographs, voice, and live video are all options for expanding the bandwidth of communication. Text, however, provides its own allure.

While Samuel Delany suggests that "sexual experience is *still* largely outside language" (28), virtual sex requires the coupling of linguistic and sexual expression, a textual representation of the loss of language. McRae writes,

> To sustain erotic pleasure while making love with words, lovers must maintain their powers of language at a moment when the power of coherent verbal expression is customarily abandoned. The speaking and experiencing selves are necessarily split by the requirement of maintaining language within sensation. Rather than a sensory void, however, the split can perhaps be described as a highly charged space, the delirious, lacerating edge of experience between the pleasure of the text and the point at which all language fails. (261)

These exchanges often begin with a back and forth description of sexual action, touching, caressing, disrobing, fondling, and exploring. As the exchange progresses, one partner may take the lead in writing the description of the sexual exchange; this can allow the other to read and masturbate, rather than write, often referred to as one-handed typing. At the moment of orgasm (virtual or carnal), cyber-lovers often resort to the textual markers that signify the loss of language and control. These can include "sounds": Ooooooooooooo, mmmmmmmmmm, aiiiiiiiiiiiiiii, ssssssssssssssssssssss, accomplished with simple keystrokes. Or in the moment of orgasm they can express themselves with mere gibberish, a literal pounding of the keys: "frsxszdevgSDZXgbzhv '[]\," a kind of textual pounding of the body of pleasure. The following exchange, lifted from the final moments of a sexual exchange, illustrates the paucity of language required for sexual interaction online, the seams of dialogue between the two participants, the flow of linguistic exchange, and the visual representation of desire through text itself:

elije: *te tumbo* [I throw you down]
tuya: *tomame* [take me]

elije: *tus piernas separadas* [your legs spread]

elije: *ummm*

elije: *me bajo los pantalones* [I lower my pants]

elije: *quiero poseerte* [I want to possess you]

elije: *estoy loco por poseerte* [I'm crazy to possess you]

tuya: *siiiiiiii amor siiiiiiii* [yes love yes]

elije: *ummmm dentro ummmm* [inside]

elije: *aaaaaiiiiiiiiii*

elije: *que placer* [what pleasure]

elije: *despacio* [slow]

tuya: *ooooooooooooooooooooooooooooooooooooo*

elije: *empuja* [push]

tuya: *aaaiiiiiiiiiii*

elije: *mas* [more]

tuya: *mas* [more]

tuya: *si amor follame, asiiiii* [yes love, fuck me like that]

elije: *mas* [more]

tuya: *follame* [fuck me]

elije: *ummmm*

elije: *o cielo* [oh heaven]

tuya: *soy tuya* [I'm yours]

elije: *como te entra* [how it fills you]

tuya: *siiiiiiiiii* [yes]

elije: *ummmm*

elije: *empuja* [push]

elije: *mas* [more]

elije: *mas* [more]

tuya: *sssssssssssssssssssssiiiiiiiiiiiiiiiii!!!!!!!!!!!* [yes]

tuya: *sdjkfWEUIIWEFBCJhisdi;fgue7808080sduoofe*

tuya: *!!!!!!!!!!!!!!!!!!!!!!!111111111111111*

elije: *asi amor* [like that love]

Despite those who find the idea of virtual sex an oxymoron, pleasure, real carnal pleasure, can and does happen. Of course, faking orgasm textually requires a great deal less effort than in physical exchanges, and ending an unsatisfactory sexual encounter is as easy as logging off. Eluding unwanted advances, avoiding lovers who have become stale, or seeking out new kinds of sexual adventures can be as easy as changing rooms, changing your nick, or changing your gender.[32] Yet the sensation of pleasure, disgust, or anxiety can linger in the imagination, even once the screen goes blank. And just as in real life, the millions of users who engage in Net sex routinely experience romantic attachment, sexual harassment, and obsessive desire.

᠊ The IRC creates the possibility for a seemingly unlimited number of anonymous sexual encounters, anytime. "Safe sex" on demand—fantasies fulfilled, instant sexual gratification, all without even brushing your teeth. #espanol and other cyberspaces provided a respite from school, work, and the complications of my real-life social and sexual adventures. While many of these relationships may have initially included sex, at some point or another most developed into other kinds of friendships. Like walking into a neighborhood bar after a long day at work, I knew I could log on and see a familiar nick, someone I could share my day with, or simply someone to swap stories with about life on or off the Net. Aside from these moments of reprieve from the sometimes solitary life of academic work, my sexual interactions online also forced me to rethink my own gender and sexuality. What I had understood as my desires, identifications, and sexual practices were all called into question. After several months of performing heterosexuality and delighting in heterosexual cyber-sex, I started to wonder if aside from being a theoretical bisexual, I could also be a practicing one. I began to toy with the possibility of sex with a carnal man, and arranged to meet a few of my male cyber-lovers F2F. In the physical world, however, smell, taste, sight, and sound carry a different presence, and the chemical-carnal charge required for physical intimacy simply never materialized. Though repeated heterosexual virtual exchanges with men did not result in any significant changes in my sexual object choice, it did transform me in other ways. It forced me to reimagine the boundaries between lesbian, bisexual, and heterosexual; between Latina femme and *una mujer latina*; between butches, boys, and men; and the transgendered bodies and identities that traverse these categories. By allowing me to participate interactively in the sexual fantasies of Latino masculinity, it also gave me a greater understanding of the erotic and emotional nuances of masculine sexuality, particularly in real-life Latin@ butches.

For some, Net sex can take on an obsessive quality, or it can become infinitely more fulfilling than the messy physicality of sexual and social relationships in the carnal world. Claudia Springer suggests,

> The appeal of computer existence for humans in the late twentieth century cannot be separated from the actual cultural crises confronting us, in particular the crises surrounding issues of sex and death. In a time when sexual contact with other humans carries the risk of AIDS, computer sex can pose an attractive alternative. . . . There is a long Western cultural tradition of associating sex with death; now, sex is being replaced by computer use, which provides the deathlike loss of self once associated with sexual pleasure. (717–18)

But the little death of orgasm, the loss of self, can also be resignified as an affirming spark of renewed life, the creation of new subjectivities. Cyberspace effects an interstitial plane between the intense physicality of carnal fruition and the possibility of exceeding the physical limitations of the body through language. This is the digital undoing of the unified scripts of subjectivity.

The lust for knowledge of the self, including the quest for insights into the mysteries of our own sexual contradictions, seduces us into thinking we can come to know desire. Yet mastery over desire, whether through the self-conscious production of the scripts of its enactment or through discursive analysis of its texts, continues to elude us. Instead these attempts at mastery form another dimension of the process of that seduction, forever teasing us with the possibility of knowing the primal sources of pleasure. Ironically, academic discourse, which has perpetuated a practice where desire is displaced from the body to the page, has also authorized the discursive valorization of desire. Here the scholarly mandate to probe, investigate, unravel, and resignify affords the justification for lingering in the sexualized embrace of the enigma that is desire.

If these narratives are read as merely confessional moments in the perverse practices of an online writer, they must also be read as exposing the queer titillation of off-line lurkers. If, however, readers reach beyond their edges for the allegorical potential of these virtual tales, these anecdotes also bear witness to the illusive quest for the fusion of subjectivity and mastery through their continual division and union. These stories recount the desire for control over representations of identity and the delights of losing control and being transformed in the process. They speak to the spastic potential for imagining the self made possible when fantasies, fetishes, and flesh are unleashed through self-inscribed texts of subjectivity, the enigmatic power that language has to transform our scripts of identity. Finally, these moments of confessional indulgence taunt us with the knowledge that the textual analysis of desire can never fully grasp or explain the pleasures that arise through their articulation.

Bytes and *Bohíos*

While some bemoan the future of a society where humans interact more with machines than with each other, my own experiences suggest that electronic connectivity generates greater, rather than less, social interaction. In fact, this increased interaction can at times be overwhelming. I now maintain regular e-mail correspondence with many friends and colleagues, some of whom I have never met. Some of these individuals have become part of my extended family, the people I rely on to keep me sane, if not sensible. E-mail provides a queer kind of stability to my life, it allows me to keep in touch with the world even when I am moving through it, connectivity is only a modem away. Today, Eudora delivered to my screen the following e-mail message:

> dear Titi
> I LOVE YOU
> >From ISIS aND dinorah
> Zoo
> ANILA RAUL ISIS ANila rAUL
> I LOVE YOU
> DOG
> CAT
> CLEo
> yo fui a la escuela

Isis, my niece, who is not yet five, sits on her mother's lap and presses the letters on the keyboard with tiny fingers to spell out the details of her world: her family, her new kitten, her love for her Titi, who sits far away, smiling. Does she wonder how her words reach me, what technology makes our communication possible? Or does she simply accept this new medium, like the telephone, or the television, as a "natural" part of her world? Just as her friends Barney and Big Bird come to her through a screen or pictures in a book, Titi Juany visits her through the computer, the telephone, or by photographs sent in the mail, the same Titi Juany that has wild sexual interfaces with technology.

My grandmother was born in 1903 in the tiny town of Soledad, in the outskirts of Cartagena, in the central valley of Cuba. She was born in a *bohío*, a wooden one-room shelter with a thatch roof. The technologies of her day included an elaborate process of combining sandy dirt, water, ashes, and sunlight to create a sturdy dirt floor; gathering and tying *pencas de palmiche*, the hard-seeded branches of royal palms, to make brooms, using the boiled water of the rhizomatic *yuca* plant as a rinse to bleach and starch clothes. Later in her life, as a working housewife who took laundry in for a living, she concocted a way to steal electricity from the local plant in order to use her newly acquired electric iron. By stopping the electric meter with a guitar string, she found a way to access a technology she needed, but could not afford. Not to be read as a narrative of development or progress, I recount these generational shifts as a way to return us to an understanding of space and time, stories and storytellers. Today somewhere on the planet, a housewife will find a way to liberate goods or services in order to accomplish her daily chores; someone else will transact a billion-dollar merger; children and old people will tell stories on the newly swept surface of a dirt floor; someone will sit in prison while others hurriedly send out electronic postings petitioning her release; and lovers will meld and come undone in the spasms of ecstatic passions. The interior and the exterior continually inform each other; swirling bits and bytes of discursive fragments spin out in search of meaning. Life on the Net is not the last word in subjectivity, it is another manifestation of how discursive spaces transform our practices of identity and the social worlds we occupy.

Epilogue

Closing the Book

> In writing this story I shall yield to emotion and I know perfectly well that every day is one more day stolen from death. In no sense an intellectual, I write with my body. And what I write is like a dank haze. The words are sounds, transfused with shadows that intersect unevenly, stalactites, woven lace, transposed organ music. . . . I swear this book is composed without words: like a mute photograph. This book is a silence: an interrogation.
>
> Clarice Lispector, *The Hour of the Star*

At this moment of factitious endings it seems fitting to return to other beginnings, to other texts that I could have produced, other rhizomatic routes I could have followed. And today, this day that I recompose this conclusion, I feel like dancing. (Like Marcelo Tenório, I like to dance.) In 1974 in Hartford, Connecticut, I walked into a dark, magical space that has never left me, and I danced and understood the yearnings of freedom and desire. It was called the Warehouse, the first of many gay bars where I have found a space to move and discover my queer latinized body. I was fourteen. There I made *familia* with lesbian prostitutes with multicolored children, with blond drag queens with butch *boricua* lovers, with Black academic dreamers and sweet white junkie players; there I danced the Latin Hustle, the Bus-Stop, and felt the desperate call of Donna Summer's "Last Dance" night after night.

In the years that have followed there have been many other bars where my dancing body has found a home, each new space requiring a moment of initiation where new rules of spaces and identities are learned and performed, each enacting a process of coding and decoding bodies and spaces.

These bars have also already crept their way into this text in ways that may not have seemed initially clear. In San Francisco Diane Felix, or Chili D, the program director of Proyecto, has hosted monthly Latin dance nights for women and their friends for the past fifteen years. The bar has changed location, changed names, changed music, and changed crowds over the years, but serves as a consistent yet mobile place where women dance salsa, merengue, cumbia, rancheras, and the latest Latin dance crazes. It was at one of these events that I conversed with Tania Alvarez, Tenório's lawyer, and began imagining the chapter on his case. My first night in Pamplona, Spain, where I met my *gallega* cyber-lover, I was taken to El Mesón de la Navarreria, located in *el casco viejo*, or old sector of the city. It is a queer-friendly, immigrant-friendly, leftist bar that plays a hot mix of *nuevo flamenco*, contemporary Cuban, old Motown, and sizzling samba. El Mesón is located at the weekend crossroads of teenage Basque-separatist guerrillas with Molotov cocktails and riot gear–suited police officers with batons and rubber bullets; getting in and out of the bar often takes careful maneuvering and comfortable shoes.

There have been other bars, which like a string of lovers have marked my life and introduced me to new ways of imaging the intersection of bodies and spaces. At La Escuelita in New York City, patrons are frisked at the door and must wait to be seated.[1] As in many bars in Latin America, you can order *un servicio*, or a bottle of liquor, soda, a bucket of ice, and glasses for the table. El Río, in San Francisco's Mission District, is a multicultural, multigender, multigenerational neighborhood "dive" that has offered live bands every Sunday from 4:00 to 8:00 during the warmer months since as long as I can remember. There I enjoyed the rare pleasure of seeing many women friends on El Río's salsa stage, including María Cora, Tami Ellis, and the all-women salsa band Azúcar y Crema; María Medina Serafín as the band leader of the group Sin Igual; the incomparable pianist Patricia Thumas; and the first all-women salsa band I ever heard, Sabrocita, led by the now deceased Mala Maña. Moving to Philadelphia after accepting an academic appointment, I immediately sought out new dance floors and discovered Latin Night at Studio Six in Atlantic City. The action there doesn't begin until midnight and the DJ offers a fiery blend of *bachata*, salsa standards, and grueling merengues. La Mega ("la que se pega"), the local Spanish-language radio station in the area, has begun advertising this once exclusively gay club, and now straight patrons have begun to remap this territory. Closer to home in Philadelphia's gayborhood, I also discovered that Thursday nights are Latin Night at Woody's, and began anew the arduous process of forming community and *familia* through music and dance. Assured of one frenzied night a week where I could press myself close to the body of my *papi chulo* and revel in the ecstasy of the rhythms that have formed me, I realized I could survive the trauma of this latest moment of dislocation.

These bars create their own sense of community and social codes, and "regulars" know the rules about how and who to invite on the dance floor; where drug consumption is permitted and where it is not; how to read dress codes in order to interpret gender and sexual preferences; and the intricacies of bathroom etiquette. These discursive dancing spaces create their own identity practices; each is haunted with its own sense of history and urgency, rhythm and desire. These spaces of *familia* have all made this moment of conclusion possible; they have taught me almost everything I now know about queer, about desire, about bodies on the margins, and dance floors creating momentary centers.

But this is not a conclusion, conclusions are not possible, the stories told within these pages have not ended. All that has ended is my role as narrator. Yet I cannot simply abandon my role and leave you, the reader who has accompanied me thus far, left holding an empty page, left on a dance floor waiting for the music to stop and the lights to turn on. Already you have followed me into dubious academic terrain: the corner of Sixteenth and Mission, where Proyecto activates for change with winsome words and delightfully perverse images; the stifling courtroom where Marcelo Tenório and his advocates and adversaries negotiate temporary legal interventions in the global crisis of international hate and violence; you have even followed me into the private world of my computer screen, where technology and sexuality collide, fornicate, and come undone in wild wantonness. What is called for, at this artificial moment of closure, is a rereading, and a rewriting of the texts that I have brought together.

As a methodological practice, archeological analysis produces rhizomatic diversification rather than unification or synthesis. Even within the confines of the physical landscape of San Francisco, within the discursive language of queer *latinidad*, there is no central subject of investigation, only authorial decisions that are always partial, subjective, self-motivated. This project has been an exercise in kaleidoscopic image-making where figures of queer *latinidad* have been shattered, brought together, and pulled apart through a twisting of the lens of discourse.

The sequence of these chapters represents neither a linear or progressional evolution. Activism, as history or as practice, is not the foundational memoir of legal interventions. Virtual identities do not represent the future of subjectivity, and are never free from the regulative injunctions of social, political, economic, cultural, and linguistic formations that subjects bring to the screen, or that the screens of technologies bring to subjects. Instead, I have attempted to demonstrate how each of these discourses—activism, law, and cyberspace—is constrained by the tensions of the spaces it occupies, and how subjects negotiate multiple, and at times contradictory, discursive dimensions to assign meanings that are legible and efficacious in specific localized sites. Preexisting discursive narratives, such as identity politics, colonialism and freedom, and the promise of liberatory subjectivity through technology, follow the speaking subject into each of these realms. These discursive forces press upon the linguistic and social imaginary and in turn, this imaginary pushes back upon social practices.

Naming as a social practice, integral to the representation of identity, has been a recurring theme throughout these chapters, and is illustrative of the challenges subjects face as they attempt to negotiate discursive terrains. Proyecto has not abandoned categorical markers of identity; it continues to name itself a Latina/o gay, lesbian, bisexual, and transgender HIV prevention agency. However, it has also sought to destabilize these terms through its practices of self-naming, multiple naming, and multilingual naming. In the context of Proyecto's self-representation, naming itself becomes a creative and political project of inscribing individual and collective subjectivity. Naming the self, the community, the daily work of political activism becomes a dynamic and conscious social practice that testifies to the continual (trans)formation of the "subject-in-process."

Under regimes of law, the singularity of a name, a country, a claim for justice marks the legal document and the judicial subject: *In re Tenorio*. The space of the courtroom cannot accommodate the accent of Tenório's name, just as there is no room for the accented realities of racialized and classed experiences. These are perceived as unnecessary excesses that disrupt the imperturbable operations of the law. In the text of the legally constructed petition for asylum, the "here" and the "there" of sexual persecution constitute an impenetrable border, patrolled by immigration officers, appellate judges, and the language of legal (un)reasoning. The immediacy of the claim and the violence that brings the subject to trial can serve as the occasion for the disavowal of global relationalities in the search for momentary resolution. But the continuing violence and injustices that exist outside the courtroom serve as reminders of the consequences of these strategic interventions.

In the ever shifting topographies of cyberspace, naming as a social and linguistic practice becomes an exercise in codification. Subjects incessantly engage in encrypting identity and breaking the codes they and others have scripted. In the chaos of the anonymous and transient spaces of the IRC, names begin to lose meaning as markers of social positionality, identities come undone from the carnal realities of individual bodies. The social significance of those bodies and the identity multiples created through them, however, continue to be regulated by the dictates of cultural narratives. What cyberspace provides is a rhizomatic diversification of cultural and social spaces, but these spaces continue to be written through regulatory conventions that inform their conceptualization and systemization. While virtual realms may provide a larger and seemingly safer playing field for the performance of subjectivity, the individual subjects who enter these digital stages are never fully divorced from the cultural narratives of racialized gender and sexuality that follow them into these new virtual realms.

The discursive coupling of sex and death has unexpectedly crept its way into my narrative of identity and subjectivity, an unforeseen haunting of sorts. In cyberspace, the physical and the psychic realms of subjectivity are undone in the "little death" of orgasm. A mirror of the virtual splitting of the mind and body, these divisions continually come together and come apart in the slippery seams of these virtual identity factories. These new shattered, mobile, and buoyant identity formations, however, are repeatedly reassembled outside the machine, springing forth in affirmations of life and pleasure. It is imperative to remember however, that the technologies that make these formations possible are constructed by other minds and bodies in other factories near and far, and continue to press on the subject inside and outside the screen.

The legal claim for political asylum is based on a fear of death and bodily harm resulting from the desires of sex and the expression of sexuality. The physical mutilations and murders of queers in both Brazil and the United States perpetually haunt the political urgency of legal and political interventions. Coexisting with this carnal death of individual human subjects is the civic death that arises as the collective queer subject is banished from civil society, losing the rights of citizenship and claims to the protection of the nation-state, set adrift in the turbulent waters of internal and external exile. Citizenship, constituted through narratives of normativity and submission to the state, detains the queer subject, who stands outside the gates of nation, seeking recognition and civil rights. The public space of civil society is reserved for those who can elect to conform to the mandates of heteronormativity. The metaphorical death of the queer citizen makes imaginable the physical death of the queer resident of the nation.

Within the space of activism, the union of sex and death in the AIDS pandemic serves as the catalyst for new forms of representation of living, resisting, surviving. Within the images and texts of Proyecto's cultural production, sex and death are accepted as conditions of life, conditions informed, regu-

lated, and defined by hegemonic forces that use both to control and limit social agency. Rather than succumbing to the fear of either, Proyecto's programming creates opportunities for individuals to grapple with their own
definitions and understandings of these culturally defined phenomena.
More important, this discursive reinscription of the social, cultural, and political significance of sex and death serves to issue a challenge for activating
the will to life, not as a natural state of being, but as a politicized project of
resistance and survivance in the face of disenfranchisement, erasure, and
politicized genocide.

The languages I have traversed over the course of this academic performance have taken me into both familiar and foreign terrains. Each discursive
space I entered imposed a different set of linguistic and literary challenges.
Writing about activism and the activists with whom I have shared much of
my life and work required me to simultaneously negotiate the body and the
footnotes of the text, the center and the margins of knowledge production.
I made the conscious decision not to conduct interviews, but to instead
demonstrate how these subjects, individually and collectively, had already
initiated the questions, answers, and dialogue that I wished to make evident
in my own textual production. In the process, I also sought to validate textual forms—flyers, films, oral presentations, creative language practices, political manifestos—not as objects of study but as other forms of theoretical
production. Furthermore, I want to encourage my readers to seek out the
works of the many talented individuals whose words and images have enriched my own intellectual formation.

The chapter on law enacted a more traditional kind of academic narrative
practice. I have never met Marcelo Tenório. I did not sit in that courtroom
where his fate was decided. Instead, I had to rely on the text that was produced
within that space, the court transcript. Legal writing enacts its own demands,
which I have disrupted and deformed in conscious and unconscious ways.

In attempting to demonstrate the identity practices deployed in cyberspace, I elected to use myself as the primary cultural subject under investigation, shifting my presence from the notes into the body of the text. The risk,

of course, is that those composed transcripts of my own engagement with queer *latinidad* will be read merely as confessional, or worse, as literal depictions of my own identity and sexuality. My hope is that these discursive disclosures will be read as an attempt at allegory, deployed through the apprehensive methodology of performative writing, an exercise in virtual representation to represent virtual worlds rather than a self-indulgent performance of my own subjectivity. The risks of exposure, misreadings, and overinterpretations are not ones that I have taken lightly. The reinscription and resignification of academic practices, however, at times require shifting the subject on trial, from those who exist as the subject of the text to the subject who produces the text under inquiry.

In fact, academic discourse has been perhaps the most influential discursive dimension operating within this text, not only as the frame that brings these other spaces together but as the provisional home of my own analytical interventions and interests. As an academic subject with complex and contradictory investments, I too have also had to navigate variegated discursive dimensions to produce articulations of subjectivity and social practice that are decipherable by multiply positioned reading audiences. I too have felt the force of regulative injunctions that demand conformity through the perpetuation of normative disciplinary practices. There is no escape, only routes of intervention, momentary seizures of subversive potential, the cautious, willful trepidation between courage and cowardice that is writing.

Perhaps it is the effects of this illegal entry into academic disciplines that I wish to underscore in these closing pages. In this text, I have demonstrated how discourses on identity and subjectivity travel, how they try to roam through different spaces, how they are stopped at discursive borders, how they are changed through that effort and that motion. Access to the competing discourses that lay claim to the bodies and voices of subjects remains at the crux of efforts to liberate them from their positional groundings. The challenge becomes finding innovative ways to access and mobilize discourses in the service of individual and social transformation. The artists and activists at Proyecto are constantly engaged in acts of appropriation, translation, and resignification, and their efforts have powerfully impacted the discursive landscape of queer *latinidad* in San Francisco and elsewhere. In law, this access to discourse is mediated by the language of the law itself, and by those groups and individuals that come to represent the judicial subject both inside and outside the courtroom. These agents of representation must be held accountable for their strategies of writing the space of resistance, particularly when they resort to the recirculation of narratives that reinscribe positions of power and privilege. In cyberspace, access to discourses is dependent on the materiality of technology, an access that must be demanded as part of a larger social agenda of the redistribution of goods and resources. Until then, users deploy other mediums of communication—gossip, storytelling, image making, and the printed word—to spin knowledge out and into the machines of technology.

When discourse is ripped from its roots, its epistemological underpinnings can be contemplated and studied, its rhizomatic potential can be set in motion. Perhaps then discourse itself can be recognized as a vehicle of transformation, allowing for other kinds of knowledge to bloom. Rather than relying on explicative narratives to inscribe and interpret subjectivity, readers and writers can begin to turn these practices into conscious engagements with knowledge production. Instead of structuralist categories that fail to account for the psychic excesses of mobile desires, identifications, and contradictions, thinkers can begin to unleash their critical imaginations in the service of perceiving and articulating the complex dimensions of subjectivity and the dramas in which they unfold. Lastly, we must not be ashamed of finding pleasure in our work, in the language games that surround us. It is this pleasure in words and deeds that can sustain us through the trials of life and the act of living on trial.

If my own words sound overly passionate, if they seem to beseech a radical reenvisioning of the project of reading, writing, and interpretation, it is because I remain foolishly invested in a vision of the future, trapped in my own temporal attachments to life. The end of this manuscript signals a kind of tiny death, and it begs remembrance. Roa Bastos ends the text that serves as the opening epigraph for my own narrative with the following parenthetical statement: "(the remainder stuck together, illegible, the rest unable to be found, the worm-eaten letters of the Book hopelessly scattered)" (424). The remainder of my own text is similarly stuck together, illegible, lost and scattered in other spaces. As I scurry off the page I leave you, my reader, with the possibilities of interpretation, interrogation, and action, and with the courage and *corazón* of the *divas, atrevidas, y entendidas* that have enriched my own understanding of queer *latinidad*.

Notes

Notes to Chapter 1

1. For useful critical commentary and analysis on the use of the word *latinidad*, see Román and Sandoval-Sánchez, "Caught in the Web: Latinidad, AIDS, and Allegory in *Kiss of the Spider Woman*, the Woman, the Musical." My own usage echoes the more "contestatory and contested" potential voiced by Aparicio and Chávez-Silverman. See specifically note 1 in the introduction to *Tropicalizations: Transcultural Representations of Latinidad*.

2. The term "(post)(neo)colonialism" has been selected as a claim to the simultaneity of these categories for understanding the relationships between nations and cultures in Latin America. I contend that these conditions function in unison to constitute one another. As we enter the twenty-first century, Latin America and the Caribbean are home to several U.S. and British colonies and "dependent territories," including Puerto Rico, Bermuda, the British and U.S. Virgin Islands, Anguilla, Turks and Caicos Islands, the Cayman Islands, the Falkland Islands, and Montserrat. Martinique, Guadeloupe, and French Guiana are governed by an overseas department of France. In addition to Puerto Rico, the U.S. Virgin Islands, Guam, and American Samoa, U.S. territories currently also include the Federated States of Micronesia, Marshall Islands, Midway Islands, Mariana Islands, Palau, and Wake Island. Other Latin American countries have been postcolonial since the late eighteenth century. As early as 1793, Toussaint L'Ouverture rebelled successfully against enslavement and colonial rule in Haiti. These historical complexities require reflection and continued critical analysis on the manifestations and uses of theories of postcoloniality in a historicized Latin American context. The volcanic eruptions in Montserrat also remind us that nature itself is a powerful force in the historic evolution of diverse geographies. Fuller investigation of these questions exceeds the scope of this project. For further reading on the uses and implications of postcolonial, postmodern, and poststructuralist theory in Latin America, see the essays in Yúdice et al., *On Edge*; Beverley et al., *The Postmodernism Debate in Latin America*; and the very influential work by García Canclini, *Hybrid Cultures: Strategies for Entering and Leaving Modernity*.

3. See Vizenor, *Manifest Manners*, and "Changing Personal Names," in *Crossbloods*, for the significance of personal names and nicknames in tribal stories. For the significance of racialized location within families and social constellations, see Moraga, "La Güera," in *Loving in the War Years*; Ortiz Cofer, "The Story of My Body," in *The Latin Deli*; Richard Rodriguez; Moreno Vega; Cortez et al.; and numerous essays in Ramos, *Compañeras*; and Moraga and Anzaldúa, *This Bridge*. The pervasiveness of authors of color who read and write the racialized and gendered body as a critical theoretical practice in many ways precedes and informs newer manifestations of this practice in Anglo queer and feminist writings.

4. For essays that analyze the contentious relationship between race and identity in Puerto Rico, Latin America, and the Caribbean, see the spring 1996 special double issue of *Centro: Journal of the Center for Puerto Rican Studies*, particularly Rodríguez-Morazzani and Santiago-Valles. Also of exceptional interest is Adrian Burgos, Jr.'s article on Caribbean baseball players in the Negro Leagues from 1910 to 1950, in which he discusses the lived consequences of Caribbean ball players negotiating the U.S. racial order.

5. See Alarcón, "*Traddutora*," for her analysis of hetero-masculinist narratives of Malinche, and McClintock for her reading of nationalism, gender, and race in South Africa. For a powerful and nuanced analysis of sexuality, citizenship, law, and postcoloniality in Trinidad and Tobago and the Bahamas, see Alexander.

6. See Halter for her analysis of how Cape Verdeans have negotiated the binary racial order in the United States.

7. These are the native language names for these territories. The Castilian names are Galicia, Cataluña, and El País Vasco.

8. Statehood received 46.5 percent; Independence 2.5 percent, ELA .1 percent, and Free Associated Republic .3 percent. The breakdown of the vote is misleading, however. The PIP splintered its vote between Independence, Free Association, and None of the Above, and some members boycotted the vote altogether. As the election drew closer, PPD supporters began advocating None of the Above as a protest vote against the PNP, which was then in control of the governor's office and which supported the costly plebiscite in the aftermath of the devastation of Hurricane Georges. Despite a small faction that boycotted the vote altogether voter turnout was 71.1 percent.

9. For an in-depth analysis of the problematics of deploying nationalist and anti-colonial discourses in Puerto Rico, see the introduction to Negrón-Muntaner and Grosfoguel, *Puerto Rican Jam*, and specifically the essay by Grosfoguel entitled "The Divorce of Nationalist Discourses from Puerto Rican People: A Sociohistorical Perspective."

10. Literally an "air bus," this term was originally coined by Luis Rafael Sánchez as a metaphor for Puerto Rican migration and the continual exchange of cultural ideas and commodities between the island and Puerto Rican communities in the United States.

11. I use this metaphor somewhat reluctantly, wishing to draw on the implicit assumptions of Cruz-Malavé's analysis yet hesitant to perpetuate the idea that being fucked or penetrated implies passivity or submission. Cruz-Malavé also problematizes the use of this metaphor in his article. Echoing one of the characters he discusses, he writes, "[O]nce the bodies of two men are joined, once they are tangled up in 'sodomy', in homosexual practice, who's to say who's the giver and who's the taker, who attacks and who surrenders, if he who gives it surrenders, or if he who takes it devours?" (240–41). For an insightful and provocative exploration of penetration and its metaphors, see Cvetkovich. In this article she analyzes how ideologies of sexuality and the body construct one another and reconceptualizes the complex physical and psychic dynamics of sexual receptivity.

12. For a more detailed discussion of the role of la Malinche in the Mexican popular imaginary, see Alarcón, *Traddutora*. See also Moraga, *Loving in the War Years*.

13. See Castañeda for an insightful psychosocial account of the role of children as translators and cultural mediators.

14. See specifically Anzaldúa's chapter "How to Tame a Wild Tongue," in *Borderlands/La Frontera*.

15. See Frances Negrón-Muntaner's essay "English Only Jamás but Spanish Only Cuidado: Language and Nationalism in Contemporary Puerto Rico," in which she describes the treacherous terrain of nationalist movements in Puerto Rico organized around language.

16. For a reading of "accents" in law, see Matsuda. In this article she chronicles the role of accents as a significant racial code in the United States. She writes, "To acquire natural, unself-conscious, and native-sounding speech with a new accent is a feat accomplished easily only by young children, who are still in the process of language acquisition. Given this near-immutability, discrimination against accent is the functional equivalent of discrimination against foreign origin" (1349).

17. For an in-depth analysis of contemporary Cuban racial politics, see Moore, *Castro, the Blacks and Africa*. Moore is highly critical of the continued political power wielded by light-skinned Cubans in the government despite official propaganda promoting racial equality.

18. In fact when the film *The Mambo Kings* was shown in the Mission District movie theater in San Francisco, the marquee read, "Starring Celia Cruz," even though she appears on-screen only briefly. In another example of typecasting, in the Univisión production of the *telenovela El Alma no Tiene Color* (The Soul Has No Color), Cruz plays a dark-skinned mother working as a maid, whose blond, blue-eyed daughter is adopted by the family for whom she works. Her "secret" and the story unravel when her fair daughter gives birth to a dark-skinned child. Another popular *novela* with the same theme, which has been adapted several times, is *El Derecho de Nacer* (The Right to Life). These latinized *telenovela* versions of the film "Imitation of Life" are contemporary productions set in modern-day México, evidencing the residual anxiety brought about by passing and the legacy of a sexualized plantation economy.

19. Again *telenovelas* serve as barometers of racialized attitudes and anxieties. *Xica*, a wildly popular Brazilian *telenovela* based on the "real life" story of an African slave woman who seduces her Portuguese master to gain power, wealth, and freedom, was a transnational phenomenon when it was dubbed into Spanish and re-aired on Telemundo, a U.S.-based Spanish-language television station (Rohter). While it signaled the rare occasion that a Black woman starred as the central protagonist, it also recirculated sexualized racial fantasies of slavery. It was so successful that after the *telenovela* ended in its prime-time slot, it was rerun at midnight. The voice-over for the commercial stated, "Acúestate con Xica, ahora todas las noches a las 12:00" (Go to bed with *Xica*, now every night at 12:00). See also the 1993 film *Xica da Silva*, which recounts the same story. The complexities of sex, race, and agency represented in this story and their intersection with the multidimensional dynamics of the popular cultural phenomena that are *telenovelas* are too convoluted to articulate in this short space and merit much fuller investigation.

20. In a taped and edited conversation between three Afro–Puerto Rican lesbians, the significance of hair formed a central theme in identity formation. See Cortez et al.

21. For contemporary studies on Latin American Jewish studies, see Sheinin and Barr, *The Jewish Diaspora in Latin America: New Studies on History and Literature*; and Elkin and Sater, *Latin American Jewish Studies: An Annotated Guide to the Literature*. See also Levine, *Tropical Diaspora: The Jewish Experience in Cuba*.

22. See Moraga, "The Breakdown of the Bicultural Mind," in *The Last Generation*. Two worthwhile anthologies are Root, *The Multiracial Experience* and Penn, *As We Are Now*. See also the many selections by bicultural or mixed-heritage women in Moraga and Anzaldúa, *This Bridge*; Anzaldúa, *Making Face*; and Ramos, *Compañeras*.

23. These are three very popular root vegetables that are a staple of Afro-Latin cooking and are consumed throughout the Caribbean and parts of Latin America. There are hundreds of varieties, and at least as many cooking methods.

24. *Cariño* means tenderness, caring, affection, but it is also a word with deep social significance that eludes translation. In the opening and closing pages of her chapbook *Suspiros*, the Mexican poet Adriana Batista repeats the following definition of the word *cariño* as a sort of mantra that opens and closes the text. Her definition captures the many implications and nuances of the word *cariño* as a culturally and politically charged symbol:

> cariño: inclinación de amor o buen afecto que se siente, expresa o cultiva hacia una persona, animal, planta o cosa; señal de que dichos sentimientos actúan con el efecto de bondad universal y hacen que el otro, otra u otros adquieran un valor definido que permite la proyección individual, mutua o colectiva de dicho valor en el equilibrio de las fuerzas del universo; esmero y voluntad en desempeño de estos sentimientos en los actos del vivir al hacer una labor o en el trato hacia los demás seres" (n.p.)

> (*cariño*: inclination of love or good sentiment that is felt, expressed, or cultivated toward a person, animal, plant, or thing; a sign that these feelings act with the effect of universal goodness and make the other or others acquire a defined value that permits the individual, mutual, or collective projection of said value in the balance of the forces of the universe; intent and desire to demonstrate these feelings in the acts of living in realizing a labor or in the treatment of other beings.)

25. This brief list is meant not to be inclusive, but instead to offer a sample of authors and their fields while recognizing that each of these individuals is already involved in fracturing the frames I have imposed. The names of many other writers, critics, and artists working in queer Latino studies are cited throughout the text.

26. Some collections worth noting are Balderston and Guy, *Sex and Sexuality in Latin America*; Bergmann and Smith, *¿Entiendes? Queer Readings, Hispanic Writings*; Chávez-Silverman and Hernández, *Reading and Writing the Ambiente: Queer Sexualities in Latino, Latin American and Spanish Culture*; Molloy and Irwin, *Hispanisms and Homosexualities*; and Foster, *Sexual Textualities: Essays on Queering Latin American Writing*. Again, I offer these titles not as a definitive compilation, but as a starting point for those interested in the field.

27. In Cuba, the rhizomatic *yuca* when boiled is almost always served with the garlicy lemon sauce called *mojo*.

Notes to Chapter 2

1. The titles and texts referenced here and throughout this chapter include Patricia Williams, *The Alchemy of Race and Rights*; Trinh T. Minh-ha, *Woman, Native, Other*; Norma Alarcón, "Chicana Feminism: In the Tracks of the Native Woman"; and the play *Shadow of a Man*, by Cherríe Moraga. The phrase "ruins of representation" is borrowed from Gerald Vizenor's *Manifest Manners. Autobiographical Myths and Metaphors* is the subtitle title of Vizenor's autobiography, *Interior Landscapes. Dead Voices* is the title of one of Vizenor's many novels. *Vivito y coleando* is a Spanish expression for alive and kicking and also the title of a song by Conjunto Céspedes. *Rituals of Survival* is a collection of short stories by the Nuyorican author Nicholasa Mohr. Avery Gordon's powerful and poetic text *Ghostly Matters: Haunting and the Sociological Imagination* productively haunts my own writing. I am indebted to her visionary language as a way to speak of the intangible forces of history and social imagination. These fragments of language sampled in my own text are my small way of paying homage to the living creative spirits that surround me. I apologize in advance for any fragments that have not been duly credited. These omissions reflect the subconscious power of language rather than any ill-intent on the part of this author.

2. For a range of interpretations on the intersections of constructions of identity and political projects, see Mohanty, "Cartographies of Struggle: Third World Women and the Politics of Feminism"; Trinh, "Not You/Like You: Postcolonial Women and the Interlocking Questions of Identity and Difference"; and Fuss, *Essentially Speaking*. For an illustrative analysis of the burden of queer/ethnic representation within identity politics, see Muñoz, *Disidentifications: Queers of Color and the Performance of Politics*; Fung, "The Trouble with 'Asians'"; Manalansan, "In the Shadow of Stonewall"; and Puar, "Transnational Sexualities." For a playful and imaginative account of the ironies and joys of identity politics, see Chang Hall, "Bitches in Solitude: Identity Politics and Lesbian Community." See also Rajchman's anthology *The Identity in Question*. This collection is particularly valuable because in many essays the writers are directly engaging each others' arguments. It is also worthwhile to look back at two early manifestos: Third World Gay Revolution (New York), "What We Want, What We Believe" (1972); and Combahee River Collective, "A Black Feminist Statement" (1977).

3. For the problematics and possibilities of multiculturalism, see the collected essays in Gordon and Newfield, *Mapping Multiculturalism*.

4. *Mujerío* is a rarely used feminine construct of the more popular term *gentío*, or group of people, from the word *gente* (people). It came into popular usage in this community, and was selected as a group name after María Cora, the Afro–Puerto Rican poet, vocalist, and educator activist, heard a Portuguese version of the word at a feminist conference in Brazil. To inaugurate the first issue of the group's newsletter, *Mujerío*, Cora wrote the following poem:

Mujerío. Somos golpe de estado, intenciones a sublevar lo imperante. Por cada una y por todas arrastramos el peso completo de nuestra existencia amenazada. Piel en el umbral de cada puerta, poseedoras de la intimidad y teniendo acceso al centro, nos lanzamos en erupción volcánica, en viento huracanado. Mujerío. Somos hembraje, unidas en afinidad concluyente. Nos distingue la osadía de haber probado lo prohibido, tan dulce la libertad de nuestra dulzura tan libre. Tomamos muy en serio el camino hacia lo esencial, creado paso por paso apasionado. Mujerío. Somos hogar y encuentro. Tambores en círculo, tonos de rojo y púrpura en nuestro telar, contestaciones que se van forjando a medida que vivimos. Compañeras de ahora y de antes, somos lesbianas de siempre" (Cora).

5. This exceptionally creative cultural worker, Ana Ruiz, also worked with Proyecto's AtreDivas program, and provided the set design for an all-drag production of *La*

169

Casa de Bernarda Alba, by Federico García Lorca, presented at the Mission Cultural Center, June 1994. With the Mexican-born artist Ralfka González, she also cowrote and illustrated a children's book of multicultural Spanish-language folk sayings, entitled *Mi Primer Libro de Dichos*.

6. "Gutting Dreams" was authored by the Argentinean writer/dancer Ana Ines Rubinstein Izé, a "Jotografía" student.

7. It seems pertinent at this point to disclose my own association with each of these groups. From 1988 to 1991 I was an active member of Mujerío and helped to organize the 1989 gathering, which took place only days after the October 1989 earthquake in San Francisco; in 1991 while studying in New York City, I participated briefly in several meetings of Las Buenas Amigas; from 1992 to 1994 I participated in various capacities in the Annual Latina/o Gay, Lesbian and Bisexual Visual Arts Exhibit; from 1989 to 1994 I formed part of the loosely organized international network associated with the biannual Encuentro de Lesbianas Feministas de América Latina y del Caribe and attended the 1992 conference held in Boquerón, Puerto Rico; from 1993 to 1996 I was part of the Collective Core of Ellas en Acción; from 1994 to 1996 I was on the editorial advisory board of *conmoción* and in 1996 served as part of a collective based in San Francisco that guest edited the Identity issue; in 1995 I attended and participated as workshop facilitator at the national conference of LLEGO held in Washington, DC. I have been involved with Proyecto ContraSIDA por Vida, the main subject of this chapter, since its inception in 1993, serving as part of the volunteer Advisory Program Committee from 1994 to 1996, as a paid and volunteer consultant on several projects, as a Colegio ContraSIDA instructor, and as a volunteer and supporter.

8. Interestingly, throughout this essay and elsewhere, Hartsock takes refuge in the selected and highly problematic readings of "feminists of color," mapping postmodernism as the revenge of "white boys," led by Michel Foucault. Yet other than colorful citations, she rarely directly engages the implications of the subjectivity these feminists of color, and others "who have been silenced," are actually articulating in their work or in their social practices. For example, she manages to ignore Anzaldúa's connection to aliens and third-sexed beings, in order to bring her into the fold of structural materialism. In "The Theoretical Subject(s) of *This Bridge Called My Back* and Anglo-American Feminism," Alarcón directly critiques the limits and implications of standpoint epistemologies in relation to the work of Anglo-Ameri-

can feminism. See also Wiegman, "Introduction: Mapping the Lesbian Postmodern." In this essay Wiegman takes on the arguments of Hartsock and others that
postmodernism will result in the disavowal of progressive political agendas. In reference to the article in question, "Foucault on Power," Wiegman writes,

> [Hartsock's] categorical others are devoid of sexuality as difference, an omis-
> sion that enables her to position Foucault as the "white boy" who "writes
> from the perspective of the dominator." In reclaiming the teleology of human
> liberation at work in modernity by trying to work out its elisions, Hartsock re-
> peats its categorical logic. Given the structure of her argument, one wonders
> what it might mean if she could read Foucault's text as gay. (n. 8)

9. To its credit, the San Francisco HIV Prevention Planning Council, in its 1997 plan,
provides statistical information on these social factors and others that form the context in which the AIDS epidemic has unfolded in San Francisco. In San Francisco
County jails, 50 percent of the inmates are African American and 27 percent are
Latino/Hispanic (86); the cumulative dropout rate in the city is 16 percent, yet for
both African Americans and those with a Spanish surname the dropout rate is 24
percent each (81); median per capita income for white San Francisco residents is
$26,222; for Latino/Hispanic residents it is $11,400 (83); 18 percent of San Francisco's children live below the poverty level (83) and 20 percent of San Francisco's
homeless population is estimated to be under twenty-one years of age (84). Although there are no accurate estimates of the number of undocumented immigrants, the 1990 census revealed that 34 percent of San Francisco's total population
was born in a foreign country (81); 45 percent of San Franciscans speak more than
one language, and 12 percent have limited or no English proficiency (82). There are
estimated to be 15,000 commercial sex workers in San Francisco (341) and although
no accurate numbers exist, it is estimated that 1 percent of San Francisco's population is transgender (68). Unlike the situation in other urban centers, 96 percent of
recent (1991–1995) AIDS cases in San Francisco are men (100) and close to 91 percent of cumulative AIDS cases (1981–1996) are among gay and bisexual men (97);
of the female AIDS cases in the city, two-thirds are among women of color: 46 percent are African American; 36 percent are white, 12 percent are Latina, 4 percent are
Asian/Pacific Islander, 2 percent are Native American (100). For clarity, let me also
state that of the 723,959 people in San Francisco at the time of the 1990 census, 47

percent identify as non-Hispanic white; 11 percent as non-Hispanic African American; 29 percent as non-Hispanic Asian/Pacific Islander; 13 percent as Latino/Hispanic; and 0.4 percent as Native American/Alaskan Native (68). The ethnic breakdown for San Francisco youth under age eighteen is quite different; only 25 percent are white (80). These are but a few of the many statistics, culled from a variety of sources, included in this hefty 700-page tome. The statistics I have selected are by no means the only salient variables necessary to understand the current social context of the epidemic in San Francisco. These numbers, however, serve to reflect a city mired in economic disparity, social injustice, and the lived manifestations of the city's cultural and sexual diversity. These statistics are compiled from a variety of studies, and the categories used to structure and determine these figures reveal their own internal contradictions and limitations. Although references to transgenders account for over forty-five indexed entries, all the statistical data on gender are structured around the binary categories of male and female. *San Francisco HIV Prevention Plan, 1997* also cites five separate studies on lesbian and bisexual women and risk behavior, yet none of the summaries indicate how gender identifications such as butch and femme operate as co-factors in understanding risk behaviors. Latinos appear in variously constructed categories: Latino, Hispanic, Latino/Hispanic, and Spanish surname. We also appear through exclusion in the categories white non-Hispanic and black non-Hispanic, demarcating the border between these differently constructed cultural and racial categories. Although my lived experience in the city suggests a large San Francisco population that claims mixed or multiple racial and cultural heritages, this reality is made invisible in the statistical data. In terms of sexual identity, studies generally rely on self-defined sexual identity and usually go on to present the contradiction between these categories and behavior. For example, it cites 1992 Women's Survey, where 52 percent of the women who identified as lesbians had also had sex with a man within the past three years (90). For the specific details on statistical sources and research paradigms, see San Francisco HIV Prevention Planning Council.

10. See Rafael Diaz, *Latino Gay Men and HIV: Culture, Sexuality, and Risk Behavior*, in which he specifically challenges clinical methodologies that look only at male-to-male sexual practices while ignoring the contributing factors of Latino gay identity. Also based on HIV prevention programs aimed at Latino gay men in San Francisco,

Díaz's text includes substantial qualitative and quantitative analyses and serves as a social science complement to my own cultural studies practice.

11. The relatively low rate of infection in San Francisco among women is a statistic worth pondering. Some variables worth considering are the early onset and effectiveness of citywide needle-exchange programs; general differences in drug culture between San Francisco and other major U.S. cities; how the emotional and social relationships of heterosexual, bisexual, and lesbian women to gay and bisexual men have impacted behavior; and local women's role in providing AIDS-related services.

12. In its promotional materials it is variously referred to by its full name, by the initials PCPV, or as Proyecto. For purposes of readability and to avoid confusion, I refer to it as Proyecto throughout the body of the text. In citation materials it is listed by its full name, and in publication data it is abbreviated by its initials for brevity.

13. My access to many of these materials would not have been possible without the help of a far-reaching network of friends, acquaintances, and allies. As part of my commitment to collaborative and responsible scholarship, I made previous drafts of this chapter available to the staff, clients, and volunteers of Proyecto. I am indebted to those who generously shared their knowledge, constructive criticism, and support. My own methodological practice has been enriched by the guidance and friendship of Patti Lather. See her creative, collaborative hypertext *Troubling the Angels*.

14. Horacio Roque Ramirez is currently completing a manuscript on the history of queer Latina/o communities in San Francisco, tentatively entitled "Communities of Desire: Memory and History from Queer Latina/o San Francisco, from the 1960s to the 1990s."

15. Origin stories are always fraught with controversy. Nevertheless, it seems appropriate to offer a narrative that accounts for the genesis of Proyecto. It initially emerged from the National Task Force on AIDS Prevention (NTFAP), where Jesse James Johnson and Juan Rodríguez worked at the time; they would be the first director and assistant director. NTFAP, the first national gay men of color HIV organization, was also Proyecto's first fiscal agent from 1993 to 1998. NTFAP was founded and led by the late Reggie Williams and was an outgrowth of Black and White Men Together, the interracialist organization. The initial founders of Proyecto included Ricardo Bracho, Diane Felix, Jesse Johnson, Hector León, Reggie Williams, and Martín Ornellas-Quintero.

16. The order cited is not intended to present a chronological, linear, or developmental progression. Many of these groups and movements emerged simultaneously and there exist both significant overlap and divergence relative to individuals, ideology, and social context.

17. Some of the groups operating in the city at the time of this research include AGUILAS (Asociación Gay/Lesbiana Unida Impactando Latinos/as a Superarse), a "Lesbian and Gay Latino organization committed to advocating and developing positive self-identities, healthy relationships and leadership skills"; Que Tal, "a Latino men's rap group"; Grupo Socio Cultural Hispano, a "Spanish-speaking gay men's social group"; Queers for Cuba, which "works to fight the US blockade of Cuba and build solidarity with Cuban people, especially queers and people with HIV/AIDS"; Latina Lesbians of the East Bay; Puerto Rican Social Group; Ellas en Acción, "a Latina lesbian and bisexual community action group"; El Ambiente; Hermanos de Luna y Sol; and LLEGO California, the "Latina/o Lesbian, Gay, Bisexual Organization of California." These various group formations appear advertised in the *San Francisco Bay Times* "Resource Guide" under various headings: "People of Color," "Social Groups," "HIV Support Services," and "Political Groups." The different categories for inclusion and the various linguistic and stylistic forms of self-representation reflect the social and political diversity operating within each of these distinctly configured groupings.

18. The Harm Reduction Coalition, with offices in Oakland, California, and New York City, states in its promotional brochure,

> The Harm Reduction Coalition believes in every individual's right to health and well-being as well as in their competency to protect and help themselves, their loved ones, and their communities. . . . Harm reduction accepts, for better and for worse, that licit and illicit drug use is part of our world and chooses to work to minimize its harmful effects rather than simply ignore or condemn them.

Proyecto's reformulation of harm reduction extends this philosophy toward the practices of safer sex, stressing reducing risk whenever possible, rather than simply condemning or ignoring unsafe sexual practices. For insights into the working practices of the harm reduction model in needle exchange programs in New York City, see Vázquez, "St. Ann's Corner of Harm Reduction: Interview with Joyce Rivera Beckman."

19. See *¡Viva 16!* by Valentín Aguirre and Augie Robles, an exceptionally well-documented, humorous, and provocative ethnographic video, which depicts the history of Latino/a queer movements in San Francisco, and specifically the role Esta Noche and La India Bonita played in the formation of community. These bars had long attracted a regular clientele of *vestidas*, *jotos*, *jotas*, and neighborhood men looking for male sexual and social partners. Much of the archival footage presented in the film was provided by Ana Berta Campos, a longtime San Francisco videographer who has devoted much of her work to documenting queer Latina/o social movements in San Francisco. As Aguirre pointed out, however, in an after screening discussion of the work, video captures a moment that has already ceased to exist (Aguirre). The area surrounding Sixteenth and Mission has in recent years undergone a process of gentrification. Older bars, restaurants, and businesses catering to the low-income Latino population are being replaced by upscale establishments as the Mission (particularly the Sixteenth Street corridor between Mission and Castro and the Valencia Street corridor between Sixteenth and Twenty-fourth Streets) has become a more desirable and chic neighborhood as the quality of life for its Latina/o residents worsens. La India Bonita, for example, is now a yuppie bar called Skylark.

20. The addition of the term "questioning" to the more traditional roster of categories of sexuality has come into popular usage mostly in promotional materials geared toward queer youth as a means to include those who may not identify with the other available labels, but who nonetheless are engaged in questioning their sexuality relative to heterosexual norms.

21. The phrase "unnatural disaster" is borrowed from Yamada, "Invisibility Is an Unnatural Disaster: Reflections of an Asian American Woman."

22. Proyecto began at Eighteenth and Dolores, then moved to its storefront offices at Sixteenth and Mission. Recently it has moved again temporarily to offices across the street in a building shared by other community organizations because its space needed to be retrofitted. It will be able to return to its previous space, but at twice the rent.

23. Ricardo Bracho is a brilliant playwright, poet, and thinker. He was selected as a National Endowment for the Arts/Theater Communications Group Playwright in Residence. He is the author of three plays and has taught courses at the University of California at Berkeley, Stanford University, Intersection for the Arts, and San Quentin Prison. For a critical review of his play *The Sweetest Hangover (and Other*

STDs), see Muñoz, "Feeling Brown: Ethnicity and Affect in Ricardo Bracho's *The Sweetest Hangover (and Other STDs)*." This chapter would not have been possible without Ricardo's many gifts of creative language and critical insight, and his dedication to creating, documenting, and theorizing this moment in *jotería* history.

24. The Diablitas class was taught by Rana Halpern with Ariana Ochoa as her assistant. Rana Halpern later served as a Proyecto board member. The team is currently on hiatus.

25. Among the many community-based programs Proyecto has worked with in the past are Mission Neighborhood Health Center, Haight Ashbury Free Clinic, Institute for Community Health Outreach, Asian and Pacific Islanders Wellness Center, New Leaf, Lavender Youth Recreation and Information Center (LYRIC), Young Brothers Program, and Tenderloin AIDS Resource Center. Arts organizations Proyecto has collaborated with include Galeria de la Raza, Folsom Street Interchange for the Arts, Mission Cultural Center, the Mexican Museum, Artists Television Access (ATA), Cine Acción, San Francisco Cinemateque, and Brava for Women in the Arts.

26. The "Escándalo" series was conceived and led by Roberto Coto, a Salvadoreño/Cubano from Los Angeles, who is also a fashion designer.

27. This popular refrain is often credited to a poem, written in the local Afro-Antillian vernacular, by the Afro–Puerto Rican poet Fortunato Vizcarrondo "¿Y tu agüela a'onde ejtá?" It is a reference to the practice of negating dark-skinned ancestors or relatives. See Giusti Cordero's essay "Afro–Puerto Rican Cultural Studies: Beyond *cultura negroide* and *antillanismo*," in which he discusses the way this phrase has gained popular currency in Puerto Rico, including its musicalization in *plenas*. Giusti Cordero also mentions a parallel construction in the Anglophone Caribbean: "Go home and look at your grandmother," cited in Eric Williams, *The Negro in the Caribbean* (New York: Haskell House, 1991) (Giusti Cordero n. 29).

28. Unless otherwise indicated, all the flyers were produced in-house at Proyecto without credits, using appropriated images from a variety of sources. Design credits listed in the captions were gleaned through personal sources, rather than through published accounts. This disinvestment in authorial ownership seems particularly significant as an expression of collective subjectivity and a commitment to collective representation.

29. Gayle Rubin's groundbreaking article "Thinking Sex: Notes for a Radical Theory of the Politics of Sexuality" (1984) continues to have resonance today in understanding the impact of ideologies of sexual normativity on these highly charged political debates.

30. A visually and conceptually bold publication entitled *Behind Our Backs: Faggot Sex/Sissy Speak: sumt'n ta say*, published by the San Francisco AIDS Foundation, was criticized and its distribution limited because of its inclusion of nonjudgmental information on drug use. Covering the range of popular drugs such as heroin, cannabis, cocaine, MDMA (Ecstasy), LSD, mushrooms, nitrates (poppers), amphetamines, and anabolic steroids, it provided information on how these drugs are used, their side effects, and problems and risk factors associated with their use. In the summary pages of the chapter devoted to drug use, a sidebar states, "If you're going to be doing drugs keep this in mind," and goes on to provide practical advise on harm reduction. Tips such as "Drink lots of liquids. It's important to keep water in your body" alert users to the risk of dehydration caused by endless hours of dancing inspired by amphetamine highs. Other tips include: "Check for cuts, tears, or any raw spots on your body that could allow blood, cum or piss into it. This is especially true if you're doing a drug that numbs pain, like speed, that may cause you not to realize that you're cut or have a raw spot"; and "Smoking pot can help cut the edge off any kind of amphetamine high." These practical suggestions for reducing harm have been interpreted by some as promoting or condoning drug use. A more realistic interpretation recognizes the role drugs play in queer culture and the need to address the health and HIV risk factors of drug users without requiring them to first give up their drug practices. The section ends by saying, "Being high is not an excuse for having unsafe sex" (56–57). Many queer Latinos were directly involved in this project: the creative director and project director for the publication is Eliot S. Ramos; the photo director is Pato Hebert; the editor of *sumt'n ta say* is Ricardo A. Bracho and the writing credit for *Behind Our Backs* is given to "I. Papi et al."

31. This class provides an example of the larger impact these classes have on students and teachers. Janelle Rodríguez, the instructor for that class, was also a Colegio student in my own writing class, "Automitografía: (W)Riting the Self." She later completed an M.F.A. in film production at San Francisco State University, and went on to work with in the private sector. Veronica Majano used the video she produced in that class to secure funding from the Film Arts Foundation. She has since completed her first film, *Calle Chula*, which has been screened in numerous festivals, and is currently working on two new video projects. Aurora Guerrero, another student from "Shoot This," used her video as part of her portfolio for admission to a multidisciplinary M.F.A. program at California Institute of the Arts, and has since graduated and completed two short films: *Ixchell* and *Madrugada*.

32. The instructors for Proyecto's classes have been too numerous to cite individually, and while fearing that any omission will be read as a snub, I also feel compelled to name several of the individual instructors who have passed through Proyecto in the hope that it will inspire readers to seek out the works of these many gifted artists and writers. Patrick "Pato" Hebert and Marcia Ochoa co-taught the "Jotografía" class; Jaime Cortez, the comic book artist, writer, and editor of *A la Brava: A Queer Latino/a Zine*, taught "La Raza Cósmica Comix"; the writer and playwright Jorge Ignacio Cortiñas taught the writing class "Bemba Bilingüe: Double Tonguing"; the visual artist Wura-Natasha Ogunji taught "girl-colored"; the photographer Laura Aguilar and Patrick "Pato" Hebert taught "Diseños de Deseo: Sexual Self-Imaging in Photography"; Horacio Roque Ramirez taught "Te Toca la Tinta"; Marcia Ochoa and Lebasi Lashley taught "Cyberspace for Women"; Ana Berta Campos taught a Spanish-language video class for women; and Al Lujan taught "Altarations," an altar making workshop. Other instructors are mentioned throughout the text.

33. As mentioned earlier, these classes are often configured around different vectors of identity. It seems noteworthy to point out that even though this class targeted HIV-positive gay Latino men, it was taught by a woman. Another course configured around gender and offered "exclusively for Chicana-Latina Butches," was given by a self-defined "fierce femme," the poet and spoken word artist Karla Rosales.

34. At the time this image was produced, Juan Rodríguez was the assistant director of Proyecto. After experiencing a lengthy period of health assisted by the AIDS cocktail, Juan, my dear friend and *tocayo*, died from AIDS-related illnesses on December 12, 1999, *el Día de la Virgen de Guadalupe*.

35. While tears and urine are considered bodily fluids and function symbolically in that capacity in my interpretation of this work, it is important to note that both contain negligible traces of the HIV virus that causes AIDS, and thus cannot function as sources of transmission. The artist, Angel Borrero, also taught a drawing class at Proyecto entitled "Dibujando Conecciones," which used watercolor to explore the relationship between color and healing within Yoruba traditions. Borrero died of complications from AIDS within a year of creating this image.

36. This class was funded by NTFAP and actually preceded Proyecto, and yet served as an inspirational and organizational model for Colegio. It also helped to bring together many of the individuals who would later become significant in the genesis of the organization, including Juan Rodríguez, Jesse Johnson, Valentín Aguirre, Augie Robles, Loras Ojeda, and Willy B. Chavarría, to name a few.

37. Marcia Ochoa was an employee of Proyecto and was responsible for the graphic design of several of its earliest flyers and promotional materials. She is a gifted photographer, graphic designer, writer, computer geek, and community activist whose works have appeared in *conmoción* and in her own chapbook, *La ofrenda*. This chapbook forms part of the works under consideration in the essay by Yarbro-Bejarano, "The Lesbian Body in Latina Cultural Production."

38. These neologisms and linguistic innovations used in both organizational names and in queer popular culture are not unique to queer Latinas/os. For a discussion on how South Asians have used Urdu and Hindi similarly to name South Asian queer identities, see Shah, "Sexuality, Identity, and the Uses of History."

39. My own use of the word has carried it to other diverse discursive sites. After presenting an earlier draft of this paper at the American Studies Association, I noticed how quickly this word was taken up by Latina academics. After I used it in Internet postings, it was also taken up by other Latina women in those cyber-communities.

40. Valencia used the stage name La Sinvergüenza (the shameless one) to perform at the monthly Latina dance party, Colors. These performances incorporated safer-sex practices into erotic dance routines and inspired considerable controversy, *coqueteo*, and debate. *Porque Usted Tiene Animo* means because you have the drive. *Sinvergüenzaventurera* combines *sinvergüenza* (shameless) with *aventurera* (adventurer).

41. These two flyers were funded by the Department of Public Health–AIDS Office.

42. The phrase "What's the T?" has apparently circulated in various cultural communities in San Francisco for many years. Several city residents remember it as a phrase used in the early 1980s, where T stood for "twisted" as a code word for queer, such as in the phrase "Is she T?" or in references to "T-parties." Other vernacular uses seem to be drug related, where T parties were associated with marijuana. Yet its uses are context-driven and defy grammatical logic. T can come to stand in for any word. This flyer, for example, ends with the phrase "Bueno, no todo es lucha. Hay placer, belleza y sabor en la vida del transgender. La T es de ¡Tremenda!" "Well, it ain't all struggle. There's pleasure, beauty and flavor to transgender living. The T is for ¡Tremenda!" (translation from text). *Tremenda* translates as tremendous, but is more closely related in queer parlance to the word "fabulous."

43. In certain cultural circles, particularly in many parts of Cuba, papaya is a reference to vagina.

44. These translations are my own. In this portion of the flyer that records participants' responses, the quotes are not translated, and instead appear in the languages in which they were recorded.

45. I have my own history of multiple names and context-derived aliases that have emerged from the possibilities of my given birth name, Juana María de la Caridad Rodríguez y Hernández, which appears in an official context only on my Cuban passport. As an amateur visual artist, I have employed the name juana maría de la caridad; my professional name (and the one that appears on my U.S. passport) is Juana María Rodríguez; my brief foray into fictional writing used the name Caridad Hernández; my preferred online computer name is caridad. In Spanish-speaking social settings I am alternately called Juanita or Juana María, while my family (and a few intimate friends) call me Juany. In most English-speaking contexts I am simply referred to as Juana.

46. *Sabrosura* has been shown at film festivals and broadcast on television nationally and internationally in New York, Miami, Chicago, San Francisco, Los Angeles, and Barcelona. While it has appeared on San Francisco public television, it has never been broadcast as a public service announcement on any local commercial television station. The two brochures that I reference in the text were also released at the premiere screening of *Sabrosura* at the Roxie Theater.

47. Despite the statistics, the sexual and drug practices of women who have sex with women should caution us against dismissing the potential risk of transmission. One study stated that "Women who had had one or more female sexual partners since 1980 (329) were nearly twice as likely to inject drugs during the same time period as women who had no female partners"; and "[t]wice as many women who identified either as exclusively homosexual or as bisexual had engaged in anal intercourse with a male partner during the last 3 years" (San Francisco HIV Prevention 197). While both of these practices—injecting drugs and heterosexual anal intercourse— can be performed in ways that reduce the risk of exposure to HIV, another study conducted among primarily lesbian and bisexual women reported that "[y]ounger women and self-identified bisexuals were more likely to have unprotected sex with men" (195).

48. Along with Jorge Ignacio Cortiñas (who led the discussion), Ricardo Bracho, Horacio Roque Ramirez, and Patrick "Pato" Hebert, I was part of the collective cell that organized this discussion. Ana Berta Campos videotaped the event. The organizational meetings and related discussions were invaluable in helping me flesh out the arguments presented in this chapter, particularly as they pertain to issues of funding and the workings of the state.

Notes to Chapter 3

1. Some notable literary texts include *Incidents in the Life of a Slave Girl, The Stranger, The Surrounded, To Kill a Mockingbird, China Men, Native Son, Jazz*, and *Revenge of the Cockroach People*. Literary critics who examine these issues include Butler, Vizenor, Gutiérrez-Jones, Trinh, and Alexander.

2. For example, see the work of Patricia Williams, Angela Harris, Kimberlé Crenshaw, Richard Delgado, Kendall Thomas, and others.

3. 189 UNTS 137, UN Doc. A/CONF.2/108 (1951), amended as 19 US T 6223, TIAS no. 6577, 606 UNTS 267 (1967), quoted in McGoldrick 206 nn. 43, 45. McGoldrick's article provides a detailed and comprehensive history of both international law relative to refugees, and the judicial discourse surrounding homosexuality in the United States. See Grider for a specific analysis of the legal implication of the Tenório case. For a history of sexual orientation based asylum law and the implications for its interpretation see Bennett. Bennett's article includes detailed discussion of an asylum case involving a Russian lesbian, Alla K. Pitcherskaia. For an examination of asylum law and transgenders see Mohyuddin.

4. Years earlier, in 1990, a case very similar to Tenório's had already been decided by an immigration review panel. That case involved Fidel Armando Toboso-Alfonso, a gay Cuban facing deportation from the United States in 1986. At the time, however, Cubans were routinely granted political asylum based on *political* persecution, complicating the legal implications of the case. The Toboso-Alfonso case went unpublished until 1994, making it unavailable to serve as precedent in the case involving Tenório (Johnston).

5. See *Discipline and Punish; Madness and Civilization;* and *History of Sexuality,* vol. 1, *An Introduction.*

6. In March 1994, INS officials in Washington chose not to appeal a decision by an asylum officer in San Francisco to grant political asylum to a gay HIV-positive Mexican man (alias Acosta) who had immigrated to the United States illegally fourteen years ago because he feared for his life in México. INS officials cited the ruling as an isolated case, and made clear that it does not suggest that all gay Mexicans will now be eligible for political asylum. See "Gay Man Who Cited Abuse." See also Doyle. For a legal analysis of the implications of HIV status as grounds for exclusion, see Somerville, Shoop, and Margulies.

7. In 1993 Community United Against Violence (CUAV) reported a total of 366 anti–gay/lesbian offenses committed in San Francisco. Thirty-five percent of the reported incidents took place in the Castro/Mission District.

8. Tenório's testimony was translated from Portuguese by George Goic, the court-authorized interpreter. Quotes taken from the court transcript have not been edited or altered with regard to spelling or punctuation.

9. For an analysis of the myth of Brazil's racial democracy, see Hanchard, chap. 3; and Winant.

10. Given how classifications of race, class, gender, and sexuality operate in contemporary U.S. law, it is understandable that legal scholars such as Crenshaw would call for their intersection; however, in practice these categories are always already constituted through each other. To suggest their intersection may affect the illusion that race, class, gender, or sexuality can ever function as discrete categories unimpacted by these other ever-present dimensions.

11. In Brazil homosexual men are pejoratively called *deado* (deer). See *Epidemic of Hate,* written by Luiz Mott and published by IGLHRC, for grisly accounts of the violence and murders directed at gay men, lesbians, and transgendered people in Brazil. Mott also gives a detailed account of the history, political and cultural ideology, and state collusion that contribute to this violence.

12. See Manalansan's pointed and incisive critique of the political mandates of "modern homosexual identity" in "In the Shadows of Stonewall: Examining Gay Transnational Politics and the Diasporic Dilemna."

13. The incident also calls to mind the testimony of Rosa Lopez, the Salvadorian domestic who served as a witness in the O. J. Simpson trial, wherein she was told to speak only in Spanish, a mandate she continually resisted, preferring instead to speak directly to the judge in her heavily accented English.

14. In the Brooke article in the *New York Times* de Santos is described as "bisexual," although the court testimony makes no reference to his bisexuality. This slippage from homosexual to bisexual seems to be the result of Mott's comments outside the courtroom.

15. The murder of an openly gay political figure also recalls the murder of Harvey Milk, the gay San Francisco city councilman who was murdered by a political rival, Dan White.

16. The average overkill involved in all of these cases is frighteningly high: 52 percent of white victims were overkilled; 71 percent of Latina/os; and 63 percent of African Americans. The writers who compiled these statistics noted, "We imposed a high standard in gauging overkill. 'Execution-style' murders, slashed throats, strangulations, or murders involving four or less stab wounds were *not* deemed overkill" (3).

17. A more recent report, coordinated by the New York City Gay and Lesbian Anti-Violence Project and published by the National Coalition of Anti-Violence Programs, cites sixteen hate-related murders in 2000, down from twenty-eight reported by the same group in 1999 (12). Specifically in San Francisco, there were 467 people reporting some form of anti-G/L/B/T attack in 2000 (47). Of the three hate-based murders that occurred in San Francisco in 2000, down from eight in 1999, the report specifically mentioned that "One man was murdered . . . after being tied and beaten by his assailants, then chopped at least thirteen times with a hatchet and an axe" (48).

18. Subsequent to this trial, Mott's house and car were attacked by unknown persons in reaction to the publication of an academic paper about the suspected homosexuality of the Brazilian Black hero Zumbi, a seventeenth-century ex-slave and freedom fighter (Buckmire, "Brazil").

19. *In re Tenorio*, appendix, Decision of the Immigration Judge, 14.

20. The ellipses in this sentence were inserted to reflect a pause in the testimony while the court reporter changed tapes.

21. The *New York Times* article caption describes Tenório as a housepainter (Brooke). He was apparently working as a lab assistant at the time of the initial trial and testimony.

22. This is not to suggest that legalizing same-sex marriage will provide the desirable legal remedy. Legalized same-sex marriage will continue to give regulatory power to the state to define the normative social, sexual, legal and economic parameters of public and private affiliations and contractual agreements. For a feminist legal critique of marriage, including same-sex marriage, see Polikoff. See Hutchinson for a critique of same-sex marriage discourse that examines the consequences of emphasizing formal equality over material betterment and exposes the racial and class privileges of same-sex marriage arguments based on equal protection. See Ertman's "Contract Sports," for legal remedies that attempt to denaturalize the heterosexual family by making all intimate relations more contractual. See also Ertman's article "Marriage as Trade."

23. Changes in the law happen daily, and while legal activists have been challenging elements of the act since its adoption, the recent events of September 11, 2001, have cast a long shadow on attempts to ensure that all individuals, regardless of civil status, are accorded the rights of due process.

24. A local reporter tracked down Tenório, currently living in the Metro East area of St. Louis, and published an interview with him in the *St. Louis Post-Dispatch*. Tenório is quoted as stating "I am happy all the time" although the interview was held in a friend's house because "his landlord doesn't want trouble." In recounting the details of his current life, the article states that Tenório "works as a personal care attendant, enjoys a tight circle of friends and adores his cocker spaniel, named Michael Jackson." (Kee)

Notes to Chapter 4

1. "Lurking" refers to the practice of reading but not writing while online. The practice of lurking is a complex and intriguing topic unto itself. For eloquent essays on the psychological dynamics of lurkers, see Zweig and Wohlblatt.

2. Many e-mail addresses come embedded with top-level domain names, which indicate the country of origin, for example, .es (Spain), .mx (Mexico), .co (Colombia), .uk (United Kingdom). Recently the *New York Times* reported that the South Pacific island nation of Tuvalu, population 10,600, sold its two-letter suffix, .tv, for $50 million, evidencing how the symbolic marker for a virtual national designation can become a transnational commodity. See Black.

3. All online posts have been reprinted as posted, in many cases without accents. While some programs facilitate the use of these and other orthographic marks, the computer program that receives the message may not always be able to decipher the code, and they may instead appear as a series of symbols. All translations are my own.

4. This line is of course a variation of the famous opening of the television series *Dragnet*, and reminds us that before the virtual stories overheard on the Internet, many of us have been the recipients of the simulations of reality depicted on television.

5. In *The War of Desire and Technology*, Stone enacts a similar discursive practice. The first note of her text begins, "This is the first instance of the collapse of fiction and fact (whatever that is), narratization and description, that the style of this essay implies" (185 n. 1). Other notes throughout the book elaborate on her methodological practice of performative writing. Stone also has a fascinating homepage, with many useful links: www.actlab.utexas.edu/~sandy.

6. For an engaging analysis of "home," "homelessness," and technologies such as homepages, see Star, "From Hestia to Home Page: Feminism and the Concept of Home in Cyberspace." I wish to extend my thanks to Susan Leigh Star for initially encouraging me to mine my online experiences for their academic potential.

7. Several valuable histories of the Internet exist online. See Sterling; Leiner et al.

8. My most sincere thanks go to Rosio Alvarez for trying to help me understand the intricate workings of digital communication. I have been a poor student, however, preferring instead to whittle away my time in chatrooms. Technical errors in describing a technology I do not fully understand are therefore my own.

9. Of course, attempts to regulate the Internet are numerous and multifaceted. For further reading on legal issues related to the Internet, including freedom of expression in cyberspace, intellectual property issues, privacy and encryption, jurisdiction and transborder issues, personal safety and equity issues, see UCLA Online Institute for Cyberspace Law and Policy.

10. See *¡Ya Basta!* Web page, www.ezln.org.

11. Newsgroups are asynchronous, structured around wide-ranging topics of interest. The initials generally give some indication of the list. Those that begin with alt., for example, generally have to do with alternative lifestyles; rec. refers to recreation and includes games, the occult, and fan-based groups; soc. refers to society and includes many newsgroups of international and cultural interest. On some of these lists, queer groups use the initials motss (members of the same sex) as a means of encrypting their content and warding off entry to potentially homophobic users.

12. Rumor functions in all news media. Minutes before the final 1998 World Cup game between Brazil and France, Univisión erroneously reported that Rolando, the Brazilian sensation, would not be in the initial lineup. After Brazil's crushing defeat, it was rumored that Nike, one of Brazil's primary sponsors, had applied pressure to start Rolando despite injury. Nike denied the rumor.

13. Of course what we should have done was go directly to Orishnet, at www.seanet.com/~efunmoyiwa/ochanet.html.

14. See *"Café, Culpa* and *Capital,"* by Ricardo Ortiz for his reading of Albita. On the cover and promotional photographs for her first U.S. album, *No Se Parece a Nada,* Albita is shown wearing men's suits and two-toned wing-tips, and several of the song lyrics have an overt lesbian subtext. Under the promotional tutelage of Emilio Estefan's record company, she has since drastically altered her image to present a more feminine persona. Rumors of her lesbian sexuality have flourished since her arrival to the U.S. Latin music scene in 1995.

15. The homepage for Arenal is www.indiana.edu/~arenal/index.html.

16. Listserves are electronic groups that circulate postings through electronic mail to all subscribed members. Different groups have different methods for administering lists. These lists, like newsgroups, are asynchronous. The IRC (Internet Relay Chat), discussed later in this chapter; MUDs (Multi-User Dungeons or Domains), text-based virtual reality most associated with games and role-playing; and MOOs (Multi-User Object Oriented), also a form of text-based virtual reality, which tend to emphasize social interaction, are synchronous modes of exchange, otherwise known as real-time interaction.

17. O'Brien details how online practices, while allowing users to manipulate gender, require a receptive audience in order for alternative gender performances to function. O'Brien also argues that attempts at gender transformation online often result in a reinscription and reification of binary gender categories.

18. IRC is comparable to other "real-time" chat venues such as those that are available through AOL and Yahoo; however, these spaces tend to be under more "community" surveillance and thus more sanitized. In contrast to these portal maintained networks, IRC links directly to an international network of servers and is thus generally able to provide less restricted content. Some of the largest networks are Efnet, Undernet, IRCnet, and Dalnet; these networks host over 50,000 users each. Smaller networks also exist, some based on subject, and others organized by region. A useful site for learning to navigate the IRC is www.IRChelp.org. It lists information in Spanish, French, German, Greek, Dutch, Indonesian, Italian, Portuguese, and Turkish, testifying to the global scope of these networks.

19. See Bechar-Israel's engaging study and analysis of nicknames and Israeli identity on the IRC.

20. Channel operators, or chanops, are those who start new channels or who have been given chanop privileges by another chanop. Privileges generally include access to the codes that allow chanops to admit and eject members. Depending on the channel, these privileges are closely guarded, given only to regular users who have gained the trust and confidence of the existing chanops. On other channels, particularly more transient spaces, or channels set up for already established members, these privileges are extended more freely.

21. According to a study reported by *Business Week*, although English remains the lingua franca of the World Wide Web, it is the mother tongue of only 49 percent of Web users. Spanish is estimated to be the native language of 5 percent of users worldwide ("Surfing in Tongues").

22. "Flooding" means sending out repeated lines of nonsensical text or graphic images. This can greatly interfere with the server's capabilities, and can often result in temporary breakdowns in the system. "Spamming" means sending advertising or other unsolicited text to users.

23. For example, a study entitled "The Social Geography of Gender Switching in Virtual Environments on the Internet," published in the journal *Information, Communication and Society* and summarized in the *New York Times*, stated that "40 percent of participants in online communities have engaged in some form of gender switching." In fact a full "21 percent were actively posing as a person of the opposite sex at the time the study was taken" (Headlam). Of course, terms such as "gender switching," "posing," and "opposite sex" all serve to reinforce the presupposition of a fixed, oppositional, and knowable dual gender system.

24. See McRae for further insightful commentary on the online gender bending practices. Among other things, McRae's article discusses the use of a spivak gender on certain MOOs. There users can employ a unique set of pronouns, e, em, eir, eirs, eirself to indicate a third gender, known as spivak (257), named after its creator, Michael Spivak (n. 6.) See also Reid's and Kendall's articles on MUDs and MOOs and "furry" characters, furries being crosses between human and animal forms.

25. Using a dildo is not equivalent to having a dick. A dildo can merely be a dildo, a tool for penetration or sexual play. And a dick can exist in the absence of a dildo in female-to-female sex. For example, "suck my dick" as a sexually charged verbal command can function as a linguistic appropriation that refers to the act of oral sex between bodies that are genitally marked as female.

26. Of course Gloria could have been biologically male. Throughout this text, it is important for readers to remember that it is gender presentation, rather than biological or genetic sex, that is referred to by gendered pronouns and words such as "male" and "female." My use of these terms in relation to gendered bodies off-line also refers to self-inscribed gender presentation rather than definitions predicated on biology, genetics, or genitalia.

27. See, for example, Plaster of Paradise at www.castroom.com/pop. This is a homepage for those who are aroused by body casts, and includes pictures of various sexual acts where the participants have arms, legs, and/or their entire bodies in casts. It describes where to get supplies and connect with others with similar interests, and provides basic how-to information for casting. It also advises users that they don't need to actually break a limb to enjoy this sexual fetish. My thanks to Daniela Wotke for directing me to this unique site.

28. Even on #espanol other languages, including English, Portuguese, Catalan, Euskera, French, Italian, and Spanglish, were written and read. Unlike many of the English-language channels I visited, #espanol did not prohibit users from chatting in languages other than Spanish. "Obscene language," however, was prohibited in public, and channel operators seemed particularly familiar with English-language curses.

29. *Piropos*, coquettish one-liners, are considered an ancient Latino male art form, a discursive display of virility or chivalry designed to attract the attention of the sexually aloof woman. My father is a master at *piropos*. Some of my favorites include the classic "Si cocina como camina me como hasta el pega'o" (If she cooks like she walks, I'll even eat the scraping off the pot). Other popular *piropos* include "Busco arroz, que aquí no falta carne" (I'm looking for rice, there is no lack of meat here), "Que Dios te guarde, y que me de a mí la llave" (May God guard you, and give me the key), "Camina en la sombra, que un bombón como tú se derrite en el sol" (Walk in the shade, a bonbon like you will melt in the sun). Though it is originally a male heterosexual discursive form, at some Latina dyke gatherings, organizers have set up *piropo* boxes for women to leave their linguistic offerings, thus queerfully transforming this time-honored tradition.

30. Terming this a transgender performance may seem inappropriate to some. I use this term to allege that lesbian femme and feminine heterosexual are not equivalent gendered identities.

31. Very little has been written on the performance and reception of race and ethnicity in cyberspace. I would direct readers to Kolko, Nakamura, and Rodman, *Race in Cyberspace*, specifically the essays by Jennifer González, David Silver, and Beth E. Kolko. See also essays by Christina Elizabeth Sharpe and Emily Noelle Ignacio. One of the first published articles on the subject, which inspired my earliest theorizations of the subject and continues to have commanding relevance, is Daniel Tsang, "Notes on Queer 'N Asian Virtual Sex."

32. Cyber-harassment and stalking can and do happen. See Brail, "The Price of Admission: Harassment and Free Speech in the Wild, Wild West."

Note to Epilogue

1. See "'Pa' la Escuelita con Mucho Cuida'o y por la Orillita': A Journey through the Contested Terrains of the Nation and Sexual Orientation," by Manuel Guzmán. This essay chronicles Guzman's initiation into this notable and notorious New York City nightclub.

Bibliography

Aguirre, Valentín. Presentation. *"Mucho Ojo*: Reel Hot," panel at *"¡Con la Boca Abierta!* Voicing Struggle and Resistance in Queer Raza Communities," University of California, Berkeley, 11 April 1997.

Aguirre, Valentín and Augie Robles, directors. *¡Viva 16!* 1994.

Alarcón, Norma. "Anzaldúa's *Frontera*: Inscribing Gynetics." In *Displacement, Diaspora, and Geographies of Identity*, ed. Smadar Lavie and Ted Swedenburg, 41–53. Durham: Duke University Press, 1996.

———. "Chicana Feminism: In the Tracks of the Native Woman." *Cultural Studies* 4 (1990): 248–56.

———. "Conjugating Subjects in the Age of Multiculturalism." In *Mapping Multiculturalism*, ed. Avery F. Gordon and Christopher Newfield, 127–48. Minneapolis: University of Minnesota Press, 1996.

———. *"Desbordes Nacionales*: For a Transdisciplinary Pedagogy." Paper presented at conference on "Displacing Borders: Interdisciplinary Methods in American Studies," American Studies Working Group, University of California, Berkeley, 13 February 1995.

———. "The Theoretical Subject(s) of *This Bridge Called My Back* and Anglo-American Feminism." In *Making Face, Making Soul: Haciendo Caras*, ed. Gloria Anzaldúa, 356–66. San Francisco: Aunt Lute Foundation, 1990.

———. *"Traddutora, Traditora*: A Paradigmatic Figure of Chicana Feminism." *Cultural Critique* 13 (1990): 57–87.

Albita. *No Se Parece a Nada*. Sony Music Entertainment, 1995.

Alegría, Margarita, Mildred Vera, Carmen Rivera, Margarita Burgos, Ann Finlinson, and Maria del C. Santos. "Puerto Rican Sex Workers: HIV Risk Behaviors and Policy Implications." *Centro: Journal of the Center for Puerto Rican Studies* 6 nos. 1–2 (1994): 86–93.

Alexander, M. Jacqui. "Not Just (Any) *Body* Can Be a Citizen: The Politics of Law, Sexuality, and Postcoloniality in Trinidad and Tobago and the Bahamas." *Feminist Review* 48 (autumn 1994): 5–22.

Anderson, Gina Violeta. "You've Got Mail! Emoticoms, Mistresses, and Cybersex." *conmoción: revista y red revolucionaria de lesbianas latinas* 2 (1995): 10.

Ansaldi, Waldo. *La búsqueda de América Latina: Entre el ansia de encontrarla y el temor de no reconocerla: Teorias e instituciones en la construcción de las ciencias sociales latinoamericanas*. Buenos Aires, Argentina: Universidad de Buenos Aires, Facultad de Ciencias Sociales, 1991.

Anzaldúa, Gloria. *Borderlands/Fronteras: The New Mestiza*. San Francisco: Spinsters/Aunt Lute, 1987.

———, ed. *Making Face, Making Soul: Haciendo Caras*. San Francisco: Aunt Lute Foundation, 1990.

Aparicio, Frances R., and Susana Chávez-Silverman. Introduction to *Tropicalizations: Transcultural Representations of Latinidad*, ed. Frances R. Aparicio and Susana Chávez-Silverman, 1–20. Hanover, NH: University Press of New England for Dartmouth College, 1997.

Arellanes, Lisa. E-mail to author. 4 September 1997.

Arguelles, Lourdes B., and B. Ruby Rich. "Homosexuality, Homophobia and Revolution: Notes towards Understanding of the Cuban Lesbian and Gay Male Experience." *Signs* 9, no. 4 (summer 1984): 683–99.

Arriola, Elvia R. "Gendered Inequality: Lesbians, Gays, and Feminist Legal Theory." *Berkeley Women's Law Journal* 3 (1994): 103–43.

Ashcroft, Bill, Gareth Griffiths, and Helen Tiffin, eds. *The Empire Writes Back: Theory and Practice in Post-Colonial Literatures*. London: Routledge, 1989.

Aspe, Virginia Armella de, and Mercedes Meade. "An Introduction: The Context of the Mexican Retablo." In *The Art of Private Devotion: Retablo Painting of Mexico*, ed. Gloria Fraser Giffords. Fort Worth: InterCultura, 1991.

Avotcja. "What They See Is What They Get." In *Compañeras: Latina Lesbians (An Anthology)*, ed. and comp. Juanita Ramos, 12–17. New York: Latina Lesbian History Project, 1987.

Balderston, Daniel, and Donna J. Guy, eds. *Sex and Sexuality in Latin America*. New York: New York University Press, 1997.

Balibar, Etienne. "Culture and Identity (Working Notes)." Trans. J. Swenson. In *The Identity in Question*, ed. John Rajchman, 173–96. New York: Routledge, 1995.

Barrera, Mario. *Race and Class in the Southwest: A Theory of Racial Inequality*. London: University of Notre Dame Press, 1979.

Barthes, Roland. *Image, Music, Text.* Trans. Stephen Heath. New York: Noonday, 1977.

———. *A Lover's Discourse.* Trans. Richard Howard. New York: Noonday, 1978.

"Basic Statistics." Centers for Disease Control and Prevention, National Center for HIV, STD, and TB Prevention, Divisions of HIV/AIDS Prevention. Online at www.cdc.gov/hiv/stats.htm (13 February 2002).

Batista, Adriana. *Suspiros.* Santa Ana, CA: Ediciones Quiero Más, 1995.

Bechar-Israel, Haya. "From <Bonehead> to <cLoNehEAd>: Nicknames, Play, and Identity on Internet Relay Chat." *Journal of Computer-Mediated Communication* 2, no. 1 (1995). Online at www.ascusc.org/jcmc/vol1/issue2/bechar.html#collective (28 April 2001).

Bennett, Alan G. "The 'Cure' that Harms: Sexual Orientation-Based Asylum and the Changing Definitions of Persecution." *Golden Gate University Law Review* 29 (1999): 279. Lexis-Nexis Academic Universe online subscription database (12 January 2002).

Bergmann, Emilie L., and Paul Julian Smith. Introduction to *¿Entiendes? Queer Readings, Hispanic Writings*, ed. Emilie L. Bergmann and Paul Julian Smith, 1–14. Durham: Duke University Press, 1995.

Beverley, John, José Oviedo, and Michael Aronna. *The Postmodernism Debate in Latin America.* Durham: Duke University Press, 1995.

Bhabha, Homi K. "The Other Question: Discrimination and the Discourse of Colonialism." In *Out There: Marginalization and Contemporary Cultures*, ed. Russell Ferguson et al., 71–87. New York: New Museum of Contemporary Art, 1990.

Black, Jane. "Tiny Tuvalu Profits from Web Name." *New York Times*, 4 September 2000, late ed., C2. Lexis-Nexis Academic Universe online subscription database (20 October 2000).

Blaut, James. *The Colonizer's Model of the World: Geographical Diffusion and Eurocentric History.* New York: Guilford Press, 1993.

Bowers v. Hardwick, 478 US 186 (1986).

Bracho, Ricardo. Memo to the author. 8 August 1997.

———. Presentation. Mission Recreational Center, San Francisco, 13 October 1994.

Brail, Stephanie. "The Price of Admission: Harassment and Free Speech in the Wild, Wild West." In *Wired Women: Gender and New Realities in Cyberspace*, ed. Lynn Cherny and Elizabeth Reba Weise, 141–57. Seattle: Seal Press, 1996.

Branwyn, Gareth. "Compu-Sex: Erotica for Cybernauts." *Flame Wars: The Discourse of Cyberculture,* ed. Mark Dery. Special issue of *South Atlantic Quarterly* 92, no. 4 (fall 1993): 779–93.

Britzman, Deborah P. "On Refusing Explication: Towards a Non-narrative Narrativity." *Resources for Feminist Research* 25, nos. 3–4 (winter 1997): 34–37. Lexis-Nexis Academic Universe online subscription database (11 August 2000).

Brooke, James. "In Live-and-Let-Live Land, Gay People Are Slain." *New York Times,* 12 August 1993, internatl. ed., A4.

Buckmire, Ron. "Brazil: News from Luiz Mott." *Queer Planet.* Online subscription news service. (23 May 1995).

———. "Iranian Gay Man Granted Political Asylum in the USA." *Queer Planet.* Online subscription news service. Online at (19 July 1995).

Burgos, Adrian, Jr. "*Jugando en el Norte*: Caribbean Players in the Negro Leagues, 1910–1950." *Centro: Journal of the Center for Puerto Rican Studies* 8, nos. 1–2 (1996): 151–69.

Butler, Judith. *Bodies That Matter: On the Discursive Limits of "Sex."* New York: Routledge, 1993.

———. "Discussion." In *The Identity in Question,* ed. John Rajchman, 129–44. New York: Routledge, 1995.

———. *The Psychic Life of Power: Theories in Subjection.* Stanford: Stanford University Press, 1997.

Calhoun, Cheshire. "Sexuality Injustice." *Notre Dame Journal of Law, Ethics and Public Policy: Symposium on Sexual Orientation* 9 (1995): 241–74.

Caraballo, David, and Joseph Lo. "IRC Prelude." Online at www.irc.help.org/irchelp /new2irc.html (28 April 2001).

Castañeda, Antonia I. "Language and Other Lethal Weapons: Cultural Politics and the Rites of Children as Translators of Culture." In *Mapping Multiculturalism,* ed. Avery F. Gordon and Christopher Newfield, 201–14. Minneapolis: University of Minnesota Press, 1996.

Castellanos, Mari. Letter. *Esto No Tiene Nombre,* spring 1992, 4.

Céspedes, Guillermo. "Vivito y Coleando." *Vivito y Coleando: Alive and Kicking.* Conjunto Céspedes. Green Linnet Records, 1995.

Chang Hall, Lisa Kahaleole. "Bitches in Solitude: Identity Politics and Lesbian Community." In *Sisters, Sexperts, Queers: Beyond the Lesbian Nation*, ed. Arlene Stein, 218–29. New York: Plume, 1993.

Chávez Leyva, Yolanda. "Listening to the Silences in Latina/Chicana Lesbian History." In *Living Chicana Theory*, ed. Carla Trujillo, 429–34. Berkeley: Third Woman Press, 1998.

Chávez-Silverman, Susana. "Tropicolada: Inside the U.S. Latino/a Gender B(l)ender." In *Tropicalizations: Transcultural Representations of Latinidad*, ed. Frances R. Aparicio and Susana Chávez-Silverman, 101–18. Hanover, NH: University Press of New England for Dartmouth College, 1997.

Chávez-Silverman, Susana, and Librada Hernández, eds. *Reading and Writing the Ambiente: Queer Sexualities in Latino, Latin American and Spanish Culture*. Madison: University of Wisconsin Press, 2000.

Clark, VèVè A. "Developing Diaspora Literacy and *Marasa* Consciousness." In *Comparative American Identities: Race, Sex, and Nationality in the Modern Text*, ed. Hortense J. Spillers, 40–61. New York: Routledge, 1991.

Combahee River Collective. "A Black Feminist Statement" (1977). In *But Some of Us Are Brave*, ed. Gloria Hull, Patricia Bell Scott, and Barbara Smith, 13–22. Old Westbury, NY: Feminist Press, 1982.

Community United Against Violence (CUAV). Press Statement. San Francisco, 8 March 1994.

Cora, María. "Mujerío." *Mujerío* 1 (1987): 1.

Cortez, Yvette, Arline Hernández, and Rebecca Rivera. "Tres Boricuas Hablando." *conmoción: revista y red revolucionaria de lesbianas latinas* 3 (1996): 12–14.

Cortiñas, Jorge Ignacio. "Nuestro América." Paper presented at closing plenary, Tercer Encuentro Nacional de LLEGO, Washington, D.C., 28 May 1995.

Crenshaw, Kimberlé. "Demarginalizing the Intersection of Race and Sex: A Black Feminist Critique of Antidiscrimination Doctrine, Feminist Theory, and Antiracist Politics." *University of Chicago Legal Forum* (1989): 139–67.

Cruz-Malavé, Arnaldo. "'What a Tangled Web!' Masculinity, Abjection, and the Foundations of Puerto Rican Literature in the United States." In *Sex and Sexuality in Latin America*, ed. Daniel Balderston and Donna J. Guy, 234–49. New York: New York University Press, 1997.

Cvetkovich, Ann. "Recasting Receptivity: Femme Sexualities." In *Lesbian Erotics*, ed. Karla Jay, 125–46. New York: New York University Press, 1995.

Davis, Tim. "The Diversity of Queer Politics and the Redefinition of Sexual Identity and Community in Urban Spaces." In *Mapping Desire*, ed. David Bell and Gill Valentine, 285–303. New York: Routledge, 1995.

Degler, Carl N. *Neither Black nor White: Slavery and Race Relations in Brazil and the United States.* 1971; Madison: University of Wisconsin Press, 1986.

Delany, Samuel. "Aversion/Perversion/Diversion." In *Negotiating Lesbian and Gay Subjects*, ed. Monica Dorenkamp and Richard Henke, 7–33. New York: Routledge, 1995.

Deleuze, Gilles. *The Deleuze Reader.* Ed. Constantin V. Boundas. New York: Columbia University Press, 1993.

Delgado, Richard. "Legal Storytelling: Storytelling for Oppositionists and Others: A Plea for Narrative." In *Critical Race Theory: The Cutting Edge*, ed. Richard Delgado, 64–74. Philadelphia: Temple University Press, 1995.

Díaz, Rafael M. *Latino Gay Men and HIV: Culture, Sexuality, and Risk Behavior.* New York: Routledge, 1998.

Diegues, Carlos, dir. *Xica da Silva.* Embrafilme, 1993.

Dixon, Melvin. "I'll Be Somewhere Listening for My Name." *Outlook*, summer 1992, 43–46.

Doyle, Jim. "Political Asylum Granted to Gay from Mexico." *San Francisco Chronicle*, 25 March 1994, A1.

Duncan, Richard F., and Gary L. Young. "Homosexual Rights and Citizen Initiatives: Is Constitutionalism Unconstitutional?" *Notre Dame Journal of Law, Ethics and Public Policy: Symposium on Sexual Orientation* 9 (1995): 93–135.

Elkin, Judith Laiken, and Ana Lya Sater, eds. *Latin American Jewish Studies: An Annotated Guide to the Literature.* New York: Greenwood, 1990.

Ertman, Martha M. "Contract Sports." *Cleveland State Law Review* 49 (2000): 31. Lexis-Nexis Academic Universe online subscription database (12 January 2002).

———. "Marriage as a Trade: Bridging the Private/Private Distinction." *Harvard Civil Rights-Civil Liberties Law Review* 36 (2000): 79. Lexis-Nexis Academic Universe online subscription database (5 March 2002).

Ferriss, Susan. "Mission Meets Castro." *San Francisco Examiner*, 1 June 1997, A1+.

Flores, Juan. *Divided Borders: Essays on Puerto Rican Identity*. Houston: Arte Público Press, 1993.

———. *From Bomba to Hip-Hop: Puerto Rican Culture and Latino Identity*. New York: Columbia University Press, 2000.

Flores, Juan, and George Yúdice. "Living Borders/*Buscando América*: Languages of Latino Self-Formation." In *Divided Borders: Essays on Puerto Rican Identity*, 199–224. Houston: Arte Público Press, 1993.

Foster, David. *Gay and Lesbian Themes in Latin American Literature*. Austin: University of Texas Press, 1991.

———, ed. *Sexual Textualities: Essays on Queering Latin American Writing*. Austin: University of Texas Press, 1997.

Foucault, Michel. *The Archeology of Knowledge and the Discourse on Language*. Trans. A. M. Sheridan Smith. New York: Pantheon, 1972.

———. *Discipline and Punish: The Birth of the Prison*. Trans. Alan Sheridan. New York: Vintage Books, 1979.

———. *Foucault Live (Interviews, 1966–84)*. Trans. John Johnston. Ed. Sylvère Lotringer. New York: Semiotext(e) Foreign Agents Series, 1989.

———. *History of Sexuality*. Vol. 1, *An Introduction*. Trans. Robert Hurley. New York: Pantheon, 1978.

———. *Madness and Civilization*. Trans. R. Howard. New York: Random House, 1965.

Fung, Richard. "The Trouble with 'Asians.'" In *Negotiating Lesbian and Gay Subjects*, ed. Monica Dorenkamp and Richard Henke, 123–30. New York: Routledge, 1995.

Fusco, Coco. *English Is Broken Here: Notes on Cultural Fusion in the Americas*. New York: New Press, 1995.

Fuss, Diana. *Essentially Speaking: Feminism, Nature, and Difference*. New York: Routledge, 1989.

Gabilondo, Joseba. "Postcolonial Cyborgs: Subjectivity in the Age of Cybernetic Reproduction." In *The Cyborg Handbook*, ed. Chris Hables Gray, 423–32. New York: Routledge, 1995.

García Canclini, Néstor. *Hybrid Cultures: Strategies for Entering and Leaving Modernity*. Trans. Christopher L. Chiappari and Silvia L. López. Minneapolis: University of Minnesota Press, 1995.

"Gay Man Who Cited Abuse in Mexico Is Granted Asylum." *New York Times*, 26 March 1994, sec. 1, 5.

Giusti Cordero, Juan A. "Afro-Puerto Rican Cultural Studies: Beyond *cultura negroide* and *antillanismo.*" *Centro: Journal of the Center for Puerto Rican Studies* 8 (1996): 57–77.

Goldberg, Suzanne. Brief of Lambda Legal Defense and Education Fund, Inc. as *Amicus Curiae* in Support of Respondent. A72 093 558. San Francisco, CA.

González, Deena J. "Speaking Secrets: Living Chicana Theory." In *Living Chicana Theory*, ed. Carla Trujillo, 46–77. Berkeley: Third Woman Press, 1998.

González, Jennifer. "The Appended Subject: Race and Identity as Digital Assemblage." In *Race in Cyberspace*, ed. Beth E. Kolko, Lisa Nakamura, and Gilbert B. Rodman, 27–50. New York: Routledge, 2000.

González, Ralfka, and Ana Ruiz. *Mi primer libro de dichos/My First Book of Proverbs*. Introduction by Sandra Cisneros. Emeryville, CA: Children's Book Press, 1995.

Gordon, Avery. *Ghostly Matters: Haunting and the Sociological Imagination*. Minneapolis: University of Minnesota Press, 1997.

Gordon, Avery, F., and Christopher Newfield, eds. *Mapping Multiculturalism*. Minneapolis: University of Minnesota Press, 1996.

Grider, Stuart. "Sexual Orientation as Grounds for Asylum in the United States." *Harvard International Law Journal* 35 (1994): 213–24.

Grosfoguel, Ramón. "The Divorce of Nationalist Discourses from the Puerto Rican People: A Sociohistorical Perspective." In *Puerto Rican Jam: Rethinking Colonialism and Nationalism*, ed. Frances Negrón-Muntaner and Ramón Grosfoguel, 57–76. Minneapolis: University of Minnesota Press, 1997.

Gutiérrez-Jones, Carl. *Rethinking the Borderlands: Between Chicano Culture and Legal Discourse*. Berkeley: University of California Press, 1995.

Guzmán, Manuel. "'Pa' la Escuelita con Mucho Cuida'o y por la Orillita': A Journey through the Contested Terrains of the Nation and Sexual Orientation." In *Puerto Rican Jam: Rethinking Colonialism and Nationalism*, ed. Frances Negrón-Muntaner and Ramón Grosfoguel, 209–30. Minneapolis: University of Minnesota Press, 1997.

Hale, C. Jacob. "Leatherdyke Boys and Their Daddies: How to Have Sex without Women or Men." *Social Text* 52–53 (fall–winter 1997): 223–35.

Halter, Marilyn. *Between Race and Ethnicity: Cape Verdean American Immigrants, 1860–1965*. Urbana: University of Illinois Press, 1993.

Hanchard, Michael George. *Orpheus and Power: The Movimento Negro of Rio de Janeiro and Sao Paulo, Brazil, 1945–1988*. Princeton: Princeton University Press, 1994.

Harm Reduction Coalition. Promotional Brochure. Oakland, CA, and New York, n.d.

Harris, Angela P. "Race and Essentialism in Feminist Legal Terms." *Stanford Law Review* 42 (1990): 581–616.

Harris, Lyle Ashton. "Revenge of a Snow Queen." *Out/Look* 13 (1991).

Hartsock, Nancy. "Foucault on Power: A Theory for Women?" In *Feminism/Postmodernism*, ed. Linda J. Nicholson, 157–75. London: Routledge, 1990.

Hasenbalg, Carlos. "Race and Socioeconomic Inequality in Brazil." In *Race, Class, and Power in Brazil*, ed. Pierre-Michel Fontaine, 25–41. Los Angeles: UCLA Center for Afro-American Studies, 1985.

Headlam, Bruce. "Boys Will Be Boys, and Sometimes Girls, in On-line Communities." *New York Times*, 25 May 2000, late ed., G8. Lexis-Nexis Academic Universe online subscription database (11 July 2000).

Higginbotham, A. Leon. *In the Matter of Color: Race and the American Legal Process: The Colonial Period*. New York: Oxford University Press, 1978.

"HIV/AIDS among Hispanics in the United States." Centers for Disease Control and Prevention, National Center for HIV, STD, and TB Prevention, Divisions of HIV/AIDS Prevention. Online at www.cdc.gov/hiv/pubs/facts/hispanic.htm (13 February 2002).

Hutchinson, Darren Lenard. "'Gay Rights' for 'Gay Whites'?: Race, Sexual Identity, and Equal Protection Discourse. *Cornell Law Review* 85 (2000): 1358. Lexis-Nexis Academic Universe online subscription database (12 January 2002).

IGLHRC (International Gay and Lesbian Human Rights Commission) et al. *Alert to Gay Men and Lesbians from Countries Other Than the United States*. Flyer. n.d.

Ignacio, Emily Noelle. "Ain't I a Filipino (Woman)?: An Analysis of Authorship/Authority through the Construction of 'Filipina' on the Net." *Sociological Quarterly* 41, no. 1 (2000): 551. InfoTrac online subscription database (28 April 2001).

In re Tenorio, no. A72 093 558, EOIR Immigration Court, 26 July 1993.

Jabès, Edmond. *The Book of Questions: El, or the Last Book*. Trans. Rosmarie Waldrop. Middletown, CT: Wesleyan University Press, 1984.

Jiménez-Muñoz, Gladys M. "¡Arráncame la vida! Masculinidad, poder y los obstáculos al sexo seguro." *Centro: Journal of the Center for Puerto Rican Studies* 6, nos. 1–2 (1994): 128–35.

Johnston, David. "Ruling Backs Homosexuals on Asylum." *New York Times*, 17 June 1994, late ed.-final, A12. Lexis-Nexis Academic Universe online subscription database (12 June 2000).

Kaplan, Caren. "Resisting Autobiography: Out-Law Genres and Transnational Feminist Subjects." In *De/Colonizing the Subject: The Politics of Gender in Women's Autobiography*, ed. Sidonie Smith and Julia Watson, 115–38. Minneapolis: University of Minnesota Press, 1992.

Kee, Lorraine. "Gay Trailblazer Prefers Label of 'Good and Compassionate'." *St. Louis Post-Dispatch*, 18 March 2002, Everyday Magazine, D1. Lexis-Nexis Academic Universe online subscription database (27 April 2002).

Kendall, Lori. "MUDder? I Hardly Know 'Er! Adventures of a Feminist MUDder." In *Wired Women: Gender and New Realities in Cyberspace*, ed. Lynn Cherny and Elizabeth Reba Weise, 217–23. Seattle: Seal Press, 1996.

Knopp, Lawrence. "Sexuality and Urban Space: A Framework for Analysis." In *Mapping Desire*, ed. David Bell and Gill Valentine, 149–61. New York: Routledge, 1995.

Kolko, Beth E. "Erasing @race: Going White in the (Inter)Face." In *Race in Cyberspace*, ed. Beth E. Kolko, Lisa Nakamura, and Gilbert B. Rodman, 213–32. New York: Routledge, 2000.

Kolko, Beth E., Lisa Nakamura, and Gilbert B. Rodman, eds. *Race in Cyberspace*. New York: Routledge, 2000.

Krieger, Nancy, and Elizabeth Fee. "Man-Made Medicine and Women's Health: The Biopolitics of Sex/Gender and Race/Ethnicity." In *Women's Health, Politics and Power: Essays on Sex/Gender, Medicine, and Public Health*, ed. Elizabeth Fee and Nancy Krieger, 11–29. Amityville, NY: Baywood, 1994.

Lather, Patricia Ann and Chris Smithies. *Troubling the Angels: Women Living with HIV/AIDS*. Boulder: Westview Press, 1997.

Leiner, Barry et al. "A Brief History of the Internet." Online at www.isoc.org/Internet-history/brief.html (4 September 2000).

Levine, Robert. *Tropical Diaspora: The Jewish Experience in Cuba*. Gainesville: University Press of Florida, 1993.

Lispector, Clarice. *The Hour of the Star*. Trans. Giovanni Pontiero. New York: Carcanet, 1987.

LLEGO: A National Latino/a Lesbian and Gay Organization. *La Guía: A Resource Guide*. Washington, D.C.: LLEGO, 1995.

López, María Milagros. "Postwork Society and Postmodern Subjectivities." In *The Postmodernism Debate in Latin America*, ed. John Beverley, José Oviedo, and Michael Aronna, 165–91. Durham: Duke University Press, 1995.

Lorde, Audre. *Sister Outsider: Essays and Speeches*. Freedom, CA: Crossing Press, 1985.

———. *Zami: A New Spelling of My Name*. Freedom, CA: Crossing Press, 1982.

Manalansan, Martin F., IV. "In the Shadows of Stonewall: Examining Gay Transnational Politics and the Diasporic Dilemma." In *The Politics of Culture in the Shadow of Capital*, ed. Lisa Lowe and David Lloyd, 485–503. Durham: Duke University Press, 1997.

Marcosson, Samuel A. "The 'Special Rights' Canard in the Debate over Lesbian and Gay Civil Rights." *Notre Dame Journal of Law, Ethics and Public Policy: Symposium on Sexual Orientation* 9 (1995): 137–83.

Margulies, Peter. "Asylum, Intersectionality, and AIDS: Women with HIV as a Persecuted Social Group." *Georgetown Immigration Law Journal* 8 (1994): 521–55.

Matsuda, Mari J. "Voices of America: Accent, Antidiscrimination Law, and a Jurisprudence for the Last Reconstruction." *Yale Law Review* 100 (1991): 1329–1407.

Mattoso, Katie M. de Quieros. *To Be a Slave in Brazil, 1550–1888*. Trans. Arthur Goldhammer. New Brunswick: Rutgers University Press, 1986.

McClintock, Anne. "'No Longer in a Future Heaven': Nationalism, Gender and Race." In *Becoming National: A Reader*, ed. Geoff Eley and Ronald Grigor Suny, 260–84. New York: Oxford University Press, 1996.

McGoldrick, Brian J. "United States Immigration Policy and Sexual Orientation: Is Asylum for Homosexuals a Possibility?" *Georgetown Immigration Law Journal* 8 (1994): 201–26.

Mclane, Daisann. "Re: Opiniones sobre el Sr. Mas Canosa." Online posting, newsgroup soc.culture.cuba (19 December 1994).

McRae, Shannon. "Coming Apart at the Seams: Sex, Text, and the Virtual Body." In *Wired Women: Gender and New Realities in Cyberspace*, ed. Lynn Cherny and Elizabeth Reba Weise, 242–63. Seattle: Seal Press, 1996.

Mohanty, Chandra Talpade. "Cartographies of Struggle: Third World Women and the Politics of Feminism." In *Third World Women and the Politics of Feminism*, ed. Chandra Talpade Mohanty, Ann Russo, and Lourdes Torres, 1–47. Bloomington: Indiana University Press, 1991.

Mohyuddin, Fatima. "United States Asylum Law in the Context of Sexual Orientation and Gender Identity: Justice for the Transgendered?" *Hastings Women's Law
Journal* 12 (2001): 387. Lexis-Nexis Academic Universe online subscription database (12 January 2002).

Molloy, Sylvia, and Robert McKee Irwin. *Hispanisms and Homosexualities.* Durham:
Duke University Press, 1998.

Montejano, David. *Anglos and Mexicans In the Making of Texas, 1836–1986.* Austin:
University of Texas Press, 1987.

Moore, Carlos. *Castro, the Blacks, and Africa.* Los Angeles: Center for Afro-American
Studies, University of California Press, 1988.

———. *Loving in the War Years: lo que nunca pasó por sus labios.* Boston: South End
Press, 1983.

Moraga, Cherríe. *The Last Generation.* Boston: South End Press, 1993.

———. *Loving in the War Years: lo que nunca pasó por sus labios.* Boston: South End
Press, 1983.

———. *Shadow of a Man.* In *Heroes and Saints and Other Plays*, 37–84. Albuquerque:
West End Press, 1994.

Moraga, Cherríe, and Gloria Anzaldúa, eds. *This Bridge Called My Back: Writings by
Radical Women of Color.* Watertown, Mass.: Persephone Press, 1981.

Moreno Vega, Marta. "Resistance and Affirmation in African Diaspora Latin Communities." *Heresies: A Feminist Publication on Art and Politics* 7, no. 3 (1993):
78–83.

Morrison, Toni. Introduction to *Race-ing Justice, En-gendering Power: Essays on Anita
Hill, Clarence Thomas, and the Construction of Social Reality.* New York: Pantheon,
1992.

Mosak, Esther. "White Mirrors: Film and Television Workers Talk about Racial Representation." *Cuba Update*, November 1991, 28–30.

Mott, Luiz Roberto. *Epidemic of Hate: Violations of the Human Rights of Gay Men,
Lesbians, and Transvestites in Brazil.* Salvador, Bahia: Grupo Gay da Brasil;
San Francisco: International Gay and Lesbian Human Rights Commission,
1996.

Muñoz, José Esteban. *Disidentifications: Queers of Color and the Performance of Politics.*
Minneapolis: University of Minnesota Press, 1999.

———. "Feeling Brown: Ethnicity and Affect in Ricardo Bracho's *The Sweetest Hangover (and Other STDs)*." *Theatre Journal* 52, no. 1 (2000): 67–79. Project Muse online subscription database (28 October 2000).

Negrón-Muntaner, Frances. "English Only Jamás but Spanish Only Cuidado: Language and Nationalism in Contemporary Puerto Rico." In *Puerto Rican Jam: Rethinking Colonialism and Nationalism*, ed. Frances Negrón-Muntaner and Ramón Grosfoguel, 257–85. Minneapolis: University of Minnesota Press, 1997.

Negrón-Muntaner, Frances, and Ramón Grosfoguel, eds. *Puerto Rican Jam: Rethinking Colonialism and Nationalism*. Minneapolis: University of Minnesota Press, 1997.

New York City Gay and Lesbian Anti-Violence Project, comp. "Anti-Lesbian, Gay, Transgender, and Bisexual Violence in 2000. A Report of the National Coalition of Anti-Violence Programs." New York: National Coalition of Anti-Violence Programs, 2001.

———. "Gay/Lesbian–Related Homicides in the United States, 1992–1994: First National Analysis and Report." New York: New York City Gay and Lesbian Anti-Violence Project, 1994.

O'Brien, Jodi. "Changing the Subject." *Women and Performance* 17 (undated). Online at www.echonyc.com/~women/Issue17/art-obrien.html (14 May 1998).

Ochoa, Marcia. *La ofrenda*. Ann Arbor, 1991.

Ortiz, Ricardo L. "*Café, Culpa* and *Capital*: Nostalgic Addictions of Cuban Exile." *Yale Journal of Criticism* 10, no. 1 (1997): 63–84.

Ortiz Cofer, Judith. *The Latin Deli: Telling the Lives of Barrio Women*. New York: Norton, 1993.

Ortiz-Torres, Blanca. "The Politics of AIDS Research and Policies and the U.S. Latino Community." *Centro: Journal of the Center for Puerto Rican Studies* 6, nos. 1–2 (1994): 108–14.

Patton, Cindy. *Inventing AIDS*. New York: Routledge, 1990.

Penn, William S., ed. *As We Are Now: Mixblood Essays on Race and Identity*. Berkeley: University of California Press, 1997.

Pérez, Emma. "Irigaray's Female Symbolic in the Making of Chicana Lesbian *Sitios y Lenguas* (Sites and Discourses)." In *The Lesbian Postmodern*, ed. Laura Doan, 104–17. New York: Columbia University Press, 1994.

¡Perra! La Revista. December 1995, 2.

Phelan, Peggy. *Unmarked: The Politics of Performance.* London: Routledge, 1993.

Pile, Steve, and Nigel Thrift. Introduction to *Mapping the Subject: Geographies of Cultural Transformation,* ed. Steve Pile and Nigel Thrift, 1–12. London: Routledge, 1995.

———. "Mapping the Subject." In *Mapping the Subject: Geographies of Cultural Transformation,* ed. Pile and Thrift, 13–56. London: Routledge, 1995.

Polikoff, Nancy D. "Why Lesbians and Gay Men Should Read Martha Fineman." *American University Journal of Gender, Social Policy and Law* 8 (2000): 167. Lexis-Nexis Academic Universe online subscription database (12 January 2002).

Proyecto ContraSIDA por Vida. Calendar of events. San Francisco: PCPV, 1994.

———. *Proyecto ContraSIDA por Vida.* San Francisco: PCPV, 1996.

———. *What's the T?* San Francisco: PCPV, 1996.

———. *¡Y QUE! Young, Queer and Under Emergency.* San Francisco: PCPV, 1996.

Puar, Jasbir K. "Transnational Sexualities: South Asian (Trans)nation(alism)s and Queer Diasporas." In *Q&A: Queer in Asian America,* ed. David L. Eng and Alice Y. Hom, 405–19. Philadelphia: Temple University Press, 1998.

Quiroga, José. *Tropics of Desire: Interventions from Queer Latino America.* New York: New York University Press, 2000.

Rajchman, John, ed. *The Identity in Question.* New York: Routledge, 1995.

Ramos, Juanita, ed. and comp. *Compañeras: Latina Lesbians (An Anthology).* New York: Latina Lesbian History Project, 1987.

Reid, Elizabeth M. "Text-Based Virtual Realities: Identity and the Cyborg Body." In *High Noon on the Electronic Frontier: Conceptual Issues in Cyberspace,* ed. Peter Ludlow, 327–44. Cambridge: MIT Press, 1996.

Roa Bastos, Augusto. *I the Supreme.* Trans. Helen Lane. New York: Vintage Books, 1987.

Rodríguez, Janelle. Presentation. "*Mucho Ojo*: Reel Hot," panel at "*¡Con la Boca Abierta!* Voicing Struggle and Resistance in Queer Raza Communities," University of California, Berkeley, 11 April 1997.

———, dir. *Sabrosura.* San Francisco: PCPV, 1996.

Rodríguez, Juan. Address at artists reception. Proyecto ContraSIDA por Vida, 18 January 1995.

Rodriguez, Richard. "Complexion." In *Out There: Marginalization and Contemporary Cultures,* ed. Russell Furguson et al., 265–78. New York: New Museum of Contemporary Art, 1990. Reprinted from *Hunger of Memory. The Education of Richard Rodriguez: An Autobiography*, 113–39. Boston: D. R. Godine, 1982.

Rodríguez-Morazzani, Roberto P. "Beyond the Rainbow: Mapping the Discourse on Puerto Ricans and 'Race.'" *Centro: Journal of the Center for Puerto Rican Studies* 8, nos. 1–2 (1996): 151–69.

Rohter, Larry. "Brazil Builds Bigger and Better Telenovelas." *New York Times*, 27 August 2000, late ed, Arts and Leisure Desk, sec. 2, 21. Lexis-Nexis Academic Universe online subscription database (23 January 2001).

Román, David. *Acts of Intervention: Performance, Gay Cultures and AIDS*. Bloomington: Indiana University Press, 1998.

———. "Tropical Fruit." In *Tropicalizations: Transcultural Representations of Latinidad*, ed. Frances R. Aparicio and Susana Chávez-Silverman, 119–38. Hanover, NH: University Press of New England for Dartmouth College, 1997.

Román, David, and Alberto Sandoval-Sánchez. "Caught in the Web: Latinidad, AIDS, and Allegory in *Kiss of the Spider Woman*, the Woman, the Musical." In *Everynight Life: Culture and Dance in Latin/o America*, ed. Celeste Fraser Delgado and José Esteban Muñoz, 255–87. Durham: Duke University Press, 1997.

Romany, Celina. "Neither Here nor There . . . Yet." *Heresies: A Feminist Publication on Art and Politics* 7, no. 3 (1993): 93–96.

Root, Maria P., ed. *The Multiracial Experience: Racial Borders as the New Frontier*. Thousand Oaks, CA: Sage, 1996.

Rothenberg, Tamar. "And She Told Two Friends: Lesbians Creating Urban Social Spaces." In *Mapping Desire*, ed. David Bell and Gill Valentine, 165–81. New York: Routledge, 1995.

Rubin, Gayle. "Thinking Sex: Notes for a Radical Theory of the Politics of Sexuality." In *The Lesbian and Gay Studies Reader*, ed. Henry Abelove, Michèle Aina Barale, and David M. Halperin, 3–44. New York: Routledge, 1993.

Said, Edward. "Reflections on Exile." In *Out There: Marginalization and Contemporary Cultures*, ed. Russell Ferguson et al., 357–66. New York: New Museum of Contemporary Art, 1990.

Sandoval, Chela. "Feminist Forms of Agency and Oppositional Consciousness: U.S. Third World Feminist Criticism." In *Provoking Agents: Gender and Agency in Theory and Practice*, ed. Judith Kegan Gardiner, 208–26. Urbana: University of Illinois Press, 1995.

Sandoval-Sánchez, Alberto. "A Response to the Representation of AIDS in the Puerto Rican Arts and Literature: In the Manner of a Proposal for a Cultural Studies Project." *Centro: Journal of the Center for Puerto Rican Studies* 6, nos. 1–2 (spring 1994): 181–86.

San Francisco AIDS Foundation. *Behind Our Backs: Faggot Sex/Sissy Speak: sumt'n ta say.* San Francisco: San Francisco AIDS Foundation, 1995.

San Francisco HIV Prevention Planning Council in Partnership with the Department of Public Health AIDS Office. *San Francisco HIV Prevention Plan, 1997.* San Francisco: Harder and Company Community Research, 1996.

Santiago-Valles, Kelvin. "Policing the Crisis in Whiteness of All the Antilles." *Centro: Journal of the Center for Puerto Rican Studies* 8, nos. 1–2 (1996): 142–57.

Shah, Nayan. "Sexuality, Identity, and the Uses of History." In *A Lotus of Another Color: An Unfolding of the South Asian Gay and Lesbian Experience,* ed. Rakesh Ratti, 113–32. Boston: Alyson, 1993.

Shahl, Joh, dir. *Imitation of Life.* 1934.

Sharpe, Christina Elizabeth. "Racialized Fantasies on the Internet." *Signs* 24, no. 4 (1999): 1089. InfoTrac online subscription database (28 April 2001).

Sheinin, David, and Lois Baer Barr, eds. *The Jewish Diaspora in Latin America: New Studies on History and Literature.* New York: Garland, 1996.

Shoop, Lyn G. "Health Based Exclusion Grounds in the United States Immigration Policy: Homosexuals, HIV Infection, and the Medical Examination of Aliens." *Journal of Contemporary Health Law and Policy* 9 (1993): 521–44.

Silver, David. "Margins in the Wires: Looking for Race, Gender, and Sexuality in the Blacksburg Electronic Village." In *Race in Cyberspace,* ed. Beth E. Kolko, Lisa Nakamura, and Gilbert B. Rodman, 133–50. New York: Routledge, 2000.

Sirk, Douglas, dir. *Imitation of Life.* 1959.

Soja, Edward. "History: Geography: Modernity." In *The Cultural Studies Reader,* ed. Simon During, 135–50. New York: Routledge, 1993.

Somerville, Margaret A. and Sarah Wilson. "Crossing Boundaries: Travel, Immigration, Human Rights and AIDS." McGill Law Journal 43 (1998): 781. Lexis-Nexis Academic Universe online subscription database (12 January 2002).

Sondheim, Alan. "Introduction to Space." *Being On Line: Net Subjectivities,* guest edited by Alan Sondheim. Special issue of *Lusitania* 8 (1996): 6–10.

Soto-Mayorga, Daniel. "Re: Jornada Astrológica." Online posting, listserve Arenal (13 August 1997).

Spivak, Gayatri Chakravorty. "Explanation and Culture: Marginalia." In *Out There: Marginalization and Contemporary Cultures*. ed. Russell Ferguson et al., 377–93. New York: New Museum of Contemporary Art, 1990.

Springer, Claudia. "Sex, Memories, and Angry Women." *Flame Wars: The Discourse of Cyberculture*, ed. Mark Dery. Special issue of *South Atlantic Quarterly* 92, no. 4 (fall 1993): 713–32.

Star, Susan Leigh. "From Hestia to Home Page: Feminism and the Concept of Home in Cyberspace." In *Between Monsters, Goddesses, and Cyborgs: Feminist Confrontations with Science, Medicine, and Cyberspace*, ed. Nina Lykke and Rosi Braidotti, 30–44. London: Zed Books, 1996.

Sterling, Bruce. "Short History of the Internet." Online at w3.aces.uiuc.edu/AIM/SCALE/nethistory.html (10 August 2000).

Stivale, Charles J. "Cyber/Inter/Mind/Assemblage." *Being On Line: Net Subjectivities*, guest edited by Alan Sondheim. Special issue of *Lusitania* 8 (1996): 119–25.

Stone, Allucquère Rosanne. *The War of Desire and Technology at the Close of the Mechanical Age*. Cambridge: MIT Press, 1996.

"Surfing in Tongues." *Business Week*, 11 December 2000, 18. InfoTrac online subscription database (28 April 2001).

Takaki, Ronald. *Iron Cages: Race and Culture in Nineteenth-Century America*. 1979; New York: Oxford University Press, 1990.

tatiana and Amy. Letter. *conmoción: revista y red revolucionaria de lesbianas latinas* 2 (1995): 6–7.

Third World Gay Revolution (New York). "What We Want, What We Believe." In *Out of the Closets: Voices of Gay Liberation*, ed. Karla Jay and Allen Young, 363–67. New York: Quick Fox, 1972.

Thomas, Kendall. "The Eclipse of Reason: A Rhetorical Reading of *Bowers v. Hardwick*." *Virginia Law Review* 79 (1993): 1805–32.

tierra, tatiana de la. "Love Me Dis-embodied." Unpublished essay, 1998.

Torres Rivera, Alejandro. "El espectáculo del coloniaje en Puerto Rico." *Areíto* 4 (1994): 22–24.

Trinh T. Minh-ha. "Not You/Like You: Postcolonial Women and the Interlocking Questions of Identity and Difference." In *Making Face, Making Soul: Haciendo*

Caras, ed. Gloria Anzaldúa, 371–75. San Francisco: Aunt Lute Foundation, 1990.

———. *Woman, Native, Other: Writing Postcoloniality and Feminism*. Bloomington: University of Indiana Press, 1989.

Trujillo, Carla. "La Virgen de Guadalupe and Her Reconstruction in Chicana Lesbian Desire." In *Living Chicana Theory*, ed. Carla Trujillo, 214–31. Berkeley: Third Woman Press, 1998.

Tsang, Daniel C. "Notes on Queer 'N Asian Virtual Sex." *Amerasian Journal* 20, no. 1 (1994): 123–30.

Tuller, David. "Gay Brazilian Claims Persecution—Wins U.S. Asylum." *San Francisco Chronicle*, 29 July 1993, A13.

———. "Gay Request for Asylum Based on Sexual Persecution." *San Francisco Chronicle*, 20 May 1993, A19.

UCLA Online Institute for Cyberspace Law and Policy. "Cases, Statutes, and Topical Highlights: Cyberspace Law and Policy." www.gseis.ucla.edu/iclp/csth.html (28 June 2000).

Valencia, Loana D. P. "Wanna Be a *Puta*?" *conmoción: revista y red revolucionaria de lesbianas latinas* 3 (1996): 38–39.

Valle Silva, Nelson do. "Updating the Cost of Not Being White in Brazil." In *Race, Class, and Power in Brazil*, ed. Pierre-Michel Fontaine, 42–55. Los Angeles: UCLA Center for Afro-American Studies, 1985.

Vazquez, Adela C. Presentation. "*De Sangre y de Amor*: HIV in Our Communities," panel at "*¡Con la Boca Abierta!* Voicing Struggle and Resistance in Queer Raza Communities," University of California, Berkeley, 11 April 1997.

Vazquez, Blanca. "St. Ann's Corner of Harm Reduction: Interview with Joyce Rivera Beckman." *Centro: Journal of the Center for Puerto Rican Studies* 6, nos. 1–2 (1994): 192–204.

Vizcarrondo, Fortunato. *Dinga y Mandinga (Poemas)*. San Juan: Instituto de Cultura Puertorriqueña, 1979.

Vizenor, Gerald. *Crossbloods: Bone Courts, Bingo, and Other Reports*. Minneapolis: University of Minnesota Press, 1990.

———. *Dead Voices: Natural Agonies in the New World*. Norman: University of Oklahoma Press, 1992.

———. *Interior Landscapes: Autobiographical Myths and Metaphors*. Minneapolis: University of Minnesota Press, 1990.

———. *Manifest Manners*. Hanover: Wesleyan University Press, 1994.

Weide, Darlene, and Rebecca Denison. "Women and AIDS: A Global Problem." *WORLD: Women Organized to Respond to Life-Threatening Diseases* 32 (1993): 2–5.

White, Emily. "Glossary." *Flame Wars: The Discourse of Cyberculture*, ed. Mark Dery. Special issue of *South Atlantic Quarterly* 92, no. 4 (fall 1993): 851–54.

Wiegman, Robyn. "Introduction: Mapping the Lesbian Postmodern." In *The Lesbian Postmodern*, ed. Laura Doan, 1–20. New York: Columbia University Press, 1994.

Williams, Linda. *Hard Core: Power, Pleasure, and the Frenzy of the Visible*. Berkeley: University of California Press, 1989.

Williams, Patricia. *The Alchemy of Race and Rights*. Cambridge: Harvard University Press, 1991.

Winant, Howard. "'The Other Side of the Process': Racial Formation in Contemporary Brazil." In *On Edge: The Crisis of Contemporary Latin American Culture*, ed. George Yúdice, Jean Franco, and Juan Flores, 85–113. Minneapolis: University of Minnesota Press, 1992.

Wockner, Rex. *News Briefs*. Web archive online at www.qrd.org/world/wockner /news.briefs (1 May 2000).

Wohlblatt, Karen. "The Sweetness of Lurking." *Being On Line: Net Subjectivities*, guest edited by Alan Sondheim. Special issue of *Lusitania* 8 (1996): 36–38.

Yamada, Mitsuye. "Invisibility Is an Unnatural Disaster: Reflections of an Asian American Woman." In *This Bridge Called My Back: Writings by Radical Women of Color*, ed. Cherríe Moraga and Gloria Anzaldúa, 2nd ed. 35–40. New York: Kitchen Table Press, 1983.

Yarbo-Bejarano, Yvonne. "Crossing the Border with Chabela Vargas: A Chicana Femme's Tribute." In *Sex and Sexuality in Latin America*, ed. Daniel Balderston and Donna J. Guy, 33–43. New York: New York University Press, 1997.

———. "Deconstructing the Lesbian Body: Cherríe Moraga's *Loving in the War Years*." In *The Lesbian and Gay Studies Reader*, ed. Henry Abelove, Michèle Aina Barale, and David M. Halperin, 595–603. New York: Routledge, 1993.

———. "The Lesbian Body in Latina Cultural Production." In *¿Entiendes? Queer Readings, Hispanic Writings*, ed. Emilie L. Bergmann and Paul Julian Smith, 181–97. Durham: Duke University Press, 1995.

Yúdice, George, Jean Franco, and Juan Flores, eds. *On Edge: The Crisis of Contemporary Latin American Culture*. Minneapolis: University of Minnesota Press, 1992.

Zweig, Ellen. "The Lurker: Outline for a Murder Mystery." *Being On Line: Net Subjectivities*, guest edited by Alan Sondheim. Special issue of *Lusitania* 8 (1996): 26–27.

Index

Academia, 3, 8, 29–31, 36, 119, 149, 159–60; and disciplinary boundaries, 3, 29–31; language of, 36, 159–60; practices of, 160

Accent(s), 165n. 16; in cyberspace, 138; marks, 86, 157, 185n. 3; removal of, 86; traces of, in cyberspace, 116; and transformation of language, 19

Activism, 34, 37, 156, 159; and AIDS, 38, 49, 50–52, 76–77, 79–80; and cyberspace, 121–23; discourse of, 156; and ghosts, 37–39, 83; and identity, 39–46, 157; and identity politics, 34, 39–46; language of, 36, 79–80; and Luis Mott, 98; and postmodern practice of, 46, 79; and power, 46; and Proyecto, 50–52, 79–80; in San Francisco, 46, 49, 76–77; and sex and death, 158–59; and Spanglish, 74; and technology, 121–23; after Tenório, 110–12. *See also* Groups

African Ancestral Lesbians United for Societal Change, 41

Afro-Latina/o: and competing demands of political and cultural movements, 21; and hair, in identity formation, 167n. 20; in U.S. entertainment media, 20; Tenório as, 93; visibility of, in representations of Latina/o community, 19–21

Aguilar, Laura, 178n. 32

AGUILAS, 77, 174n. 17

Aguirre, Valentín, 175n. 19, 179n. 36

AIDS: demographic statistics on, 38, 46–47, 171–72n. 9; and funding, 80; and ghosts, 38, 83; and identity, 47, 65, 172n. 10; and immigration, 89, 182n. 6; in San Francisco, 38, 171–72n. 9, 172n. 10; and spirituality, 61; and women, 47, 80, 173n. 11, 180n. 47

Alarcón, Norma, 6–7, 9, 32–33, 45, 164n. 5, 170–71n. 8; and "horizon of meanings," 7, 29, 88; and "not yet," 7; and "subject-in-process," 6–7, 31, 33, 157

Albita, 124, 186n. 14

Alvarez, Rosio, 185n. 8

Alvarez, Tania, 85, 89–90, 94–96, 98, 111–12, 154

Amantes de La Luna, Las, 77

Ambiente, El, 174n. 17

Ambiguity: in naming, 26; within the text, 2

Anderson, Gina Violeta, 136

Annual Latina/o Gay, Lesbian and Bisexual Visual Arts Exhibit, 43, 170n. 7

Ansaldi, Waldo, 9; *La busqueda de AmÈrica Latina*, 9

Anzaldúa, Gloria, 3, 23, 30, 165n. 14, 170–71n. 8; and "mestiza consciousness," 23

Arellanes, Lisa, 55

Arenal, 123, 125–26, 186n. 15

Arguelles, Lourdes, 30

Arriola, Elvia, 95

Conquest: and colonialism, 15, 18; and
nation, 14; and resistance, 15; sexual,
141, 144; and submission, 18; of
technology, 117; and translation, 18;
and tribal deterritorialization, 14
Contradictions, 6–9, 44; and Caribbean
cultural identity, 13; in constructions
of *latinidad*, 9–23; and cultural identity, 21–23; of cyberspace as "global
space," 130; and feminism, 9; in
Proyecto's relation to the state, 82; as
refuge from homosexual persecution,
109; as sites of knowledge, 8; as
"spaces of dissension," 9; of United
States
Cora, María, 154, 169n. 4
Cortez, Jamie, 178n. 32
Cortiñ as, Jorge Ignacio, 111, 178n. 32,
181n.48
Coto, Roberto, 176n. 26
Crenshaw, Kimberlé, 95, 182n. 10
Criminalization: of drug culture and
prostitution in San Francisco, 50; of
homosexuality, 106–7; of men of
color, 89; and regulative power, 107;
of underage sex, 176n. 29
Cruz, Celia, 19–20, 123, 166n. 18
Cruz, Sor Juana Inéz de la, 27
Cruz-Malavé, Arnaldo, 17, 18, 165n. 11
Cuba: in cyberspace, 123–25; and iden-
tity, 140, 180n. 45; and language, 26,
28, 180n. 45; and media depictions
of race, 19–20; and political asylum,
88, 181n. 4; and race, 19–20, 140,
166n. 17; and stereotypes, 140; and
technology, 150–51
Cultural identity, 11–13; and
Chicanismo, 11; in cyberspace, 138; in
geopolitical sites, 10; and language,

18–19, 138; and *mestizaje*, 12; and
mixed cultural heritages, 21, 167n.
22; and national identity, 11–13; per-
meability of, 75
Cyber-sex, 115, 129, 141–49; and the
body, 142, 144; and discipline, 136;
and exoticization of lesbian sex, 133;
and gender performance, 134,
138–41; and guilt, 137–138; and heteronormativity, 139; and intimacy,
143; and language, 142–45; and off-
line sexual practices, 129, 147–48;
and orgasm, 145; and pleasure, 147;
and queering, 142; and routine, 143;
and S/M, 135–36; and safety, 136,
147; and sexual conquest, 141; and
submission, 136; and text, 144; and
the transgender body, 134–135, 140;
and visual media, 144
Cyberspace, 117–19, 121–23, 133–34; ac-
cessibility of, 122; and the body, 115,
117, 120, 127, 137, 141–42, 144; and
coming out, 124, 142; and desire,
116–117; discourse of, 157, 159–60;
and gender, 130–33, 140; and gender
"passing," 130, 133–35, 139, 187nn.
23, 24; and gender binary, 132; and
gender performance, 131–35, 139,
186n. 17; as a "global space," 130;
and identity, 32, 34, 127–28, 156; and
identity patrol, 130–33; and identity
production, 127–28; and ideology,
122–23, 157; and illusion of privacy,
129; and intimacy, 120, 140, 143; and
language, 123, 126, 131–132, 140,
142, 187n. 21, 188n. 22; and naming, 128, 157, 164n. 3, 187n. 19; and
performance, 119, 127; and queer
communities, 115, 185–86n. 11; and

Lopez, Rosa, 182n. 13
Lorde, Audre, 9
Lujan, Al, 178n. 32
Lupe, La, 30
Lurking, 114, 149, 184n. 1

Macha/o(s): in "Asi somos," 50–51; and author(ity), 52–53, 73; and homosexual violence, 100; and "machismo," 99–100, 102; and *"marimacha,"* 26; traces of violence in, 53; and translation, 100
Majano, Veronica, 177n. 31
Mala Maña, 154
Malinche, La, 18, 165n. 12
Mambo Kings, The, 20, 166n. 18
Margins, 1–2, 3, 155
Mariel boatlift, 30, 76
Martin, Ricky, 30
Martinez, Jacqueline, 67
Mastery: and desire, 148–49; and submission, 52; of technology, 117
Mayans, 10, 185n. 10
Mclane, Daisann, 124
McRae, Shannon, 118, 127, 145
Meade, Mercedes, 63
Mestizaje, 12–14; in Brazil, 97; and Chicana/o identity, 11; and *mulatismo*, 12–13, 97; and the state, 12–13
Metaphor: of *arroba* (@) sign, 126; dance as, 93; and death of the queer citizen, 158; and ghosts, 37; and myths, 37; names as, 12; of papaya, 70; of penetration, 165n. 11; of Puerto Rican *"guagua aérea,"* 165n. 10; of sexual submission, 18; of *tortillera*, 26; of "trans-creation" as Latino self-formation, 74; translation as, 3

Methodology, 8–9, 22, 31–32, 33–36, 48, 156, 173n. 13; and archeology, 8–9, 156
Mexican Museum, 176n. 25
México, 10–11, 49, 64, 77, 84; and Aztlán, 11; and immigration, 84, 182n. 6; and *latinidad*, 10; and the Mayans, 10, 185n. 10; and *mestizaje*, 14; and national identity, 10–11; *retablos* in, 61; and *telenovelas*, 166n. 18; and Marcelo Tenório, 84
Migration, 15–17, 165n. 10. *See also* Immigration
Milk, Harvey, 183n. 15
Mirabal, Nancy, 67
Mission Cultural Center, 49, 169–70n. 5, 176n. 25
Mission District, 34, 35, 49–51, 82, 154; gentrification of, 82, 175nn. 19, 22; and Proyecto, 34, 49–51, 175n. 22; racial/ethnic composition of, 50; violence against homosexuals in, 182n. 7. *See also* San Francisco
Mission Neighborhood Health Center, 176n. 25
Mohr, Nicholasa, 168n. 1
Moraga, Cherríe, 9, 30, 61, 164n. 3, 168n. 1
Mott, Luiz, 85, 96–104, 112, 122, 182n. 11, 183n. 18
Mujerío, 42, 49, 169n. 4, 170n. 7
Mulatismo: in Brazil, 97; and exoticization, 140; and *mestizaje*, 12–13, 97; and racial categories, 13; and resistance, 12; and the state, 13
Multilingualism, 18–19; and navigation of discursive spaces, 75
Muñoz, José Esteban, 29, 168–69n. 2, 175–76n. 23

Postcolonialism, 32, 163n. 2; and *la-tinidad*, 10; (post) (neo) colonialism, 10, 32, 113, 163n. 2; and representation, 65

Postmodernism: and activism, 39, 45–46, 79–80, 161; in Latin America, 163n. 2

Power, 82; and activism, 46; and *activismo*, 74; of attorney, 108; of discourse over the body, 21; and empowerment, 24, 55, 73, 79, 80; of heterosexuality, 107–9; of language, 21, 149, 161, 168n. 1; regulatory, 5, 107, 109, 184; in the service of radical justice, 46; and sex, 59, 67; of social categories, 81; of the state, 44, 53, 82, 184n. 22; of stories and storytellers, 37; and technology, 117; in *tetatúd*, 67

Project Muse, 123

Proyecto ContraSIDA por Vida, 34–35, 47–85, 154–55, 158–60, 169–170n. 5, 170n. 7, 173nn. 12, 13, 15, 174n. 18, 175n. 22, 176nn. 24, 25, 26, 28, 177–78n. 31, 178nn. 32, 33, 34, 179nn. 36, 37, 41, 181n. 48; approach to HIV prevention and treatment, 53–55; audience of, 50, 56, 79, 80; and Colegio ContraSIDA, 59–60; and collectivity, 48, 54, 59, 65, 79–80, 157, 176n. 28; and "community-in-process," 80; and community dialogues, 57; and *familia*, 56, 79; and food, 56; and harm reduction, 174n. 18; and identity "in-progress," 34; and identity politics, 48–49; and language, 51–54, 69, 72–75; mission statement ("Asi somos") of, 50–54, 76; and programming, 55–57, 59–60;

and promotional materials, 57–59, 65–74, 77–80, 159, 176n. 28; and refusal of explication, 48, 78; and *retablos*, 61–65; and self-representation, 48, 50, 60–65, 80, 157; and state funding, 80–82; and strategies of intervention, 59, 73, 79, 159; and translation, 54, 69, 73

Puerto Rican Social Group, 174n. 17

Puerto Rico, 14–15, 17, 164n. 8, 165n. 9; and *des-tierro*, 17–18; and migration, 17; and Nuyorican literature, 17–18; and plebiscites, 16–17, 164n. 8; political parties of, 16–17; and political status in United States, 16; and race, 164n. 8. *See also* Nuyorican (Diasporican) identity

Puta, 67, 144; name, 76; and "Wanna be a Puta?," 68

Que Tal, 174n. 17

Queer, 2, 23–25, 35, 115, 155; in "Asi somos," 50–52; and categories, 24; and coming out, 124; critical uses of, 24; and heterosexual cyber-sex, 142; and refusing explication, 24; and representation, 168–69n. 2; and "sex-positive," 67; spaces, 24, 91–92, 106

Queer language, 25–28, 68; and *arroba* (@) sign, 126; and Spanish, 24, 25–27; and "*tetatúd*," 67; and traces of violence, 53; and "*tremenda*," 179–80n. 42; and "What's the T?," 69, 179–80n. 42. *See also* Butch(es); Femme(s); *Jota/o(s)*; *Macha/o(s)*; *Vestida(s)*

Queer *latinidad*, 8–9, 31, 36, 41, 119, 156, 160–62; and academia, 29–30,

168n. 26; and activism, 46, 49, 81; and bars, 50, 153; and community, 27, 34, 44, 49, 76, 79, 81, 173n. 14, 174n. 17, 175n. 19; as object of study, 30; performance of, 36; as a "space of dissension," 9

Queer Latino studies, 29–30, 168nn. 25, 26

Queer Planet, 115

Queers for Cuba, 174n. 17

Quiroga, José, 29, 31; *Tropics of Desire*, 29

Race, 12–14, 19–21, 93–98, 140–41, 164n. 4, 166nn. 17, 18, 19, 176n. 27; and accents, 165n. 16; in Brazil, 92–93, 95–98, 100–101, 182n. 9; in cyberspace, 137, 140–41, 189n. 31; and exoticization, 19–20, 137, 140, 166n. 19; and homophobia, 95, 97, 101, 157, 182n. 10; and language, 12, 93; in Latin America, 12–14, 19–21; and the racialized body, 12, 20–21, 93–94, 137, 164n. 3, 167n. 20; in U.S. Latina/o communities, 20–21; and violence, 92–93, 97, 100–101

Ramirez, Horacio Roque, 173n. 14, 178n. 32, 181n. 48

Ramos, Eliots S., 177n. 30

Reno, Janet, 108

Rhizomatic readings, 22, 31, 153, 156; of cyberspace, 121; of *latinidad*, 22; of sexual orientation, 90; and temporality, 150–51

Rich, B. Ruby, 30

Rio de Janeiro, 104–6; gay ghettos of, 91; mythologized geography of, 104–5; and San Francisco, 105; Marcelo Tenório and, 84, 94–95; violence against homosexuals in, 84, 91, 104

Roa Bastos, Augusto, 1–2, 161; *Yo/El Supremo*, 2

Robles, Augie, 175n. 19, 179n. 36

Rodríguez, Celia Herrera, 61

Rodríguez, Janelle, 77–78, 177–78n. 31

Rodríguez, Juan, 63–65, 173n. 15, 178n. 34, 179n. 36

Román, David, 29, 163n. 1

Romany, Celina, 16

Rosales, Karla, 178n. 33

Rubinstein Izé, Ana Ines, 170n. 6

Ruiz, Ana, 169–70n. 5

Sábado Gigante, 20

Sabrocita, 154

Sabrosura, 77–79, 180n. 46

Salamandras de Ambiente, 42

Salpafuera, 27

SalsaSoul Sisters, 41

San Francisco: and AIDS, 38, 47, 49, 171–72n. 9, 172–73n. 10, 173n. 11, 174n. 17, 182n. 6; and gentrification, 82, 175nn. 19, 22; ghosts of, 38; and liberalism of the court, 89; mythologized geography of, 105–6; and queer Latina/o activism, 46–47, 49, 76, 174n. 17; urban geography of, 49, 78, 119, 175n. 19; violence against homosexuals in, 91, 182n. 7, 183nn. 15, 17. See also Mission District

San Francisco AIDS Project, 77

San Francisco Cinemateque, 176n. 25

San Francisco Gay and Lesbian Historical Society, 76

Sandoval, Chela, 7, 31

Sandoval-Sánchez, Alberto, 37, 47, 65, 163n. 1

Santos, Reinaldo Jose de, 99, 183n. 14

About the Author

Juana María Rodríguez is an assistant professor of English at Bryn Mawr College.

CPSIA information can be obtained
at www.ICGtesting.com
Printed in the USA
JSHW030154100322
23729JS00009B/8